The Party Train

# The Party Train

## A COLLECTION OF
## North American Prose Poetry

EDITED BY

## Robert Alexander
## Mark Vinz
## & C. W. Truesdale

NEW RIVERS PRESS

1996

Copyright © 1996 by New Rivers Press
Library of Congress Catalog Card Number 95-069349
ISBN 0-89823-165-5
All Rights Reserved
Edited by Robert Alexander, C. W. Truesdale, Mark Vinz
Editorial Assistance by Mary Roen
Book Design and Typesetting by Peregrine Graphics Services

New Rivers Press is a non-profit literary press dedicated to publishing the very best emerging writers in our region, nation, and world.

The title itself derives from a piece by Jack Anderson (included here). The cover art is by Charles Simic, who is also included in this anthology.

The publication of *The Party Train* has been made possible by generous financial support of The Elmer L. And Eleanor J. Andersen Foundation, The Bush Foundation, General Mills Foundation, Liberty State Bank, The McKnight Foundation, The Minnesota State Arts Board (through an appropriation by the Minnesota Legislature), The National Endowment for the Arts (through an appropriation by the Congress of the United States), Star Tribune/ Cowles Media Company, Scott Tankenoff and The Alex and Mollie Tankenoff Foundation, the Tennant Company Foundation, the United Arts Fund, and the contributing members of New Rivers Press. New Rivers Press also wishes to acknowledge the Minnesota Non-Profits Assistance Fund for its invaluable support.

*The Party Train* has been manufactured in the United States of America for New Rivers Press, 420 N. 5th Street/Suite 910, Minneapolis, MN 55401 in a first edition of 5,000 copies.

## IF MY FATHER WERE TO ASK,

"What's a prose poem?" I would turn my face and look into the distance away from our farm house, into a wild copse of trees which runs from the road's edge and on up the hill to the far fields. Box elder, green ash, and black locust tangle in a net of branches, tied together by thorny greenbrier. I know of a coyote den beneath one old box elder tree, on the edge of a gully cutting through the copse. If I were to stick my hand into the hole, I could feel cool wet air and perhaps the playful teeth of pups.

"Remember when you plowed the fields in the spring," I say to my father, "and the air behind you filled suddenly with sea gulls?" I can see him inhale the aroma of memory: the green and yellow tractor, the motor exhaust and dust, steel blades of the plow sinking into the earth and turning it, the smell all sexual and holy, worms and grubs uncovered into sunlight, then an unexpected slash of white as the gulls materialize behind the plow, a thousand miles and more from any ocean.

S. C. Hahn

# CONTENTS

~

THE PARTY TRAIN

# C. W. Truesdale
## PUBLISHER'S PREFACE

The task of putting together this anthology of prose poems was both exciting and daunting. Exciting because the three editors found such richness and variety in the many submissions we received. And daunting just because of the enormous number of them—over five hundred submissions of up to fifteen pages each—far more than New Rivers Press has ever received for one of its anthologies. In fact, we received so many submissions of such high quality that we could easily put together another such anthology of similar length and excellence.

This is a testament to the attraction of a form of poetry (by established as well as beginning poets) that has never received its critical due despite the excitement the form has generated among poets themselves.

Why this critical neglect—and even hostility—has occurred is a mystery to me. One of the editors, Robert Alexander, in a letter to me explained it in these terms: "All the discussion now about the prose poem reminds me quite a bit of the critical controversy around the turn of the century about free verse. Many, many people (most of them editors of magazines, unfortunately) thought free verse merely a bastardized prose that had no place in the world of 'poetry.' Alice Corbin Henderson, Associate Editor of *Poetry*, is one of the strongest exceptions—but, of course, the champions of free verse were mainly the poets themselves: Pound, Amy Lowell, John Gould Fletcher, Carl Sandburg, William Carlos Williams, H. D., Gertrude Stein, etc. (Each of these poets, significantly, also experimented with prose forms.) To me the question is, Why all this critical brouhaha about the prose poem now, at the end of the century—when I thought all these questions had been settled once and for all at the beginning of it?" Alexander goes on to say, "I think the answer lies somewhere in the dominance of free verse for the last seventy-five years or so. In essence, in America at any rate (though not in Europe or South America or Asia), free verse has forced the prose poem (along with various metrical forms like sonnets and villanelles) to the sidelines, has marginalized it as a genre. The prose poem, however, unlike the sonnet, or free verse, was never accepted by this country's reading public, or by the critics—so rather than a return to old verities (as poets are flocking these days back to meter and—dare we say it—rhyme), we have a critical discourse concerning the prose poem that has totally forgotten its past."

Almost every review of a prose poem collection or essay on the subject begins with the difficulty of defining the genre, or dismissing it as a bastard or hybrid form. Seldom does a review or essay on "regular poetry" begin this way. Actually, though the prose poem has come down to us in many varieties, it is no more varied than its lineated counterpart, for which that question of definition seldom, if ever, arises. We hope this anthology will go a long way toward redressing these problems. If nothing else, we have put together a volume that ought to provide a stunning and varied demonstration of some of the things it is possible to do in this genre.

As to why a poet chooses to write in prose rather than in lineated form—this would probably generate as many responses as there are prose poets. I suspect that even among the three editors themselves the answer would not be the same at all. Robert Alexander seldom writes lineated verse at all these days; Mark Vinz has written a good deal of both; and I, though much attracted to the form as a poet and publisher, have written relatively few prose poems compared to the others. Both Alexander and Vinz are accomplished prose poets and eloquent defenders of the genre, yet in their own work they differ considerably from one another. Alexander tends to be a spare (though not minimalist) writer, given to subtle yet powerful intonations. Vinz introduces a broader variety of character and humor, and an excitement which is often subtly and skillfully moderated by irony and reflectiveness. As for myself, I don't really know why I sometimes feel impelled to use prose rather than lineated verse—perhaps it results simply from intuition or impulse, and I think that this is probably true of many poets who have explored the form. It simply feels right to use prose rather than verse sometimes, and they will, often, freely mix prose and lineated poetry in the same volumes.

~

Without wishing to be too specific or restrictive about the varieties of prose poems we came across in putting this anthology together (and one must note that many of the pieces we have included could conceivably be put in more than one category), I would identify some of the following kinds of prose poem:

1. *The Object Poem* is well-illustrated in this anthology by some of Vern Rutsala's poems (especially the ones about brooms, mops, ironing boards, etc.).

2. *The Surreal Narrative* was very popular among poets in the 1960s but is still widely used. Some of these are best described by using Dr. Johnson's definition of "the metaphysical conceit": the violent yoking together of unexpected elements. This is also quite apparent in many dreams, and, not surprisingly, many dream-like poems have been included here. Among the best known poets who often create "surreal narratives" are Russell Edson, Jack Anderson, and Marie Harris. All of them have done this consistently and often to bizarre comic effect, though surreal narrative can certainly sometimes be serious or even tragical in its dimensions.

3. *The "Straight" Narrative:* What often distinguishes such poems from short stories or short, short stories (though the line is sometimes a pretty thin one, as Vinz points out in his introduction) is that the emphasis tends to be on feeling or affect, rather than on narrative or plot per se. Sometimes a prose poem will just record an incident rather than a full-blown story and the effect of it will come through the details of what is observed. Robert Alexander's "Finding Token Creek" is a good example of this: it is a narrative poem but the action described in it is of no great importance; it is in the amazing descriptions of what the poet sees as he and his dog are boating through a rather ordinary marsh and stream area near Madison, Wisconsin, that makes it a true poem.

4. *The "Character" Poem:* This is similar in kind (if not quality) to the old series we used to find in *The Reader's Digest* called "The Most Unforgettable Character I've Ever Met." Character-drawing also used to be very popular in the novel and short story, where it most often consisted of a paragraph or two of sometimes comic portraiture (as in Dickens or Trollope). In the prose poem, such characters abound often without any narrative element, or very little. A person may be fleetingly

glanced at in passing, or a relationship existing over a long period of time but in no definite set of specific actions (as in the many mother/son, father/daughter relationships depicted in these poems). One of the best examples of such poems I can think of is Sesshu Foster's untitled piece beginning "Sometimes I'm dragged. . . ."

5. *The Landscape or Place Poem:* This is one of the most common forms of prose poetry, whether familiar landscapes are being described (as in many of Mark Vinz's poems) or unique and even exotic ones (as in the travel poems of James Wright). Often (but not always, of course) such material comes out of journal entries (as in Henry David Thoreau or Nathaniel Hawthorne) or letters.

6. *The Meditative Poem:* Many of the poems included in this volume are meditations (on place, character, incidents, etc.). Jane Brox's brief meditations on her New England landscape and aspects of farming are excellent examples. Donald Hall's long, multi-sectioned poem "Flies" is another splendid example. And John Minczeski's poem called "My Name" is a short but powerful meditation on the significance of his own name, treated virtually as an object moving from one continent to another.

7. *The "Hyperbolic" or "Exaggerated" Poem:* To a certain extent, exaggeration of some sort can be found in a great many prose poems from different categories. In its purest form, this sort of verbal play and exaggeration can be found in the work of Michael Benedikt (as in "The Voyage of Self-Discovery") or in Philip Dacy's "The Elephant."

∼

At New Rivers Press, we like to use writers themselves as editors of our anthologies—as much as possible. Both Robert Alexander (*White Pine Sucker River*) and Mark Vinz (*The Weird Kid* and *Late Night Calls*) have published engaging volumes of prose poems with New Rivers. And Alexander also wrote a Ph.D. dissertation on the subject at the University of Wisconsin–Milwaukee from which many of the prose poems in the historical section were selected. Both of these editor/writers have a strong, critical interest in the field and the good judgment to select only material of the highest quality.

Our first task was to publish announcements of this upcoming anthology in *Poets and Writers, AWP*, and other writing venues (which we did in the spring of 1993). We also established a loose deadline (1 March 1994). Early on, we settled on 1960 as our approximate starting date, but also decided to present a separate historical overview of the form as practiced in America from the time of Walt Whitman on to 1960).

In addition to unsolicited contributions, we also asked for submissions from those established prose poem writers whose work one or more of us especially admired. We also received valuable suggestions from Peter Johnson, editor of *The Prose Poem: An International Journal*. Mark Vinz wrote to his many friends in Canada for examples of their work, since early on we decided to include that country in *The Party Train*. He also supplied us with work by many other poets he knew personally and whose work he admired. I invited many New Rivers poets who had worked in this form to submit. Some of the authors who submitted work also suggested others who might be included. Thus John Minczeski, for instance, sent us prose poems by Jane Brox, whom none of the editors was familiar with.

By early August, each of the three editors had read all of the submissions. We met and decided what authors to include. In November, we met again to decide which poems by these authors we wanted to use. More often than not, we decided not to use work that has or will be included in other prose poem anthologies because we all wanted *The Party Train* to be full of surprises and unexpected pleasures. In fact, all of us were delighted to discover so much fine work by poets none of us had heard of—a fact which testifies to the continuing vitality of American literature. The last thing in the world that any of us wanted to put together was another predictable academic anthology of the prose poem. Still, we all feel that we have created a collection of such high quality and comprehensiveness that it might easily attract classroom use—which we certainly hope will happen.

Lastly, we hope to encourage many other poets to take advantage of this neglected, undervalued, but exciting form.

# Robert Alexander
## PROSE/POETRY

*What is poetry and if you know what poetry is what is prose.*
—GERTRUDE STEIN

More than a hundred years ago Walt Whitman wrote: "In my opinion the time has arrived to essentially break down the barriers of form between prose and poetry."[1] Counting down now to the close of yet another century—indeed, a millennium—it seems appropriate to take stock of what American writers have accomplished in the light of Whitman's admonishment. In putting together this anthology the editors have attempted to do just that: to collect some of the best examples of work Americans have produced in the continuing endeavor of the prose poem.

Many readers have long been taken aback by the term *prose poetry*, or *prose poem*, thinking, along with T. S. Eliot, that it doesn't make a whole lot of sense:

> The distinction between 'verse' and 'prose' is clear; the distinction between 'poetry' and 'prose' is very obscure.... I object to the term 'prose-poetry' because it seems to imply a sharp distinction between 'poetry' and 'prose' which I do not admit, and if it does not imply this distinction, the term is meaningless and otiose, as there can be no combination of what is not distinguished.[2]

This objection, it seems to me, can be answered by a brief discussion of the terms themselves.

When we enter into a conversation with another person, we have—as the phenomenologist Julius Laffal reminds us—certain "implicit expectations based on long experience in learning the language and in engaging in conversations with others."[3] Similarly, when we open a book, we approach the piece of writing in the context of our knowledge of literature. This knowledge serves as the frame within which we see the particular book we're reading.

For different kinds of writing, furthermore, we have quite different expectations. We expect a poem to behave differently from a short story—after all, it comes from a different tradition. But just what are these different expectations? What is it we expect from a poem? And what is it we expect from a piece of prose? If we can answer those two questions, we might have some idea of what it is we're looking for in a poem which also happens to be a piece of prose—that is, a "prose poem."

For a moment, let's consider the poem in a spoken rather than a written form. This is, after all, the origin of poetry. In her definitive study, *Oral Poetry,* Ruth Finnegan has this to say:

> The first and most important point is that in written literature poetry is normally *typographically* defined. . . . Obviously this rule will not, by definition, work for unwritten poetry. One is thus forced to look for other, apparently more 'intrinsic' characteristics by which something can be delineated as 'poetry' within oral literature. . . . What we must look for is not one absolute criterion but a range of stylistic and formal attributes—features like heightened language, metaphorical expression, musical form or accompaniment, structural repetitiveness (like the recurrence of stanzas, lines or refrains), prosodic features like metre, alliteration, even perhaps parallelism. So the concept of 'poetry' turns out to be a relative one, depending on a combination of stylistic elements no one of which need necessarily and invariably be present.[4]

This sort of definition, in biology (taxonomy) and anthropology (kinship relations), is called a *polythetic* classification, one that depends on a preponderance of various characteristics, with no single element essential. From this point of view, there are many qualities or features that we associate with poetry as a written form *besides* lineation. The reader will find, for example, a lot of poems in this book that concern themselves with traditionally 'poetic' subjects—what Whitman in *Leaves of Grass* refers to as "night, sleep, death and the stars."

Brevity is another characteristic of poetry. No less an authority than Edgar Allen Poe said that there's no such thing as a long poem, because any such work is really just a succession of shorter pieces strung together: "What we term a long poem is, in fact, merely a succession of brief ones—that is to say, of brief poetical effects."[5] Hence the brevity of the pieces in this anthology is, in some cases, partly what distinguishes them from short stories. Robert McAlmon's "Village," for example, first published in 1921, has almost a novelistic feel to it—a *one-page novel*, as Carol Bergé calls some of her own work.

Another traditional feature of poetry, which often forms a striking aspect of the prose poem, involves how poems end. As Barbara Smith says in *Poetic Closure*:

> The devices of closure often achieve their characteristic effect by imparting to a poem's conclusion a certain quality that is experienced by the reader as striking validity, a quality that leaves him with the feeling that what has just been said has the "conclusiveness," the settled finality, of apparently self-evident truth.[6]

The closing couplet from one of Shakespeare's sonnets will illustrate this point: "This thou perceiv'st, which makes thy love more strong, / To love that well, which thou must leave ere long" (Sonnet 73). Among prose poems there are likewise many examples where the last sentence or two seem fraught with more significance than the rest of the piece— including what I consider to be perhaps the first American prose poem, a piece of writing by Hawthorne:

AUTUMNAL CHARACTERISTICS
In sunny spots of woodland, boys are gathering walnuts, and shouting to one another from among the yellow foliage. There is something in the atmosphere of these warm autumnal afternoons, that gives a peculiar effect to laughter and joyous voices—it makes them far more elastic and gladsome than at other seasons. Grasshoppers, flies, and winged insects of all sorts, are more abundant now, in the middle of October, than I have seen them at any other season. Yellow butterflies flutter about in the sunshine, singly, or by pairs; but they seem to fly more feebly than in summer, and are blown out of their course by the stirring of every breeze. The crickets begin to sing early in the afternoon; and sometimes a locust may be heard. In sheltered nooks and hollows, where there is sunshine but no wind, the buzz of the many insects, congregated there, is an indescribably pleasant and cheerful sound. What a pity, that the frosty night will so soon stop their music![7]

This single leaf by Hawthorne was apparently written for a collector, or perhaps for an auction. What makes this passage particularly interesting is that, except for the last sentence, the entire piece is lifted from two entries in Hawthorne's *American Notebooks* (October 14 and 16, 1837). There are places where Hawthorne has either condensed or expanded the text from which the paragraph is constructed—but the last sentence has no counterpart in the *Notebooks*. Other than that one sentence, Hawthorne merely dressed up observations and details that he'd noted in his journal. But when it came to the final statement, he presumably felt he had to do more. Why? In all likelihood, he wasn't content to leave the piece seeming "merely" like a passage from his notebooks—and so he created the last sentence with its intimation of mortality.

Many of the pieces in this anthology conclude with a statement that, in essence, casts the entire piece in a different light—upping the ante, so to speak. W. S. Merwin's "The Permanent Collection," for example, is a traditional fable up until the last sentence. Then: "Could he have foreseen those who emerge from time to time in silence, with their faces shining." The last phrase turns the whole thing upside down. If their faces had been blank, this would fit with the Absence of the collection. But the unexpected Radiance casts a changed light, so to speak, on the preceding paragraphs. Why are the viewers' faces shining? What Merwin does is introduce a *new* ambiguity into the piece—which is, for this reader, enough to reframe it as a poem.

These examples have given some indication of how prose pieces can fulfill expectations we have of poetry. But now I'd like to look at something equally fundamental—that is, the expectations we have of prose. What, in other words, is the perceived nature of prose? In his exhaustive work, *From Script to Print,* H. J. Chaytor discusses the historical record:

> Until the end of the twelfth century literature produced for public entertainment or edification was almost entirely written in verse. . . . Prose made its way by slow degrees, as education advanced and as people learned to read for themselves; prose versions of earlier poems began to appear at the end of the twelfth century to meet the taste of readers who wanted a story devoid of the padding and prolixity which delayed the action in the verse narratives. . . . It was seen that prose allowed a writer to give attention to the subject in hand without the distraction of hunting for rimes and other forms of decoration or padding. Prose became distinguished as dealing with matters of fact and not of fancy; it was a scientific medium. Therefore, to tell a story in prose was to invest it with an air of realism which verse dissipated

in the first few couplets; it became clear that a family chronicle, written in verse, would vastly gain in authority and dignity, if it were rewritten in prose; it would, in fact, become real history.[8]

The impulse of prose, it seems, is to tell a story—a story grounded in the real world—and this is true whether we are reading a newspaper, a letter, a biography, or a novel. Prose can therefore speak of everyday experience in ways difficult if not impossible for free verse. As Karl Shapiro explains it:

> What I was searching for was a medium in which I could say anything I wanted—which for poets is something like finding the philosopher's stone or the elixir vitae. For one thing, I wanted to be able to use the ridiculous, for another the nonsensical, for another the "obscene." I wanted to be as personal as I liked, as autobiographical when I felt like it, editorializing or pompous, in short, to be able to drop into any intensity of language at any time. None of this was particularly original, but it was new to me.[9]

This ability of the prose poem to take on various registers of language, its ability to masquerade as different sorts of literary or non-literary prose, is one of its distinguishing characteristics—what Margueritte Murphy calls (after Mikhail Bakhtin) its *heteroglossia*.[10] Some of the poems in this anthology seem therefore like brief memoirs, or travelogues, or. . . .

In this way, prose contains the language of the everyday—but a poem is something else again. A poem is language-as-art-object, something set on a pedestal, meant to be viewed or read (or heard) as a work of art—with all that implies about the gulf between "art" and the "real world," all the cultural baggage works of art carry with them. When we break a paragraph up into lines, creating free verse, the text immediately does more than simply tell a story. The context has shifted. The poem takes on airs, it has pretensions. Prose says: "Come listen. I alone have survived to tell this tale." But a poem entices us: "Come listen. No one else can tell this tale as artfully as I."

To get an idea of how this distinction actually works, it's instructive to look at a poem that has appeared in print as *both* poetry and prose. In *Empty Mirror: Early Poems*, Allen Ginsberg published "The Bricklayer's Lunch Hour" as free verse, but in Charles Henri Ford's "Little Anthology of the Prose Poem," the poem is written as prose:

THE BRICKLAYER'S LUNCH HOUR

Two bricklayers are setting the walls of a cellar in a new dug-out patch of dirt behind an old house of wood over with ivy on a shady street in Denver. It is noon and one of them wanders off. The young subordinate bricklayer sits idly for a few minutes after eating a sandwich and throwing away the paper bag. He has on dungarees and is bare above the waist; he has yellow hair and wears a smudged but still bright red cap on his head. He sits idly on top of the wall on a ladder that is leaned up between his spread thighs, his head bent down, gazing uninterestedly at the paper bag on the ground. He draws his hand across his breast, and then slowly rubs his knuckles across the side of his chin and rocks to and fro on the wall. A small cat walks to him along the top of the wall. He picks it up, takes off his cap, and puts it over the kitten's body for a moment to try it out. Meanwhile it is darkening as if to rain.[11]

And here's the (original) free-verse version of the same poem:

THE BRICKLAYER'S LUNCH HOUR

Two bricklayers are setting the walls
of a cellar in a new dug out patch
of dirt behind an old house of wood
with brown gables grown over with ivy
on a shady street in Denver. It is noon
and one of them wanders off. The young
subordinate bricklayer sits idly for
a few minutes after eating a sandwich
and throwing away the paper bag. He
has on dungarees and is bare above
the waist; he has yellow hair and wears
a smudged but still bright red cap
on his head. He sits idly on top
of the wall on a ladder that is leaned
up between his spread thighs, his head
bent down, gazing uninterestedly at
the paper bag on the grass. He draws
his hand across his breast, and then
slowly rubs his knuckles across the

side of his chin, and rocks to and fro
on the wall. A small cat walks to him
along the top of the wall. He picks
it up, takes off his cap, and puts it
over the kitten's body for a moment.
Meanwhile it is darkening as if to rain
and the wind on top of the trees in the
street comes through almost harshly.[12]

When he rewrote the poem as prose, Ginsberg left it largely un-changed, except for deleting the final clause—and thereby strengthen-ing the poem, it seems to me. While eliminating one element of tradi-tional poetry (line-breaks), Ginsberg presumably perceived the need to emphasize the poetic quality of closure by tightening the ending. But what is the effect on the reader of the line-breaks? How, in this respect, does free verse differ from prose?

In my opinion, we "hear" Ginsberg's poem differently—or, if we were to read it aloud, we might in fact read it quite differently. As free verse, the piece seems much jerkier to me; the prose version, on the other hand, seems to flow without interruption, one sentence after another, the whole paragraph and its parts moving easily from beginning to end. For me, the prose piece is a far more successful *poem*.

As Alice Corbin Henderson wrote in 1913, when she was assistant editor of *Poetry*, "The essential difference between prose and poetry is in the quality of the rhythmic phrase."[13] Investigating just this differ-ence in a dissertation study at the University of Wisconsin–Milwaukee, Prudence Byers examined how people read aloud different kinds of non-metrical texts. She measured, among other things, the number of stressed and unstressed syllables in each sample. As it turns out, the ratio of stressed to unstressed syllables in free verse is, not surprisingly, higher than in prose.[14] Thus it's possible to say that one characteristic which distinguishes free verse rhythms from those of prose is an increased fre-quency of stress.

This makes sense when you think about it. One of the effects of line-breaks is often to throw an extra stress into the sentence, which then al-ters the rhythmic quality of the poem. As Denise Levertov says in her oft-quoted essay, "On the Function of the Line":

The most obvious function of the line-break is rhythmic: it can record the slight (but meaningful) hesitations between word and word that are characteristic of the mind's dance among perceptions but which are not noted by grammatical punctuation. . . . The line-break is a form of punctuation *additional* to the punctuation that forms part of the logic of completed thoughts.[15]

In this way, breaking a paragraph up into free verse actually superimposes rhythms that might otherwise lie unheard beneath the flow of the sentences. The paragraph begins to sound incantatory, more like blank verse than like prose.

Besides sounding more traditionally "poetic," highly stressed language also sounds more British than American. As Mencken says in *The American Language*: "In general, the speech-tunes of the Englishman show wider melodic curves than those of the American, and also more rapid changes."[16] In effect, this comes across as speech with a greater number of stressed syllables—again, more like blank verse than prose.

But a poetic form that contains English, as spoken in England, won't suffice in America. "We do not speak English—remember that," said William Carlos Williams: "We speak our own language."[17] And therefore we need a poetry of our own, one that contains the American voice as well as blank verse (together with its free verse variations) contains the English voice. What we have in the prose poem is a piece of writing grounded in the real world, whose rhythms and intonations embody not a traditional English prosody, but rather the speech patterns of everyday America. The prose poem is therefore a form particularly suited to American poetry in the closing years of the twentieth century.

In this view, the American prose poem is important precisely because it serves as a vehicle for the development of an American voice. And that's why, in my opinion, so many writers are attracted to it—because it frees them from what Morton Marcus has called the Tyranny of the Line. As Whitman went on to say, more than a century ago, "The Muse of the Prairies, of California, Canada, Texas, and of the peaks of Colorado . . . soars to the freer, vast, diviner heaven of prose."

## NOTES

1. Walt Whitman, "Notes Left Over," *Collected Prose* , pref. Malcolm Cowley, Vol. 2 of *Complete Poetry and Prose* (1892; New York: Farrar, Straus & Giroux, 1968), pp. 332. The final quote of this introduction is from this same source, p. 333.

2. T. S. Eliot, "Prose and Verse," *The Chapbook, A Monthly Miscellany,* No. 22 (April, 1921), pp. 4-9.

3. Julius Laffal, "Two Modes of Language and Thought," in *Language and Language Disturbances*, ed. Erwin W. Straus, M.D., Ph.D. (Pittsburgh: Duquesne Univ. Press, 1974), p. 243.

4. Ruth Finnegan, *Oral Poetry, Its Nature, Significance and Social Nature* (Cambridge: Cambridge Univ. Press, 1977), p. 25.

5. Edgar A. Poe, "The Philosophy of Composition," in *Essays and Miscellanies, Works, Vol. 14,* ed. James A. Harrison (New York: AMS Press, 1965), p. 196.

6. Barbara Smith, *Poetic Closure* (Chicago: Univ. of Chicago Press, 1968), p. 152.

7. Nathaniel Hawthorne, *American Notebooks*, ed. Claude M. Simpson (Columbus: Ohio State Univ. Press, 1972), pp. 554-55.

8. H. J. Chaytor, Litt. D., *From Script to Print: An Introduction to Vernacular Medieval Literature* (Cambridge, U.K.: W Heffer & Sons, 1945), pp. 83-85.

9. Karl Shapiro, "American Poet?" in *The Poetry Wreck* (New York: Random House, 1975), pp. 342-43.

10. Margueritte S. Murphy, *A Tradition of Subversion: The Prose Poem in English from Wilde to Ashbery* (Amherst: U Mass, 1993), p. 90

11. Allen Ginsberg, *New Directions 14* (1953), p. 342.

12. Allen Ginsberg, *Empty Mirror: Early Poems* (New York: Totem/Corinth, 1961), p. 31.

13. Alice Corbin Henderson, "Poetic Prose and Vers Libre," *Poetry*, 2, No. 2 (May, 1913), p. 70.

14. Prudence P. Byers, "The Contribution of Intonation to the Rhythm and Melody of Non-Metrical English Poetry," Ph.D. diss., Univ. of Wisconsin—Milwaukee 1977, pp. 41-42.

15. Denise Levertov, "On the Function of the Line," *Chicago Review*, 30, No. 3 (Winter, 1979), p. 31.

16. H. L. Mencken, *The American Language*, Fourth Edition (New York: Alfred A. Knopf, 1936), p. 322.

17. William Carlos Williams, "Briarcliffe Junior College Talk," as quoted in Linda Welsheimer Wagner, *The Prose of William Carlos Williams* (Middletown: Wesleyan Univ. Press, 1970), p. 8.

# Mark Vinz
## NOTES ON THE PROSE POEM

A number of years ago, I began to come across references to something called "the workshop poem"—a highly recognizable stance in many of the pieces appearing in literary magazines. Perhaps it was that kind of formulaic sameness (which to some extent I had begun to recognize in my own work) that led me to the prose poem, which seemed so fresh and challenging by comparison. Perhaps it was the urge to explore and develop narrative (I had begun writing short fiction after a hiatus of several years) or to explore, as a writing teacher, the ways a story and poem can spring from the same source. Perhaps it was the openness and associative nature of the form, which, as Robert Bly has said, encourages the writer to get at "feelings of half-buried thoughts" that would otherwise "remain beneath consciousness, unsure of themselves, unable to break through."

Whatever it was, reading Bly's prose poems and those of several others—Russell Edson, Denise Levertov, Roland Flint, Dave Etter, Maxine Chernoff, Keith Gunderson, Louis Jenkins, and my good friends Tom McGrath and James L. White, to name a few—certainly spurred my interest, as did Michael Benedikt's wonderful anthology *The Prose Poem*, Howard Schwartz's *Imperial Messages*, and Greg Kuzma's *Pebble* anthology. There were a wealth of models available—historical, contemporary, international—although when I began seriously writing prose poems and sending them out I found very few magazines editors who expressed any kind of interest in the prose poem in general, much less in my own work—E.V. Griffith of *Poetry NOW* was the first, and later, David Pichaske, Jay Meek and Orval Lund not only tolerated prose poems as something other than literary bastard children but actively sought them out. Then, in 1983, my first collection of prose poems, *The Weird Kid*, not only found a publisher in Bill Truesdale but an enthusiastic supporter. More than ten years later, after I had worked closely with Bill on the publication of another collection of my prose poems, *Late Night Calls*, I eagerly accepted his offer to co-edit this anthology with himself and Robert Alexander—a project which seemed an especially good way to give some added recognition to a kind of literature that has sustained so many strong voices, so much interesting exploration and dialogue.

Working with Bill and Robert has indeed continued my education in the prose poem, expanded the dialogue, bringing about more joys than frustrations, though there indeed have been some of the latter. Like the lyric "workshop poem," it appears to me there is a very recognizable prose poem stance—derived largely, it would seem, from European and South American models and much influenced by American writers such as Edson—what Dana Gioia has called "a kind of absurdist parable." Even though the quality of such work is often quite good, I've found myself resisting what sometimes seems all-too-familiar sameness. The manuscripts we have received, and others suggested for inclusion by the editors, have also continued to re-open the question about what exactly a prose poem *is*. If we start with Denise Levertov's statement that "one doesn't wish it written otherwise—as prose or as poetry," than I have often found myself thinking that what I am reading should indeed have been written *otherwise*—that it is really a short story, or a fragment of fiction, or an essay, or a lyric poem—that while it may have, in Michael Benedikt's terms, "the *intense* use of virtually all the devices of poetry," what finally shapes and sustains it is something else entirely.

If on one hand we are currently experiencing a revival of interest in popular verse traditions and forms, and on the other a peaking interest in various kinds of short short stories ("sudden fiction," "four-minute fiction," "blasters," etc.), it seems to me that the prose poem should somehow maintain a distinct middle ground, a clear option. I know, of course, that this tends to be impossible (indeed, one of my own prose poems, "Fireworks," was reprinted in *Stiller's Pond*, a fiction anthology), but I have also discovered that in the collaborative editorial process we have experienced a series of highly productive exchanges, a remarkable level of agreement. This, more than anything else, is what I should emphasize here. Like lyric poems, prose poems proceed in a variety of ways, and in spite of the debates they may provoke, there is health and strength in that fact—in the editorial give-and-take behind this anthology, and in the exciting range of work represented in it.

Just as heartening to me is reading Brooke Horvath's statements (in *American Poetry Review* and *Denver Quarterly*) that today "poets seem increasingly drawn to the form," especially because of its openness and intimacy, its freedom from self-consciousness and expectations, its function as a home for "fugitive content: a place where one may give voice to the otherwise no longer sayable, as well as to the yet-unsaid." Indeed, as Donald L. Soucy has written in *The Prose Poem: An International Journal*, what sustains this work is "not its outward form, but its inevitable, inner arc . . . the inner tension of its language." It is *voice* which dominates here—one so often driven to confrontation, to exorcism, by the sense of dread that saturates contemporary life.

Soucy's metaphor of the prose poem as "a flying trapeze act without a net" is what, finally, defines its fascination for me personally. Like the trapeze artist who risks everything, the prose poet cannot escape the need to test boundaries. And if this kind of challenge can bring about frustrations to editors, it can also produce real breakthroughs, exhilarating acrobatics—for writer and reader alike.

### PART I

# Pathfinders and Desperadoes

# Robert Alexander
## PATHFINDERS AND DESPERADOES:
## AN INTRODUCTION


In America the earliest prose poems were journal entries, as can be seen in the work of Nathaniel Hawthorne and H. D. Thoreau. Though many of Whitman's pieces in *Specimen Days* also began life as journal entries, the germ of this book can be found in a series of newspaper articles, entitled "City Photographs," which Walt Whitman wrote pseudononymously for the New York *Leader* in the early 1860s.[1] (Photography itself was a recent development, so Whitman's title suggests by association an innovative writing technique.) A number of these articles, basically sketches of place and character, centered about the staff and patients at New York Hospital.

Soon thereafter, Whitman moved to Washington, where he helped tend the growing numbers of wounded from the Civil War. He continued jotting down notes from his work in the hospitals, and these became the central focus of *Memoranda During the War*, which Whitman published in 1875, and which became essentially the first part of *Specimen Days*. The second part of *Specimen Days*, written over a decade later, Whitman calls "hints and data of a Nature-poem that should carry one's experience a few hours."[2] *Specimen Days* is in my opinion the first extensive, self-conscious manifestation of the American prose poem. Whitman himself called it "the most wayward, spontaneous, fragmentary book ever printed."[3]

The close connection between newspaper writing and the prose poem can be seen in the work of another nineteenth century writer, Lafcadio Hearn. As a matter of fact, Hearn first received critical attention for his series of "Fantastics," which appeared in the New Orleans *Item* in the early eighties. The piece included here reveals Hearn's familiarity with Baudelaire's *Petits poèmes en prose*.

Approaching the start of the twentieth century, the little magazine becomes exceedingly important in the history of the American prose poem. I'm referring here to publications from the nineties such as the

*Fly Leaf* (in Boston), the *Chap-Book* (in Chicago), and the *Lark* (in San Francisco). In the first few decades of the twentieth century any such list of little magazines would include *Poetry*, the *Little Review*, *Others*, the *Double Dealer*, *Broom*, and *transition*, to name but a few. As William Carlos Williams says in his *Autobiography*, "It was the springtime of the little magazines and there was plenty for them to do."[4] A number of the prose poems in this historical section first saw the light of day in these publications—some of them, indeed, never to appear elsewhere in print . . . until now.

One exception to this obscurity is Gertrude Stein's book *Tender Buttons*, which was first published in 1914, and whose influence was widespread and lasting. Upon reprinting it in 1928, the editors of *transition* called it an "epochal" work. As Kenneth Rexroth would say later, "The explosively liberating effect of *Tender Buttons* on an adolescent modernist at the beginning of the Twenties is quite impossible to convey."[5] For Stein it was "my first conscious struggle with the problem of correlating sight, sound and sense, and eliminating rhythm."[6]

An interesting footnote in the history of one variety of prose poem (or what's now called the "short short") is provided by a book, *365 Days*, edited by Kay Boyle and others, which comprises one story, each about a page long, for each day of the year 1934. Somewhat disingenuously, the editors state that "in specifying that the stories be so compactly done we were not so much seeking an experimental vehicle as indicating necessary limits of space."[7] Boyle's piece, "January 24, New York," is from this book. When I first took *365 Days* out of the library, in 1982, it hadn't been checked out for thirty years. This to me is emblematic of the forgetfulness which has descended on many of the more radical innovations of the American Renaissance, including the prose poem itself. The Great Depression and the Second World War put an end to a great deal of literary experimentation.

In 1951 there appeared a rather anomalous work, *Chicago: City on the Make*, which Nelson Algren himself referred to as a prose poem. Portions of this book first appeared in *Holiday* magazine, a slick cousin to *Life*. A couple of years later, in 1953, Charles Henri Ford put together "A Little Anthology of the Poem in Prose" (included as a separate section in *New Directions* 14), which contained work by more than forty poets, some in translation. The oldest poem is by Sung Yu, dating from the fourth century, B.C. One of the youngest poets included is Allen Ginsberg, whose piece, "The Bricklayer's Lunch Hour," I discuss in my preface to this present anthology. Finally, no mention of the fifties would be complete without Kenneth Patchen, whose work includes an assortment of prose. In 1959 Kenneth Rexroth said, "He is the most widely read younger poet in the country."[8] Included here are several examples of Patchen's remarkable inventiveness.

In the sixties, things start heating up for the prose poem—which seems, as in the early years of the century, to be a barometer of literary and social energy. Probably the most significant single event is the publication, in 1964, of Russell Edson's *The Very Thing That Happens*. After that, little magazines once again begin publishing a profusion of prose poems. A decade later, in 1974, Michael Benedikt becomes poetry editor of the *Paris Review*. The prose poem then becomes, in Donald Hall's words, "a dominant American literary form."[9]

Another twenty years pass—and finally you, dear reader, have the opportunity to sample some of the best American prose poetry of the last two centuries. *So eat*, as my grandmother used to say. *Enjoy*.

—R. A.

NOTES

1. Walt Whitman, "City Photographs," contained in *Walt Whitman and the Civil War: A Collection of Original Articles and Manuscripts*, ed. Charles I. Glicksberg (New York: A.S. Barnes, 1963), pp. 24–62.

2. Walt Whitman, *Specimen Days*, in *Collected Prose*, pref. Malcolm Cowley, Vol. 2 of *Complete Poetry and Prose* (1892; New York: Farrar, Straus & Giroux, 1968), pp. 196–97.

3. Walt Whitman, *Specimen Days*, p. 3.

4. William Carlos Williams, *Autobiography* (New York: New Directions, 1951), p. 175.

5. Kenneth Rexroth, *An Autobiographical Novel* (Garden City, N.Y.: Doubleday, 1966), p. 145.

6. As quoted by editors in Gertrude Stein, "Tender Buttons," *transition*, No. 14 (Fall, 1928), p. 13n.

7. *365 Days*, ed. Kay Boyle, Laurence Vail, and Nina Conarain (New York: Harcourt Brace, 1936), p. xii.

8. Kenneth Rexroth, "Kenneth Patchen, Naturalist of the Public Nightmare," in *Bird in the Bush* (New York: New Directions, 1959), p. 100.

9. Donald Hall, "On Russell Edson's Genius," *American Poetry Review*, 6, No. 5 (Sept.–Oct., 1977), p. 12.

# Nathaniel Hawthorne
## AUTUMNAL CHARACTERISTICS

In sunny spots of woodland, boys are gathering walnuts, and shouting to one another from among the yellow foliage. There is something in the atmosphere of these warm autumnal afternoons, that gives a peculiar effect to laughter and joyous voices—it makes them far more elastic and gladsome than at other seasons. Grasshoppers, flies, and winged insects of all sorts, are more abundant now, in the middle of October, than I have seen them at any other season. Yellow butterflies flutter about in the sunshine, singly, or by pairs; but they seem to fly more feebly than in summer, and are blown out of their course by the stirring of every breeze. The crickets begin to sing early in the afternoon; and sometimes a locust may be heard. In sheltered nooks and hollows, where there is sunshine but no wind, the buzz of the many insects, congregated there, is an indescribably pleasant and cheerful sound. What a pity, that the frosty night will so soon stop their music!

[1837]

# Henry David Thoreau

*from the* Journal

*Aug. 18. Rain again.*
P.M.—*to Great Fields.*

Many leaves of the cultivated cherry are turned yellow, and a very *few* leaves of the elm have fallen,—the dead or prematurely ripe. The abundant and repeated rains since this month came in have made the last fortnight and more seem like a rainy season in the tropics,—warm, still copious rains falling straight down, contrasting with the cold, driving spring rains. Now again I am caught in a heavy shower in Moore's pitch pines on edge of Great Fields, and am obliged to stand crouching under my umbrella till the drops turn to streams, which find their way through my umbrella, and the path up the hillside is all afloat, a succession of puddles at different levels, each bounded by a ridge of dead pine-needles. An Irishman, getting out stumps and roots in Moore's Swamp, at first squatted behind a wood-pile, but, being wet to his skin, now stands up and moves about for warmth. Melons crack open before they are sweet. Is not that variety of the ambrosia going to seed by Brown's bars in Sleepy Hollow the *heterophylla?*\* with short, pyramidal purplish spikes and dark-green entire lanceolate leaves above.

What means this sense of lateness that so comes over one now,—as if the rest of the year were down-hill, and if we had not performed anything before, we should not now? The season of flowers or of promise may be said to be over, and now is the season of fruits; but where is our fruit? The night of the year is approaching. What have we done with our talent? All nature prompts and reproves us. How early in the year it begins to be late! The sound of the crickets, even in the spring, makes our hearts beat with its awful reproof, while it encourages with its seasonable warning. It matters not by how little we have fallen behind; it seems irretrievably late. The year is full of warnings of its shortness, as

---

\*No; one form of the common.

is life. The sound of so many insects and the sight of so many flowers affect us so,—the creak of the cricket and the sight of the prunella and autumnal dandelion. They say, "For the night cometh in which no man may work."

[1853]

～

## *from* Walden

Then to my morning work. First I take an axe and pail and go in search of water, if that be not a dream. After a cold and snowy night it needed a divining rod to find it. Every winter the liquid and trembling surface of the pond, which was so sensitive to every breath, and reflected every light and shadow, becomes solid to the depth of a foot or a foot and a half, so that it will support the heaviest teams, and perchance the snow covers it to an equal depth, and it is not to be distinguished from any level field. Like the marmots in the surrounding hill, it closes its eyelids and becomes dormant for three months or more. Standing on the snow-covered plain, as if in a pasture amid the hills, I cut my way first through a foot of snow, and then a foot of ice, and open a window under my feet, where, kneeling to drink, I look down into the quiet parlour of the fishes, pervaded by a softened light as through a window of ground glass, with its bright sanded floor the same as in summer; there a perennial waveless serenity reigns as in the amber twilight sky, corresponding to the cool and even temperament of the inhabitants. Heaven is under our feet as well as over our heads.

Early in the morning, while all things are crisp with frost, men come with fishing reels and slender lunch, and let down their fine lines through the snowy field to take pickerel and perch; wild men, who instinctively follow other fashions and trust other authorities than their townsmen, and by their goings and comings stitch towns together in parts where else they would be ripped. They sit and eat their luncheon in stout fear-naughts on the dry oak leaves on the shore, as wise in natural lore as the citizen is in artificial. They never consulted with books, and know and can tell much less than they have done. The things which they practice are said not yet to be known. Here is one fishing for pickerel with grown perch for bait. You look into his pail with wonder as into a summer pond, as if he kept summer locked up at home, or knew where she had retreated. How, pray, did he get these in mid-winter? Oh, he got worms out of rotten logs since the ground froze, and so he caught them. His life itself passes deeper in Nature than the studies of the naturalist penetrate, himself a subject for the naturalist. The latter raises the moss and bark gently with his knife in search of insects; the former lays open logs to their core with his axe, and moss and bark fly far and wide. He gets his living by barking trees. Such a man has some right to fish, and I love to see Nature carried out in him. The perch swallows the grub-worm, the pickerel swallows the perch, and the fisherman swallows the pickerel; and so all the chinks in the scale of being are filled.

[1854]

～

## *from* Walking

We hug the earth,—how rarely we mount! Methinks we might elevate ourselves a little more. We might climb a tree, at least. I found my account in climbing a tree once. It was a tall white pine, on the top of a hill; and though I got well pitched, I was well paid for it, for I discovered new mountains in the horizon which I had never seen before,—so much more of the earth and the heavens. I might have walked about the foot of the tree for three-score years and ten, and yet I certainly should never have seen them. But, above all, I discovered around me,—it was near the end of June,—on the ends of the topmost branches only, a few minute and delicate red cone-like blossoms, the fertile flower of the white pine looking heavenward. I carried straightway to the village the topmost spire, and showed it to stranger jurymen who walked the streets,—for it was court-week,—and to farmers and lumber-dealers and wood-choppers and hunters, and not one had ever seen the like before, but they wondered as at a star dropped down. Tell of ancient architects finishing their works on the tops of columns as perfectly as on the lower and more visible parts! Nature has from the first expanded the minute blossoms of the forest only toward the heavens, above men's heads and unobserved by them. We see only the flowers that are under our feet in the meadows. The pines have developed their delicate blossoms on the highest twigs of the wood every summer for ages, as well over the heads of Nature's red children as of her white ones; yet scarcely a farmer or hunter in the land has ever seen them.

Above all, we cannot afford not to live in the present. He is blessed over all mortals who loses no moment of the passing life in remembering the past. Unless our philosophy hears the cock crow in every barnyard within our horizon, it is belated. That sound commonly reminds us that we are growing rusty and antique in our employments and habits of thought. His philosophy comes down to a more recent time than ours. There is something suggested by it that is a newer testament,—the gospel according to this moment. He has not fallen astern; he has got up early, and kept up early, and to be where he is is to be in season, in the foremost rank of time. It is an expression of the heath and soundness of Nature, a brag for all the world,—healthiness as of a spring burst forth, a new fountain of the Muses, to celebrate this last instant of time. Where he lives no fugitive slave laws are passed. Who has not betrayed his master many times since last he heard that note?

The merit of this bird's strain is in its freedom from all plaintiveness. The singer can easily move us to tears or to laughter, but where is he who can excite in us a pure morning joy? When, in doleful dumps, breaking the awful stillness of our wooden sidewalk on a Sunday, or, perchance, a watcher in the house of mourning, I hear a cockerel crow far or near, I think to myself, "There is one of us well, at any rate,"—and with a sudden gush return to my senses.

[1862]

# Walt Whitman

## *from* Specimen Days

### PATENT-OFFICE HOSPITAL

*February 23.*—I must not let the great hospital at the Patent-office pass away without some mention. A few weeks ago the vast area of the second story of that noblest of Washington buildings was crowded close with rows of sick, badly wounded and dying soldiers. They were placed in three very large apartments. I went there many times. It was a strange, solemn, and, with all its features of suffering and death, a sort of fascinating sight. I go sometimes at night to soothe and relieve particular cases. Two of the immense apartments are fill'd with high and ponderous glass cases, crowded with models in miniature of every kind of utensil, machine or invention, it ever enter'd into the mind of man to conceive; and with curiosities and foreign presents. Between these cases are lateral openings, perhaps eight feet wide and quite deep, and in these were placed the sick, besides a great long double row of them up and down through the middle of the hall. Many of them were very bad cases, wounds and amputations. Then there was a gallery running above the hall in which there were beds also. It was, indeed, a curious scene, especially at night when lit up. The glass cases, the beds, the forms lying there, the gallery above, and the marble pavement under foot—the suffering, and the fortitude to bear it in various degrees—occasionally, from some, the groan that could not be repress'd—sometimes a poor fellow dying, with emaciated face and glassy eye, the nurse by his side, the doctor also there, but no friend, no relative—such were the sights but lately in the Patent-office. (The wounded have since been removed from there, and it is now vacant again.)

[1863]

$\sim$

## ABRAHAM LINCOLN

*August 12th.*—I see the President almost every day, as I happen to live where he passes to or from his lodgings out of town. He never sleeps at the White House during the hot season, but has quarters at a healthy location some three miles north of the city, the Soldiers' home, a United States military establishment. I saw him this morning about 8½ coming in to business, riding on Vermont avenue, near L street. He always has a company of twenty-five or thirty cavalry, with sabres drawn and held upright over their shoulders. They say this guard was against his personal wish, but he let his counselors have their way. The party makes no great show in uniform or horses. Mr. Lincoln on the saddle generally rides a good-sized, easy-going gray horse, is dress'd in plain black, somewhat rusty and dusty, wears a black stiff hat, and looks about as ordinary in attire, &c., as the commonest man. A lieutenant, with yellow straps, rides at his left, and following behind, two by two, come the cavalry men, in their yellow-striped jackets. They are generally going at a slow trot, as that is the pace set them by the one they wait upon. The sabres and accoutrements clank, and the entirely unornamental *cortège* as it trots toward Lafayette square arouses no sensation, only some curious stranger stops and gazes. I see very plainly ABRAHAM LINCOLN'S dark brown face, with the deep-cut lines, the eyes, always to me with a deep latent sadness in the expression. We have got so that we exchange bows, and very cordial ones. Sometimes the President goes and comes in an open barouche. The cavalry always accompany him, with drawn sabres. Often I notice as he goes out evenings—and sometimes in the morning, when he returns early—he turns off and halts at the large and handsome residence of the Secretary of War, on K street, and holds conference there. If in his barouche, I can see from my window he does not alight, but sits in his vehicle, and Mr. Stanton comes out to attend him. Sometimes one of his sons, a boy of ten or twelve, accompanies him, riding at his right on a pony. Earlier in the summer I occasionally saw the President and his wife, toward the latter part of the afternoon, out in a barouche, on a pleasure ride through the city. Mrs. Lincoln was dress'd in complete black, with a long crape veil. The equipage is of the plainest kind, only two horses, and they nothing extra. They pass'd me once very close, and I saw the President in the face fully, as they were moving slowly, and his look, though abstracted, happen'd to be directed steadily in my eye. He bow'd and smiled, but far beneath his smile I noticed well the expression I have alluded to. None of the artists or pictures has caught the deep, though subtle and indirect expression of this man's face. There is something else there. One of the great portrait painters of two or three centuries ago is needed.

[1863]

∾

DEATH OF A WISCONSIN OFFICER

Another characteristic scene of that dark and bloody 1863, from notes of my visit to Armory-square hospital, one hot but pleasant summer day. In ward H we approach the cot of a young lieutenant of one of the Wisconsin regiments. Tread the bare board floor lightly here, for the pain and panting of death are in this cot. I saw the lieutenant when he was first brought here from Chancellorsville, and have been with him occasionally from day to day and night to night. He had been getting along pretty well till night before last, when a sudden hemorrhage that could not be stopt came upon him, and to-day it still continues at intervals. Notice that water-pail by the side of the bed, with a quantity of blood and bloody pieces of muslin, nearly full; that tells the story. The poor young man is struggling painfully for breath, his great dark eyes with a glaze already upon them, and the choking faint but audible in his throat. An attendant sits by him, and will not leave him till the last; yet little or nothing can be done. He will die here in an hour or two, without the presence of kith or kin. Meantime the ordinary chat and business of the ward a little way off goes on indifferently. Some of the inmates are laughing and joking, others are playing checkers or cards, others are reading, &c.

I have noticed through most of the hospitals that as long as there is any chance for a man, no matter how bad he may be, the surgeon and nurses work hard, sometimes with curious tenacity, for his life, doing everything, and keeping somebody by him to execute the doctor's orders, and minister to him every minute night and day. See that screen there. As you advance through the dusk of early candle-light, a nurse will step forth on tip-toe, and silently but imperiously forbid you to make any noise, or perhaps to come near at all. Some soldier's life is flickering there, suspended between recovery and death. Perhaps at this moment the exhausted frame has just fallen into a light sleep that a step might shake. You must retire. The neighboring patients must move in their stocking feet. I have been several times struck with such mark'd efforts—everything bent to save a life from the very grip of the destroyer. But when that grip is once firmly fix'd, leaving no hope or chance at all, the surgeon abandons the patient. If it is a case where stimulus is any relief, the nurse gives milk-punch or brandy, or whatever is wanted, *ad libitum*. There is no fuss made. Not a bit of sentimentalism or whining have I seen about a single death-bed in hospital or on the field, but generally impassive indifference. All is over, as far as any efforts can avail; it is useless to expend emotions or labors. While there is a prospect they strive hard—at least most surgeons do; but death certain and evident, they yield the field.

[1863]

～

## THE REAL WAR WILL NEVER GET IN THE BOOKS

And so good-bye to the war. I know not how it may have been, or may be, to others—to me the main interest I found, (and still, on recollection, find,) in the rank and file of the armies, both sides, and in those specimens amid the hospitals, and even the dead on the field. To me the points illustrating the latent personal character and eligibilities of these States, in the two or three millions of American young and middle-aged men, North and South, embodied in those armies—and especially the one-third or one-fourth of their number, stricken by wounds or disease at some time in the course of the contest—were of more significance even than the political interests involved. (As so much of a race depends on how it faces death, and how it stands personal anguish and sickness. As, in the glints of emotions under emergencies, and the indirect traits and asides in Plutarch, we get far profounder clues to the antique world than all its more formal history.)

Future years will never know the seething hell and the black infernal background of countless minor scenes and interiors, (not the official surface-courteousness of the Generals, not the few great battles) of the Secession war; and it is best they should not—the real war will never get in the books. In the mushy influences of current times, too, the fervid atmosphere and typical events of those years are in danger of being totally forgotten. I have at night watch'd by the side of a sick man in the hospital, one who could not live many hours. I have seen his eyes flash and burn as he raised himself and recurr'd to the cruelties on his sur-render'd brother, and mutilations of the corpse afterward. (See, in the preceding pages, the incident at Upperville—the seventeen kill'd as in the description, were left there on the ground. After they dropt dead, no one touch'd them—all were made sure of, however. The carcasses were left for the citizens to bury or not, as they chose.)

Such was the war. It was not a quadrille in a ball-room. Its interior history will not only never be written—its practicality, minutiae of deeds and passions, will never be even suggested. The actual soldier of 1862–'65, North and South, with all his ways, his incredible dauntlessness, habits, practices, tastes, language, his fierce friendship, his appetite, rankness, his superb strength and animality, lawless gait, and a hundred unnamed lights and shades of camp, I say, will never be written—perhaps must not and should not be.

The preceding notes may furnish a few stray glimpses into that life, and into those lurid interiors, never to be fully convey'd to the future. The hospital part of the drama from '61 to '65, deserves indeed to be recorded. Of that many-threaded drama, with its sudden and strange surprises, its confounding of prophecies, its moments of despair, the dread of foreign interference, the interminable campaigns, the bloody battles, the mighty and cumbrous and green armies, the drafts and boun-ties—the immense money expenditure, like a heavy-pouring constant rain—with, over the whole land, the last three years of the struggle, an unending, universal mourning-wail of women, parents, orphans—the marrow of the tragedy concentrated in those Army Hospitals—(it seem'd sometimes as if the whole interest of the land, North and South, was one vast central hospital, and all the rest of the affair but flanges)—those forming the untold and unwritten history of the war—infinitely greater (like life's) than the few scraps and distortions that are ever told or writ-ten. Think how much, and of importance, will be—how much, civic and military, has already been—buried in the grave, in eternal darkness.

[1865]

⤳

## A JULY AFTERNOON BY THE POND

The fervent heat, but so much more endurable in this pure air—the white and pink pond-blossoms, with great heart-shaped leaves; the glassy waters of the creek, the banks, with dense bushery, and the picturesque beeches and shade and turf; the tremulous, reedy call of some bird from recesses, breaking the warm, indolent, half-voluptuous silence; an occasional wasp, hornet, honey-bee or bumble (they hover near my hands or face, yet annoy me not, nor I them, as they appear to examine, find nothing, and away they go)—the vast space of the sky overhead so clear, and the buzzard up there sailing his slow whirl in majestic spirals and discs; just over the surface of the pond, two large slate-color'd dragon-flies, with wings of lace, circling and darting and occasionally balancing themselves quite still, their wings quivering all the time, (are they not showing off for my amusement?)—the pond itself, with the sword-shaped calamus; the water snakes—occasionally a flitting black-bird, with red dabs on his shoulders, as he darts slantingly by—the sounds that bring out the solitude, warmth, light and shade—the quawk of some pond duck—(the crickets and grasshoppers are mute in the noon heat, but I hear the song of the first cicadas;)—then at some distance the rattle and whirr of a reaping machine as the horses draw it on a rapid walk through a rye field on the opposite side of the creek—(what was the yellow or light-brown bird, large as a young hen, with short neck and long-stretch'd legs I just saw, in flapping and awkward flight over there through the trees?) the prevailing delicate, yet palpable, spicy, grassy, clovery perfume to my nostrils; and over all, encircling all, to my sight and soul, the free space of the sky, transparent and blue—and hovering there in the west, a mass of white-gray fleecy clouds the sailors call "shoals of mackerel"—the sky, with silver swirls like locks of toss'd hair, spreading, expanding—a vast voiceless, formless simulacrum—yet may-be the most real reality and formulator of everything—who knows?

[1876]

～

## LOAFING IN THE WOODS

*March 8.*—I write this down in the country again, but in a new spot, seated on a log in the woods, warm, sunny, midday. Have been loafing here deep among the trees, shafts of tall pines, oak, hickory, with a thick undergrowth of laurels and grapevines—the ground cover'd everywhere by debris, dead leaves, breakage, moss—everything solitary, ancient, grim. Paths (such as they are) leading hither and yon—(how made I know not, for nobody seems to come here, nor man nor cattlekind.) Temperature to-day about 60, the wind through the pine-tops; I sit and listen to its hoarse sighing above (and to the *stillness*) long and long, varied by aimless rambles in the old roads and paths, and by exercisepulls at the young saplings, to keep my joints from getting stiff. Bluebirds, robins, meadowlarks begin to appear.

*Next day, 9th.*—A snowstorm in the morning, and continuing most of the day. But I took a walk over two hours, the same woods and paths, amid the falling flakes. No wind, yet the musical low murmur through the pines, quite pronounced, curious, like waterfalls, now still'd, now pouring again. All the senses, sight, sound, smell, delicately gratified. Every snowflake lay where it fell on the evergreens, holly-trees, laurels, &c., the multitudinous leaves and branches piled, bulging-white, defined by edge-lines of emerald—the tall straight columns of the plentiful bronze-topt pines—a slight resinous odor blending with that of the snow. (For there is a scent to everything, even the snow, if you can only detect it—no two places, hardly any two hours, anywhere, exactly alike. How different the odor of noon from midnight, or winter from summer, or a windy spell from a still one.)

[1880]

# Lafcadio Hearn
## SPRING PHANTOMS

The moon, descending her staircase of clouds in one of the "Petits Poèmes en Prose," enters the chamber of a newborn child, and whispers into his dreams: "Thou shalt love all that loves me—the water that is formless and multiform, the vast green sea, the place where thou shalt never be, the woman thou shalt never know."

For those of us thus blessed or cursed at our birth, this is perhaps the special season of such dreams—of nostalgia, vague as the world-sickness, for the places where we shall never be; and fancies as delicate as arabesques of smoke concerning the woman we shall never know. There is a languor in the air; the winds sleep; the flowers exhale their souls in incense; near sounds seem distant, as if the sense of time and space were affected by hashish; the sunsets paint in the west pictures of phantom-gold, as of those islands at the mere aspect of whose beauty crews mutinied and burned their ships; plants that droop and cling assume a more feminine grace; and the minstrel of Southern woods mingles the sweet rippling of his mocking music with the moonlight.

There have been sailors who, flung by some kind storm-wave on the shore of a Pacific Eden, to be beloved for years by some woman dark but beautiful, subsequently returned by stealth to the turmoil of civilization and labor, and vainly regretted, in the dust and roar and sunlessness of daily toil, the abandoned paradise they could never see again. Is it not such a feeling as this that haunts the mind in springtime;—a faint nostalgic longing for the place where we shall never be;—a vision made even more fairylike by such a vague dream of glory as enchanted those Spanish souls who sought, and never found El Dorado?

Each time the vision returns, is it not more enchanting than before, as a recurring dream of the night in which we behold places we can never see except through dream-haze, gilded by a phantom sun? It is sadder each time, this fancy; for it brings with it the memory of older apparitions, as of places visited in childhood, in that sweet dim time so long ago that its dreams and realities are mingled together in strange confusion, as clouds with waters.

Each year it comes to haunt us, like the vision of the Adelantado of the Seven Cities—the place where we shall never be—and each year there will be a weirder sweetness and a more fantastic glory about the vision. And perhaps in the hours of the last beating of the heart, before sinking into that abyss of changeless deeps above whose shadowless sleep no dreams move their impalpable wings, we shall see it once more, wrapped in strange luminosity, submerged in the orange radiance of a Pacific sunset—the place where we shall never be!

And the Woman that we shall never know!

She is the daughter of mist and light—a phantom bride who becomes visible to us only during those magic hours when the moon enchants the world; she is the most feminine of all sweetly feminine things, the most complaisant, the least capricious. Hers is the fascination of the succubus without the red thirst of the vampire. She always wears the garb that most pleases us—when she wears any; always adopts the aspect of beauty most charming to us—blonde or swarthy, Greek or Egyptian, Nubian or Circassian. She fills the place of a thousand odalisques, owns all the arts of the harem of Solomon: all the loveliness we love retrospectively, all the charms we worship in the present, are combined in her. She comes as the dead come, who never speak; yet without speech she gratifies our voiceless caprice. Sometimes we foolishly fancy that we discover in some real, warm womanly personality, a trait or feature like unto hers; but time soon unmasks our error. We shall never see her in the harsh world of realities; for she is the creation of our own hearts, wrought Pygmalionwise, but of material too unsubstantial for even the power of a god to animate. Only the dreams of Brahma himself take substantial form: these are worlds and men and all their works, which shall pass away like smoke when the preserver ceases his slumber of a myriad million years.

She becomes more beautiful as we grow older—this phantom love, born of the mist of poor human dreams—so fair and faultless that her invisible presence makes us less reconciled to the frailties and foibles of real life. Perhaps she too has faults; but she has no faults for us except that of unsubstantiality. Involuntarily we acquire the unjust habit of judging real women by her spectral standard; and the real always suffer for the ideal. So that when the fancy of a home and children—smiling faces, comfort, and a woman's friendship, the idea of something real to love and be loved by—comes to the haunted man in hours of disgust with the world and weariness of its hollow mockeries—the Woman that he shall never know stands before him like a ghost with sweet sad eyes of warning—and he dare not!

[1881]

# Gelett Burgess
## THE CONFESSIONS OF A YELLSTER:
### *CHACUN À SON GOÛT*

I was boisterous and turbulent as a youth, a loud mouthed, impossible sort of a boy;—one to be kept out of doors as long as possible, and to be suppressed at night by every means in a mother's power. I was sent to boarding school, but was speedily expelled for my noise. I managed to get into college at last, and there I was perfectly happy, rooting on the campus and on the football field at all hours, with the more enthusiastic of my mates. Where there was a yell, there was I, the king-pin of the hullabaloo; a shouting mania possessed me, and I was the leader in all the celebrations of the University. I invented new cries and captained that vocal patriotism by which classes triumph, and battles are supposed to be won upon the gridiron. I had a large chest-expansion, and was known far and wide as a man of mighty lungs.

After I was graduated, I obtained a clerkship in a wholesale-house, and attempted to gain a mastery over my madness, but the effort was terrible. After every day of silence, I sought the unfrequented suburban districts, and screamed to the moon and all the planets, to relieve the tension of my desire. How I envied the retail-counter clerks, who were privileged to vociferate "Cash!" till the windows rattled! I often woke myself, and all the neighbors, by my midnight shrieks, breaking through dreams, happy dreams, where I trumpeted at fires or on shipboard, whooped with wild Apaches, or bawled with frenzied negroid Voodoos.

So things went from bad to worse. I dared not trust myself in society, lest I should explode with my pent-up feelings, and breed a scandal among my respectable friends. But at last the climax came, on a Sunday when I made a final attempt to calm myself in the odour of sanctity at a neighbouring church. The dim light of the edifice and the peaceful serenity of the congregation sobered me when I entered, and I thanked God that I was, for once, like other men. When I had begun to tire of the stillness, the harsh blare of the organ and the raucous notes of the tenor soothed me again; I delighted in the discords, for it was an ill-paid choir, and I settled myself in content. But alas, I had not calculated upon the agony of that Rector's voice! His first low and solemn words began the torture, and at each succeeding droning sentence, the barb of annoyance sunk deeper into my spirit. I itched all over, with the monotony of his whining modulations. I held up first one foot, and then the other, to distract my mind from the drawling moan of the voice; I counted the windows and the nodding heads of the worshippers; I began to wonder what would happen if I should give way under the strain, and the temptation grew suddenly like a cyclone, blowing down every barrier of decency. I held my breath in terror of the demon that possessed me, while the congregation swayed before my eyes in a dull blur. Still the Rector's voice murmured unceasingly, and like an earache that grows more and more intense, at last my desire boiled up and overflowed my soul. I rose to my feet and yelled aloud! One mad, hoarse shriek, that echoed back from the chancel, raced up and down the aisles, leaped to the vaulted roof, and swept down upon the drowsy audience. An hundred heads swung round to me, an hundred white faces confronted me with staring eyes. The Preacher stopped suddenly; there was a crescendo of astonished exclamations; a woman screamed, two grey-bearded deacons hurried toward me, and I reeled into the arms of a verger.

I am happy now, thanks to the wise services of the physician that attended me; and all day long I have the blessed right to yell "*Fresh Mackerel!*" upon the highways and byways of the town. No one stares at me as I pass, scream loudly as I may; and at night, after a day of indescribable ecstacy, I retire to my little garden and practice upon my trombone. And when I go to sleep, my dreams are full of peace.

[1897]

# Gertrude Stein

## from Tender Buttons

### A PIANO

If the speed is open, if the color is careless, if the selection of a strong scent is not awkward, if the button holder is held by all the waving color and there is no color, not any color. If there is no dirt in a pin and there can be none scarcely, if there is not then the place is the same as up standing.

This is no dark custom and it even is not acted in any such a way that a restraint is not spread. That is spread, it shuts and it lifts and awkwardly not awkwardly the centre is in standing.

~

### IN BETWEEN

In between a place and candy is a narrow foot-path that shows more mounting than anything, so much really that a calling meaning a bolster measured a whole thing with that. A virgin a whole virgin is judged made and so between curves and outlines and real seasons and more out glasses and a perfectly unprecedented arrangement between old ladies and mild colds there is no satin wood shining.

~

### COLORED HATS

Colored hats are necessary to show that curls are worn by an addition of blank spaces, this makes the difference between single lines and broad stomachs, the least thing is lightening, the least thing means a little flower and a big delay a big delay that makes more nurses than little women really little women. So clean is a light that nearly all of it shows pearls and little ways. A large hat is tall and me and all custard whole.

[1911]

# William Carlos Williams
## THE DELICACIES

The hostess, in pink satin and blond hair—dressed high—shone beautifully in her white slippers against the great silent bald head of her little-eyed husband!

Raising a glass of yellow Rhine wine in the narrow space just beyond the light-varnished woodwork and the decorative column between dining-room and hall, she smiled the smile of water tumbling from one ledge to another.

We began with a herring salad: delicately flavoured saltiness in scallops of lettuce-leaves.

The little owl-eyed and thick-set lady with masses of gray hair has smooth pink cheeks without a wrinkle. She cannot be the daughter of the little red-faced fellow dancing about inviting lion-headed Wolff the druggist to play the piano! But she is. Wolff is a terrific smoker: if the telephone goes off at night—so his curled-haired wife whispers—he rises from bed but cannot answer till he has lighted a cigarette.

Sherry wine in little conical glasses, dull brownish yellow, and tomatoes stuffed with finely cut chicken and mayonnaise!

The tall Irishman in a Prince Albert and the usual striped trousers is going to sing for us. (The piano is in a little alcove with dark curtains.) The hostess's sister—ten years younger than she—in black net and velvet, has hair like some filmy haystack, cloudy about the eyes. She will play for her husband.

My wife is young, yes she is young and pretty when she cares to be—when she is interested in a discussion: it is the little dancing mayor's wife telling her of the Day Nursery in East Rutherford, 'cross the track, divided from us by the railroad—and disputes as to precedence. It is in this town the saloon flourishes, the saloon of my friend on the right whose wife has twice offended with chance words. Her English is atrocious! It is in this town that the saloon is situated, close to the railroad track, close as may be, this side being dry, dry, dry: two people listening on opposite sides of a wall!—The Day Nursery had sixty-five babies the week before last, so my wife's eyes shine and her cheeks are pink and I cannot see a blemish.

Ice-cream in the shape of flowers and domestic objects: a pipe for me since I do not smoke, a doll for you.

The figure of some great bulk of a woman disappearing into the kitchen with a quick look over the shoulder. My friend on the left who has spent the whole day in a car the like of which some old fellow would give to an actress: flower-holders, mirrors, curtains, plush seats—my friend on the left who is chairman of the Streets committee of the town council— and who has spent the whole day studying automobile fire-engines in neighbouring towns in view of purchase,—my friend, at the Elks last week at the breaking-up hymn, signalled for them to let Bill—a familiar friend of the saloon-keeper—sing out all alone to the organ—and he did sing!

Salz-rolls, exquisite! and Rhine wine *ad libitum*. A masterly caviare sandwich.

The children flitting about above stairs. The councilman has just bought a National eight—some car!

For heaven's sake I mustn't forget the halves of green peppers stuffed with cream cheese and whole walnuts!

[1917]

⌒

## A MATISSE

On the french grass, in that room on Fifth Ave., lay that woman who had never seen my own poor land. The dust and noise of Paris had fallen from her with the dress and underwear and shoes and stockings which she had just put aside to lie bathing in the sun. So too she lay in the sunlight of the man's easy attention. His eye and the sun had made day over her. She gave herself to them both for there was nothing to be told. Nothing is to be told to the sun at noonday. A violet clump before her belly mentioned that it was spring. A locomotive could be heard whistling beyond the hill. There was nothing to be told. Her body was neither classic nor whatever it might be supposed. There she lay and her curving torso and thighs were close upon the grass and violets.

So he painted her. The sun had entered his head in the color of sprays of flaming palm leaves. They had been walking for an hour or so after leaving the train. They were hot. She had chosen the place to rest and he had painted her resting, with interest in the place she had chosen.

It had been a lovely day in the air.—What pleasant women are these girls of ours! When they have worn clothes and take them off it is with an effect of having performed a small duty. They return to the sun with a gesture of accomplishment.—Here she lay in this spot today not like Diana or Aphrodite but with better proof than they of regard for the place she was in. She rested and he painted her.

It was the first of summer. Bare as was his mind of interest in anything save the fullness of his knowledge, into which her simple body entered as into the eye of the sun himself, so he painted her. So she came to America.

No man in my country has seen a woman naked and painted her as if he knew anything except that she was naked. No woman in my country is naked except at night.

In the french sun, on the french grass in a room on Fifth Ave., a french girl lies and smiles at the sun without seeing us.

[1921]

∿

## *from* For Bill Bird

It was getting kinda late. We'd been talking cars. I wanted them to come in on a new model we had just unloaded. He seemed interested but she wouldn't let him buy it. So I kept talking, stalling along hoping for a break.

Pretty soon I hears a car pull up in front of the house and stop. I thought someone was coming in. I waited a while then I ast them if they'd heard it too.

Oh, yes, she says, that's our daughter coming home from the movies.

That was all right but after another half hour and nobody comin in I spoke up again. I guess you were wrong, I says, about that being your daughter.

No, she says, she usually sits out there with her boy friend for a while before coming in. I suppose she sees the light and knows we're up.

A little after twelve o'clock the car starts up and I could hear it fade out down the street. Then someone comes runnin up the front steps. The door flings open and in comes the girl. A peach, take it from me. As soon as she sees me she stops and stands there swinging her panties around on the finger tips of her left hand.

Hello folks, she says then, and lets her underwear go onto a couch. How's everybody?

Evelyn! says her mother, I hope you're not going to bring disgrace and scandal into this house.

Oh don't worry, Mother, she says, we're careful.

[1932]

∽

## EXULTATION

The rain surpasses itself. It has gone beyond itself to the contours of a happy day. A day of sunshine, a June day, a day when the old gardener is arrested by a scent of roses wakens to the small sounds of the driving rain.

It is a week-end holiday the first of the year in the good weather, when everyone has gone to the lake. The cottage has to be cleaned, the windows opened, the roof, broken by last February's ice storm, repaired. The mice that have built a nest in the rags back of the kitchen door, routed. But it is too lovely to spend all our time indoors.

Bill is in the garden. "Come on out, Daphne, and look at this sky and this water. It does something to you. It really does!" He has been raking dead oak leaves from the almost buried arena of the summer's anticipated operations for leisure and going back and forth: to the float, back entry. Everything has to be cleared and put in order.

The rain continues to fall. It penetrates to the bones. This dampness and this chill is a foretaste of the grave.

But it is in the rain, the rain, friend of the seeds, friend of all budding things that in the microscopy of its attention puts my dejection to shame. Without the rain—without this rain, without this dejection, the humor of the quicksilver lizard would not inhabit the breathing sand. He scampers, his throat, as he lifts his head to watch me, pulsing rapidly. I shift my eyes and he is gone.

Which is he?

If he is not the rain, what is he? In the microscopy of its attention exists also a pulse of oars, the slow dip and withdrawal. And the talk. And the intent of the talk. And the silences. The slow forward and back. The smell of the fishy lakewater. The heat of the day. The shores equidistant from the shallow boat as it moves in leisurely fashion upon the hardly rippled lake. There are the cries of the splashing children swimming at the place set aside for them.

The time is ripe. Now is the time. There is no other time in which to exult at the brilliant fulfillment of a summer day.

[1953]

# Jane Heap
WHITE

I

Sharp, empty air. . . . Out of the black mouths of engines white smoke rises on thin stems into white ghosts of ancient trees; together they rise into ghosts of ancient forests, sway and surge and are gone again a million years.

II

The hot air of the day stays in the city until night. The long slope of my roof presses the heat down upon me. Soon it will rain. But there is no rest in me: my heart is wandering too far. My friends may still be in the city, but I do not seek them. I go to the animals in the park. Within their enclosures black shadows of camels lie in the darkness. A great white camel broods in the moonlight, apart from the rest. His lonely eyes are closed and he moves his head slowly from side to side on his long neck, swaying in pain, searching in a dream for his lost world. I have seen a Norwegian ship carrying its carved head through the waters of a fjord with such a movement. . . .

Now the high clouds cover the moon. Out on the lake a wind assails the layers of heat. A white peacock sits in a tree, aloof, elegant, incorruptible. . . . A light green spirit. . . . Across the first thunder he lifts his long white laugh at us like a maniac.

[1917]

31

# Fenton Johnson

## AUNT HANNAH JACKSON

Despite her sixty years Aunt Hannah Jackson rubs on other people's clothes.

Time has played havoc with her eyes and turned to gray her parched hair.

But her tongue is nimble as she talks to herself.

All day she talks to herself about her neighbors and her friends and the man she loved.

Yes, Aunt Hannah Jackson loved even as you and I and Wun Hop Sing.

"He was a good man," she says. "But a fool."

"So am I a fool and Mrs. Lee a fool and this Mrs. Goldstein that I work for a fool."

"All of us are fools."

For rubbing on other people's clothes Aunt Hannah Jackson gets a dollar and fifty cents a day and a worn-out dress on Christmas.

For talking to herself Aunt Hannah Jackson gets a smile as we call her a good-natured fool.

≈

## THE GAMBLER

I am a gambler. Golden are my teeth. My head is shining like a cabaret floor and my hands are gleaming with stones from the mines of Kimberly.

I am the house. Who dares defeat the house?

Good friend, throw the dice! I live by chance and chance rewards me well.

≈

## THE BARBER

I wield the razor, sling hot towels and talk.

My daily newspaper is the racing chart and my pastime making bets on fleet-footed horses.

Whatever is left from betting I divide with my wife and a yellow woman who lives in an apartment on Wabash Avenue.

(Poor Wife! She gets very little.)

I love gay clothes, a good supply of Fatimas and the fire in gin and whiskey.

I love life. Who doesn't?


∼


## THE DRUNKARD

I had a wife, but she is gone. She left me a week ago. God bless her!

I married another in the rear of Mike's saloon. It was a gallon jug of the reddest liquor that ever burned the throat of man. I will be true to my new wife. You can have the other.


[1919]

# Robert McAlmon
VILLAGE


The saloons are all closed now. Boards are across their doorways. Spiderwebs hang across the broken panes of glass.

Al Wilson would not have cared though if he were alive today. Long before prohibition was ever considered his wife had him blacklisted at all the saloons, and told the grocers not to sell him extracts of any sort; not to sell him anything in fact. She forced him to the cornsilos.

Poor gentile Mrs. Wilson! She had no cornsilo to make her forget her straits. She was a desolate figure, not made for desolation either. To the last she would wear gloves, neatly patched; would go to church every Sunday and march with dignity up the aisle to sing with her quavery soprano in the choir. To the last she would make calls and ask ladies to call upon her. She at least could do the correct thing if Alfred was a town character.

Other men—the tobacco chewers spitting from their benches at the livery stable, the church Deacon Davis whose walk home was ceremonial with hat lifting and circumspect gallantry, and with talks about the new minister for there was never a time when there was not a new minister—the other men, drinkers too but not "addicts" would, between their pool games, and talk about getting a new postoffice for the town, reminisce about the time when the Wilsons were first married. Everybody was so sure Alfred would make Congress—so fine a gentleman, and so brilliant a young attorney, "promising, Ha, Ha, Ha, but promises ain't allus kept" Gus the horseshoer would blow out over his tongue of snuff. Poor Al! no gitting around the fact that Mrs. Wilson was a charming woman, soft voice and so accomplished a musician—too nice; the ruination of Al!

Now all the Wilsons had was five children, and one of them not quite right. Alfred drunk, it was said, when—O yes, a sad case, a sad case.

The saloons are closed now. Last summer one young attorney shot himself because life was so dull in the old town, and a living so hard to make. "He didn't have likker to cheer him oop like Al Wilson did in his young days" Gus told me, as always, over his cud of Copenhagen snuff.

There may be other restless ones. One boy used to tell me that I was the only one "to understand." Understand? I could see that he was becoming one more of the restless ones—to what end?—but what is the end of an end?

Cobwebs and dusty broken window panes are in so many deserted buildings in the old town. Even the mudhole in which I learned to swim is dry, life is so dry, dusty dry there.

[1921]

# Jean Toomer
## KARINTHA

Her skin is like dusk on the eastern horizon,
O cant you see it, O cant you see it,
Her skin is like dusk on the eastern horizon
. . . When the sun goes down.

Men had always wanted her, this Karintha, even as a child, Karintha car-
rying beauty, perfect as dusk when the sun goes down. Old men rode
her hobby-horse upon their knees. Young men danced with her at frol-
ics when they should have been dancing with their grown-up girls. God
grant us youth, secretly prayed the old men. The young fellows counted
the time to pass before she would be old enough to mate with them.
This interest of the male, who wishes to ripen a growing thing too soon,
could mean no good to her.

Karintha, at twelve, was a wild flash that told the other folks just what
it was to live. At sunset, when there was no wind, and the pine-smoke
from over by the sawmill hugged the earth, and you couldnt see more
than a few feet in front, her sudden darting past you was a bit of vivid
color, like a black bird that flashes in light. With the other children one
could hear, some distance off, their feet flopping in the two-inch dust.
Karintha's running was a whir. It had the sound of the red dust that
sometimes makes a spiral in the road. At dusk, during the hush just
after the sawmill had closed down, and before any of the women had
started their supper-getting-ready songs, her voice, high-pitched, shrill,
would put one's ears to itching. But no one ever thought to make her
stop because of it. She stoned the cows, and beat her dog, and fought the
other children. . . . Even the preacher, who caught her at mischief, told
himself that she was as innocently lovely as a November cotton flower.
Already, rumors were out about her. Homes in Georgia are most often
built on the two-room plan. In one, you cook and eat, in the other you
sleep, and there love goes on. Karintha had seen or heard, perhaps she

had felt her parents loving. One could but imitate one's parents, for to follow them was the way of God. She played "home" with a small boy who was not afraid to do her bidding. That started the whole thing. Old men could no longer ride her hobby-horse upon their knees. But young men counted faster.

> Her skin is like dusk,
> O cant you see it,
> Her skin is like dusk,
> When the sun goes down.

Karintha is a woman. She who carries beauty, perfect as dusk when the sun goes down. She has been married many times. Old men remind her that a few years back they rode her hobby-horse upon their knees. Karintha smiles, and indulges them when she is in the mood for it. She has contempt for them. Karintha is a woman. Young men run stills to make her money. Young men go to the big cities and run on the road. Young men go away to college. They all want to bring her money. These are the young men who thought that all they had to do was to count time. But Karintha is a woman, and she has had a child. A child fell out of her womb onto a bed of pine-needles in the forest. Pine-needles are smooth and sweet. They are elastic to the feet of rabbits. . . . A sawmill was nearby. Its pyramidal sawdust pile smouldered. It is a year before one completely burns. Meanwhile, the smoke curls up and hangs in odd wraiths about the trees, curls up, and spreads itself out over the valley. . . . Weeks after Karintha returned home the smoke was so heavy you tasted it in water. Some one made a song:

> Smoke is on the hills. Rise up.
> Smoke is on the hills, O rise
> And take my soul to Jesus.

Karintha is a woman. Men do not know that the soul of her was a growing thing ripened too soon. They will bring their money; they will die not having found it out. . . . Karintha at twenty, carrying beauty, perfect as dusk when the sun goes down. Karintha. . . .

Her skin is like dusk on the eastern horizon,
O cant you see it, O cant you see it,
Her skin is like dusk on the eastern horizon
. . . When the sun goes down.

Goes down. . . .

[1922]

# Ernest Hemingway
L'ENVOI

*from* In Our Time

The king was working in the garden. He seemed very glad to see me. We walked through the garden. "This is the queen," he said. She was clipping a rose bush. "Oh, how do you do," she said. We sat down at a table under a big tree and the king ordered whisky and soda. "We have good whisky anyway," he said. The revolutionary committee, he told me, would not allow him to go outside the palace grounds. "Plastiras is a very good man, I believe," he said, "but frightfully difficult. I think he did right, though, shooting those chaps. If Kerensky had shot a few men things might have been altogether different. Of course, the great thing in this sort of an affair is not to be shot oneself."

It was very jolly. We talked for a long time. Like all Greeks he wanted to go to America.

[1924]

# Kay Boyle

## MONASTERY

Petalless vines of light stain the window with tendrils. Walls stretch their bleached dark-fibred limbs across the hill.

On the blue lake in his hair, his palms, white-throated, fold their wings and linger. Evening shuffles in as he walks, breaking radiant foliage on the sunset, bearing great bunches of rich black and seedless grapes.

∾

## WHORE STREET

Street bruised blue from the nudge of the wind, artery clogged with the setting sun. A white curtain trembles like a blade undrawn from the quick. Bed, baring firm iron limbs, scars the approach of darkness.

Breasts swing in slow delirious rhythm, caressing the odors that twitch unslaked in the gutter. Eyes press upon the withered mandarin of sun.

The night resmoothes his hair . . . memory dangling hot tongues . . . behind his eyes the white ripe fruit, the wine that crouches at the core . . . a white arm lifted, odor from the pit staining the sagging mattress of the sea.

[1925]

∾

## JANUARY 24, NEW YORK

### I

In one corner of the dormitory, near the roof, was a pigeon-cote in which more than fifty birds were cooing. The chief prisoner was a pigeon-fancier, the warden said with an apologetic smile. The detectives shifted their cigars in their mouths and looked wearily around the room. "Why, he's so soft-hearted he has to leave the building when the cook's killing one of the birds for his supper," the warden went on. "You know what he's in for?" snapped the commissioner. "Burglary, felonious assault, and homicide."

### II

The detectives went through the first tier of cells in the west wing, throwing out everything they found. The prisoners were driven out and they huddled at the end of the flats, some of them rouged, their eyebrows painted, two holding blankets around their naked shoulders. Out from the cells sailed corsets, compacts, perfume bottles, a blonde wig, nightgowns, high-heeled slippers and ladies' underwear. The detectives went up to the second tier and herded the prisoners out. "I wouldn't work here for a thousand berries a week," a detective said. "I'm just not that kind of a girl."

### III

The commissioner remarked that such characteristics were common in prison, but that it was disgusting to see them flaunted in this way. He didn't think he'd ever get over the shame of what he'd seen. The king-pin had a great weakness for lemonade, said the warden with an indulgent smile. The detectives pried open the locker in his cell: it was filled with tinned peaches, olives, pickled herrings, malted milk, copies of *The New Yorker*, and a deck of heroin. "If you lay a finger on my rosary," said the kingpin in a high falsetto, "I warn you I'll scream."

[1936]

# William Faulkner
## THE PRIEST

Evening like a nun shod with silence, evening like a girl slipping along the wall to meet her lover. . . . The twilight is like the breath of contented kine, stirring among the lilacs and shaking spikes of bloom, ringing the soundless bells of hyacinths dreaming briefly of Lesbos, whispering among the pale and fronded palms.

Ah, God, ah, God. The moon is a silver sickle about to mow the rose of evening from the western sky; the moon is a little silver boat on green and shoreless seas. Ave, Maria, dream. . . . How like birds with golden wings the measured bell notes fly outward and upward, passing with clear and faint regret the ultimate slender rush of cross and spire; and how like the plummet lark the echo, singing, falls. Ave, Maria. . . . Ah God, ah God, that night should come so soon.

Orion through the starry meadows strays, the creaking Wain breaks darkly through the Milky Way's faint dewed grass. Sorrow, and love that passeth away. Ave, Maria! a little silver virgin, hurt and sad and pitiful, remembering Jesus' mouth upon her breast. Mortification, and the flesh like a babe crying among dark trees . . . "hold my hair fast, and kiss me through it—so: Ah, God, ah God, ah God, that day should be soon!"

Ave, Maria; deam gratiam . . . tower of ivory, rose of Lebanon. . . .

[1925]

# Sherwood Anderson
## THE LAME ONE

At night when there are no lights my city is a man who arises from a bed to stare into darkness.

In the daytime my city is the son of a dreamer. He has become the companion of thieves and prostitutes. He has denied his father.

My city is a thin old man who lives in a rooming house in a dirty street. He wears false teeth that have become loose and make a sharp clicking noise when he eats. He cannot find himself a woman and indulges in self-abuse. He picks cigar ends out of the gutter.

My city lives in the roofs of houses, in the eaves. A woman came to my city and he threw her far down out of the eaves on a pile of stones. Nobody knew. Those who live in my city declare she fell.

There is an angry man whose wife is unfaithful. He is my city.
My city is in his hair, in his eyes. When he breathes his breath is the breath of my city.

There are many cities standing in rows. There are cities that sleep, cities that stand in the mud of a swamp.
I have come here to my city.
I have walked with my city.
I have limped slowly forward at night with my city.

My city is very strange. It is tired and nervous. My city has become a woman whose mother is ill. She creeps in the hallway of a house and listens in the darkness at the door of a room.

I cannot tell what my city is like.
My city is a kiss from the feverish lips of many tired people.
My city is a murmur of voices coming out of a pit.

[1930]

# Kenneth Patchen
## FAMILY PORTRAIT

Great tarry wings splatter softly up out of the rotting yolk of sun. In the millyard the statue of an old bastard with a craggy grin is turning shit-colored above the bowed heads of the new shift crunching in between the piles of slag. . . . That's my father washing at the kitchen sink. The grimy water runs into the matted hair of his belly. The smell of Lava soap and sweat adds its seasoning to the ham and cabbage. On the other side of town a train whistles. Tearing shadows fill the steaming room. Wind rushes out of my old man with the sound of a thunderclap, and my sister vigorously rattles the lid of a pot. In the parlor my grandfather lies, two days dead. "Aye, and the only statue for him's a spade in 'is stumpy teeth now."—"A lapful of withered nuts to make the muckin grasses grow. . . ."—"Hush you are, for here be the priest with his collar so tidy and straight."—"Liked his bit of drink, he did, God take the long thirst out of his soul and all." I remember once after a brush with Mrs. Hannan, who happened to be passing hard under his window one morning, he told me, "Ah, there's only one thing worse than the rich, my lad . . . and that's the poor, and that's the ruckin, lyin, unmannerin, snivelin poor, my lad!" and a great whip of tobacco juice lashed out into the dust of the road. On, on into the small hours went the singing and the laughing and the gay, wonderful story-telling . . . and the wax of the candles dripping slowly down on his stiff, dark clothes.

[1949]

∾

# THERE *ARE* TWO

Ways about it. In fact, that only scratches the surface; for—well, had you seen the weeds, the weeds—even those weeds growing just below the outer edge of the wall! that would fix you! Crested . . . tubular . . . a few with—well, sort of hands. . . .

In fact, I told my friend Flip, "Flip, you've got to do something about those weeds, especially those weeds down there just under the stains along the wall by the gate." But as usual he was monkeying around the car. It was almost dark by the time he got downstairs again, and the first thing he said was: "Do you want that other set of pipes inside, or do you want them curled around the hood?"

I told him curled around would be just dandy as a pair of little pink panties.

So. You know how it is. Sure, I had come there looking for that elusive oyster, happiness. Yep, that's what I was after, that goddam little sad-faced, buck-toothed oyster, happiness. And what had I got? Do I *really* have to tell you?

After a while I went out and climbed up on top of the wall. It had started to rain again. Pretty soon it was coming down in the large economy size buckets. I tore up all my identification papers and stripped down to where I had only one shoe and my hat on. Then I stood up on my hind legs and shouted: "So! Enough's enough, you lousy, scrounging bastards! I'm off to join the Indians, see!" Then taking my other shoe off, I added: "And while you're about it, to hell with the Indians too, for that matter!"

[1949]

⌇

## WHEN WE WERE HERE TOGETHER

When we were here together in a place we did not know, nor one another.

A bit of grass held between the teeth for a moment, bright hair on the wind. What we were we did not know, nor ever the grass or the flame of hair turning to ash on the wind.

But they lied about that. From the beginning they lied. To the child, telling him that there was somewhere anger against him, and a hatred against him, and only for the reason of his being in the world. But never did they tell him that the only evil and danger was in themselves; that they alone were the poisoners and the betrayers; that they—they *alone*—were responsible for what was being done in the world.

And they told the child to starve and to kill the child that was within him; for only by doing this could he safely enter their world; only by doing this could be become a useful and adjusted member of the community which they had prepared for him. And this time, alas, they did not lie.

And with the death of the child was born a thing that had neither the character of a man nor the character of a child, but was a horrible and monstrous parody of the two; and it is in his world now the flesh of man's spirit lies twisted and despoiled under the indifferent stars.

When we were here together in a place we did not know, nor one another. O green this bit of warm grass between our teeth—O beautiful the hair of our mortal goddess on the indifferent wind.

[1957]

# Nelson Algren
## NOBODY KNOWS WHERE O'CONNOR WENT

*from* Chicago: City on the Make

An October sort of city even in spring. With somebody's washing always whipping, in smoky October colors off the third-floor rear by that same wind that drives the yellowing comic strips down all the gutters that lead away from home. A hoarse-voiced extry-hawking newsie of a city.

By its padlocked poolrooms and its nightshade neon, by its carbarn Christs punching transfers all night long; by its nuns studying gin-fizz ads in the Englewood Local, you shall know Chicago.

By nights when the yellow salamanders of the El bend all one way and the cold rain runs with the red-lit rain. By the way the city's million wires are burdened only by lightest snow; and the old year yet lighter upon them. When chairs are stacked and glasses are turned and arc-lamps all are dimmed. By days when the wind bangs alley gates ajar and the sun goes by on the wind. By nights when the moon is an only child above the measured thunder of the cars, you may know Chicago's heart at last:

You'll know it's the place built out of Man's ceaseless failure to overcome himself. Out of Man's endless war against himself we build our successes as well as our failures. Making it the city of all cities most like Man himself—loneliest creation of all this very old poor earth.

And Shoeless Joe, who lost his honor and his job, is remembered now more fondly here, when stands are packed and a striped sun burns across them, than old Comiskey, who salvaged his own.

On hot and magic afternoons when only the press box, high overhead, divides the hustler and the square.

For there's a left-hander's wind moving down Thirty-fifth, rolling the summer's last straw kelly across second into center, where fell the winning single of the first winning Comiskey team in thirty-two seasons.

Thirty-two American League seasons (and Lord knows how many

swindles ago), Nephew is doing thirty days again for the fifteenth or the thirty-ninth time (this time for defacing private property), nobody knows where O'Connor went and a thousand Happy-Days-Are-Here-Again tunes have come and gone. And the one that keeps coming back softest of all, when tavern lights come on and the night is impaled by the high-tension wires, goes:

It's only a paper moon
Hanging over a cardboard sea

For everybody takes care of himself under this paper moon, and the hustlers still handle the cardboard. Joe Felso doesn't trouble his pointy little head just because somebody tossed a rock through some other Joe Felso's window two doors down. It wasn't his window and it wasn't his rock and we all have our own troubles, Jack.

The big town is getting something of Uncle Johnson's fixed look, like that of a fighter working beyond his strength and knowing it. "Laughing even as an ignorant fighter laughs, who has never lost a battle," the white-haired poet wrote before his hair turned white.

But the quality of our laughter has altered since that appraisal, to be replaced by something sounding more like a juke-box running down in a deserted bar. Chicago's laughter has grown metallic, the city no longer laughs easily and well, out of spiritual good health. We seem to have no way of judging either the laughter of the living or the fixed smirk of the dead.

The slums take their revenge. How much did he *have,* is what we demand to know when we hear good old Joe Felso has gone to his reward. Never what was he, in human terms. Was his income listed publicly? Was there a Ford in his future at the very moment he was snatched? And whether he was of any use or any joy to himself, when he had his chance for use and joy, we never seem to wonder. It's hustle and bustle from day to day, chicken one day and feathers the next, and nobody knows where O'Connor went.

Nobody will tell how Tommy got free.

Nor whether there are well-springs here for men beneath the rubble of last year's revelry.

The pig-wallows are paved, great Diesels stroke noiselessly past the clamorous tenements of home. The constellations move, silently and all unseen, through blowing seas above the roofs. Only the measured clatter of the empty cars, where pass the northbound and the southbound Els, comes curving down the constant boundaries of night.

The cemetery that yet keeps the Confederate dead is bounded by the same tracks that run past Stephen A. Douglas' remains. The jail where Parsons hung is gone, and the building from which Bonfield marched is no more. Nobody remembers the Globe on Desplaines, and only a lonely shaft remembers the four who died, no one ever understood fully why. And those who went down with the proud steamer *Chicora* are one with those who went down on the *Eastland*. And those who sang "My God, How the Money Rolls In" are one with those who sang, "Brother, Can You Spare a Dime?"

And never once, on any midnight whatsoever, will you take off from here without a pang. Without forever feeling something priceless is being left behind in the forest of furnished rooms, lost forever down below, beneath the miles and miles of lights and lights. With the slow smoke blowing compassionately across them like smoke across the spectrum of the heart. As smoky rainbows dreaming, and fading as they dream, across those big fancy Southside jukes forever inviting you to put another nickel in, put another nickel in whether the music is playing or not.

As the afternoon's earliest juke-box beats out rumors of the Bronzeville night.

A rumor of neon flowers, bleeding all night long, along those tracks where endless locals pass.

Leaving us empty-handed every hour on the hour.

Remembering nights, when the moon was a buffalo moon, that the narrow plains between the billboards were touched by an Indian wind. Littered with tin cans and dark with smoldering rubble, an Indian wind yet finds, between the shadowed canyons of The Loop, patches of prairie to touch and pass.

Between the curved steel of the El and the nearest Clark Street hockshop, between the penny arcade and the shooting gallery, between the basement gin-mill and the biggest juke in Bronzeville, the prairie is caught for keeps at last. Yet on nights when the blood-red neon of the tavern legends tether the arc-lamps to all the puddles left from last night's rain, somewhere between the bright carnival of the boulevards and the dark girders of the El, ever so far and ever so faintly between the still grasses and the moving waters, clear as a cat's cry on a midnight wind, the Pottawattomies mourn in the river reeds once more.

The Pottawattomies were much too square. They left nothing behind but their dirty river.

While we shall leave, for remembrance, one rusty iron heart.

The city's rusty heart, that holds both the hustler and the square.

Takes them both and holds them there.

For keeps and a single day.

[1951]

# Walter Lowenfels
## JUKEBOX IN THE COALFIELDS

It's Rosefield Gardens, Richeyville, teen-age coke bar in this Appalachian coalfield. You dance here or not at all. Unless you are older and go to Bentleyville, and mix on the crowded floor where the Polka Dots are making jive and the admission is 85 cents at the door.

The girls come into the coke bar from the cold night with kerchiefs on their heads. They swish behind a partition and emerge with freshly fluffed hair, to the tunes of *St. Louis Blues* or *Kisses Sweeter than Wine*. And Bill steps off with Hannah, and Ed puts his cigarette aside. What does the jukebox say?

You will hear its song on winter avenues or where the wolves prowl on Rocky Mountain snows. It vibrates in the submerged nine-tenths of icebergs floating down the Atlantic from the Spitzbergen side of the pole.

Drown Bill and Hannah in coke, pour coal dust over them like a shower bath—they will go down once, twice—but the third time you will find them coming up like Venus on a sea shell, singing and swaying away. There is no silence here, and the miners young and old have a language that draws black music from the earth and keeps the world in a singing boil.

It is within giant peripheries that choices of action protrude like stalactites among the icy caverns of the mines. You will not know the coal miner from a word, only in some secret crevice of his blind will-to-be.

[1964]

### PART II

# The Party Train

# Duane Ackerson
## THE CHAMELEON AT HOME

The chameleon is at home everywhere but in its own house. There, all threats removed, no need for camouflage, it feels bled of everything but itself. It isn't blending with anything; whether chair, table, mirror, or bed; and, affecting these by its presence, it feels invisible in its very visibility. Each time a chameleon sees itself in the mirror, it sees nothing there to mimic, and feels like a vampire would feel seeing its own reflection. Rising from the bed, seeing an imprint on the mattress and sheets, the chameleon feels like a footprint emptied of its food, standing there, not knowing where to go.

~

## FIRE

Once, fire was used to put out water. When a house was drowning, buckets of fire were heaped on water till the house was dry. Two-thirds of the earth, scholars say, was once covered with fire; when the sun went down in the sea, it came up even hotter; when sailors saw all that fire, they thought dragons lived on the other side of the seas, and never went there. The people on the other side thought the same, and stayed home boiling potatoes in kettles of fire by turning on the water on the stove. With only water to heat their kettles of fire, a lot of houses drowned, a lot of fire that couldn't be spared was used in bailing out homes. The seas shrank enough so people could cross them, and when they didn't find dragons, the seas went away altogether. Now we have to gather up every lightning bolt that breaks for enough fire to water our gardens.

~

## THE MINUS TOUCH

A man developed a magic word that would turn gold into lead. He tried it first on cufflinks; at the mention of the word, all the gold cufflinks in the world turned to lead. Then on old people's fillings, next jewelry, both with the same results. Feeling ambitious, he tried it on lost Aztec and Spanish treasure, Swiss bankers, and finally Ft. Knox. What an abundance of wealth in the world! At last, an international monetary standard based on what everyone had: those heavy shoes with which they shuffled to school or work, the lead the boss was always telling them to get out of their seats, those toy soldiers, cherished from long ago childhoods, still at their posts, bayonets fixed, guarding golden moments.

# Steven Ajay
## MORNING SHIFT IN BANARAS

*"For Hindus, death is not the opposite of life, it is rather the opposite of birth."*
—*Diana Eck*, Banaras: City of Light

I

They say this is the fast track for Hindus; here the river is more full of air than anywhere, coming from such a height in the Himalayas to heal itself, flowing north through Banaras but south everywhere else. When you feel the fading you head this way. Of course, I have come to see it happen, am sitting on the steps of the burning ghat but this is not happening for me to see. I try to write it down: the oldest story in the oldest city, the only place in India where there's a queue.

II

The first sight becomes memory and is lost; 11:53, I look again: the noon heat and the heat of the two burning pyres holding me in my place, the water buffalo casting great pools of shade beside themselves, small birds scattering and moving, chattering silhouettes of school children. I see them from where I sit, I see them singing, playing in the cool basements of buildings; the doms staggering under their headloads of wood, spilling them down like thunder into the scooped out burning grounds, the four hollows packed hard with ash and earth and shadows. This is the doms' work, the untouchable craft of the dead, only theirs—passed on; father to son and further and held.

III

Fifteen feet from me, in the Ganges, hundreds of brilliant garlands of marigolds hug the barges that come across the river with sand, sand to build; the barges parked beneath the sweet smoke of bone and flesh where the doms' work is split precisely, split into the wood, the tax and the fire; the headloaders who sell the wood, those who collect and the fire attendants who poke, stir and reset, give their attention to the dead lying in their small but bright orange flames, to the smoking, blazing, smoldering stages of fires—and there are the final hunters who rake through the cooling ash and embers.

IV

As the temperature rises—the flames mixing with the high sun—a white goat steps onto the stone slab in front of me, punches her mother's teat as the morning shift comes to an end and the doms begin to bathe in the river only one arm's length below the burning pyres, their movements meticulous, their undressing unselfconscious, always covering the genitals, always squatting down, always turning away as they piss into the river. But this is not the end; there is no stopping with this graceful washing. A one-legged man is standing watching the bodies; he leans into his crutch, shields his eyes from the heat.

V

There is no wind today; four boats are being rowed, slowly; cows sit still in the sun smart as carvings as the corpses keep coming without commotion like snakes winding out of stone through the narrow streets to the top of the ghat, keep coming wrapped in red and gold silk; are carried down the steps, are gently lowered and left on the steps, their feet at an angle to the river.

VI

On the platform above me a family argues the tax but no grieving, no tears, no wailing to pain the dead while other bodies arrive covered with flowers, are brought down and dipped in and set on their wood, in the still warm hollows.

VII

While flecks of ash are falling on my pants and shirt and in the thick, sweet smoke of bone and flesh, an eldest son completes his circles counterclockwise around his father, everything backwards at the time of death, as he takes the flaming Kusha grass from the doms' eternal fire and reaches towards his father, smoke beginning, the straw lighting under the body, igniting the ghee, lighting the kindling and the silk, the sandalwood oil, the precious timber arched over the chest; his father now an offering to the fire, the fire conveying the offering to heaven before the escalating crackle of fat and finally the weightlessness: the rite of the skull, the long bamboo stick cracking the skull releasing the soul and all of this while the men from the morning shift are still washing themselves with both hands, rubbing each muscle, drying and oiling themselves. So, after all their hauling of wood, the haggling, after all the heat and ash and hunting, dressed in egg-white tops and rich red lunghis, the men are ready to walk home, to eat, to rest, to live until tomorrow.

# Robert Alexander
## AT THE PARTY

Ralph has just bought himself a new pair of red sneakers. The catalpa tree beyond his porch has fragrant trumpet-shaped flowers among the huge leaves. When Ralph looks closely at the catalpa flowers, he sees on the pale blooms red streaks the same color as his new sneakers.

Across the street spring pigeons call each other names. She sat there, the window was open and the surf of traffic mixed with the warm air.

Saturday night, at the party, Fred asks him, Why red? They were on sale, says Ralph, the only ones left. When Ralph gets home the night air is still warm and, falling asleep, he can smell the catalpa flowers.

$\sim$

## FINDING TOKEN CREEK

> *Oh, and I have watched you, fish of*
> *heaven, here in Wisconsin.*
> —Jim Hazard

Before the Yahara enters Lake Mendota, it widens out and flows through Cherokee Marsh. The marsh surrounds a fairly wide river there, in some places nearly a hundred yards from shore to shore. From a canoe on the water there are of course some houses visible, but often it appears that you are paddling out in the wilderness, blue water and sky surrounding you, green trees and marsh-grass, low hills down where the river flows into the marsh. Along the shore are reeds and cattails, pickerelweed with its large arrowhead leaves, wild bergamot.

Yesterday was one of the last true spring days around here before summer comes along and fills the air with moisture, the sun too hot at midday to stay out in for the two or three hours it takes to paddle to the river at the head of the marsh from the gravel parking lot down at the end of the dirt road that School Street becomes if you follow it long enough, way off behind the shed where the highway department stores its winter plows. The marsh is protected, no cars allowed for its entire length—and that's why from out on the water few houses are visible. The wide buffer of marsh between the river and subdivisions is nearly impenetrable this late in June with blackberry patches poison ivy and interwoven willows and oaks.

Yesterday the wind was blowing from the northeast. The wind very rarely blows from the northeast around here, only when there's a strong weather system sitting right over Hudson Bay, turning the air down upon us after it passes over the thirty-five degree water of Lake Superior three hundred or so miles to the north. This makes it especially a pleasure to be out paddling around—my dog sitting in front of me in the bow—since it means that returning I won't have to fight the prevailing northwesterlies that at ten or twenty knots can make the return trip something to think about. Nothing of that sort this afternoon, just the prospect of a pleasant tailwind going home, easing me along. The sky clear. Air cool in the hot sun. Smell of sun-hot skin.

In falling the willow blocked what could have been the mouth of a stream, but off to one side, what I'd missed on previous trips, is a small break in the cattails—and through it I can see water. I gather speed and slip through, my dog ahead of me unsure of what I'm doing shrinks back from the cattails coming at her from both sides of the canoe, and then we're out into open water, another flowing stream, nearly invisible from the Yahara. Barely ten feet across but deeper than the Yahara, faster flowing and colder. Willows and cattails to the sides, blue sky overhead.

It has rained heavily in the last couple of days, and the surface of Token Creek is filled with bits of mud moving downstream. The river here twists in doglegs around which I sweep in my short and maneuverable canoe, keeping to the inside though not so far as to get hung up on the little sandbars that form on the inside of the curves. I cross one such bar, sweeping around into the new stretch of the creek, and upstream I see that a willow has dropped a branch or two onto the water's surface, so that mud and flotsam is piled up against the upstream side. And it's here that my dog and I see something remarkable.

What it looks like is a kind of underwater flower, about ten of them strung out just upstream of the willow branches—ten or so flowers the bright orange color of daylilies. And there's a sound like very small pebbles dropping into water. As we drift closer, slowing against the current (I am careful not to paddle, not even to move), I see that these flowers are in fact the mouths of carp just breaking the surface, then moving underwater to swallow. These delicate orange flowers are the mouths of feeding carp, huge fish the color of murky water visible just beneath the surface. My dog is watching all this too; she too sees the large fish with complacent faces opening their orange mouths to the creek's surface. While the wind blows uncommonly from the cloudless northeast.

～

## A JOE PASS GUITAR SOLO

I've fallen asleep in the afternoon. It's November and the radio is playing a jazz program from the local public radio station. But my father and I are in Fenway Park. It's June and the outfield grass is dark green (darker than the huge green left-field wall) and my father has just bought one of those ten-cent paper bags of peanuts (it must be close to a full pound of peanuts for a dime). We're both eating peanuts. My father's hands—which seem huge to me, the back covered with veins "like a roadmap" as he used to say—are deft as hell with the peanuts. Crack, and he tosses them into his mouth, the shells drop through the green slats of the seat.

It's the eighth inning and the Red Sox are behind by five runs. Ted Williams is batting and my father points out to me how perfect his swing is. "Look at that bastard swing," my father says, "level as Nebraska." I don't think my father was ever in Nebraska. "But remember, Rob," he says, "he only hit .400 in his really good years. . . . Even at his best Ted Williams missed the ball six times out of ten."

It's getting to the end of my dream. I'm in that funny place where you're dreaming but you're also aware of the room around you. There's late-afternoon sun through the plants in my window and it sounds like Joe Pass on the radio, bass and piano comping in the background. Joe Pass's left hand is going all over the fingerboard of his arch-top Gibson and his right hand is in perfect time. The notes are like tropical birds flying from the small speaker of my radio . . . and suddenly all these bright yellow and blue and orange birds come circling and wheeling into Fenway Park. My father and I look up amazed at the bird-filled June sky.

# Bert Almon
## THE CLEMATIS SEMINAR

While my colleagues were listening to Dr. Christopher Norris of the University of Cardiff deflating Derrida's detractors, I was in St. Albert, Alberta, at Hole's Nurseries, sneaking into a nurseryman's workshop with a purloined invitation, listening to Raymond Evison, late of Wales now of Guernsey, talk about clematis.

Clematis can climb a high trellis like a convoluted argument, holding on with tendrils that snap if you try to help them wrap around the wood. The growing range is great, from Guernsey in the Gulf Stream to the cold mountains of China. "These would be hardy for you," he kept telling the Alberta nurserymen, "but these would not be hardy for you."

Not being at the deconstruction seminar, I can assure you that Dr. Norris deconstructed Derrida's deconstructors, but I can't tell you how many minuses make a plus.

Mr. Evison showed slides of his trip to Szechuan on a quest for new varieties of clematis. Bad roads and dysentery couldn't stop him, but altitude sickness finally turned him back. Dr. Norris can breathe the most rarefied atmosphere. Evison took only seeds, leaving the local plants undisturbed. Now his gardeners are growing them under glass in Guernsey.

Typical enemies of the cultivar: wilt, cultural materialism, slugs and snails, the insinuation of speech-acts, mice and rabbits, power-brokers and neopragmatists, not to mention winds toppling a top-heavy growth. But the root is very thick and the plant should never be given up for dead. It likes to keep its feet wet and out of the direct sun.

For the literary the varieties include Daniel Deronda and Fair Rosamond. For the French speaker, Etoile de Paris. The empirically British will savor Mrs. Cholmondelay, Sir Garent Wolseley, and Guernsey Cream. Mr. Evison has named one plant for his daughter. My notes do not contain the name, not even in the margins.

I do not think that Dr. Norris will winter-over in Alberta.

≈

## LOMBARD STREET

I am charmed by Lombard Street, the ancient center of the Italian money-lenders who replaced the exiled Jews under the first three Edwards. Now the street is filled with banks and insurance companies but antique signs hang high over the pavements, like the golden grasshopper of the Banque Paribas. If I wanted to save here I would prefer a bank with a golden ant to tide me over the winters of recession. The grasshopper came from the coat of arms of Sir Thomas Gresham, founder of the Royal Exchange one street over, the author of Gresham's Law: bad money drives out good. Pope was born on a cul-de-sac off Lombard Street and Lloyd's Coffeehouse buzzed with culture till a delirium of caffeine transmuted it into an insurance consortium.

My favorite sign is the golden Cat & the Fiddle, another fabular frivolity, home of the Mitsubishi Trust House, heirs of the Lombardy bankers and the newest scapegoats for the decline of the West. I half expect Ezra Pound to wander by chanting "usury, usury." Other signs that once hung over the street were The Golden Fleece & Artichoke, The Hat & Feathers, and The Queen's Head & Sun. Over the door of Mitsubishi Trust House are carved three entwined buxom women, but they never represented a brothel. Emblems of the insurance industry, the woman with the griffin's head represents the hazards of foreseeing the future, the woman with the torch symbolizes fire, and the woman with the caduceus beside the anchor stands for hazards of the ocean. Lloyd's of London has shipwrecked in the Gulf War and other disasters. The new gesture of English tellers and clerks is to hold the big notes up to the light to check for the hologram and the silver thread, but bad money drives out good money in an endless cycle. Nowhere do I see a great sign with the golden serpent Ourobouros swallowing his own tail.

～

## PERSEID SHOWER

The whole family reclines in wicker chairs on the patio, eyes up for the shower, debris of a comet. Last year the full moon in the southeastern sky blocked the view but picked out the white clematis on the trellis while leaving the purple ones invisible. This year the lights of cars and buses carry over the fence once in a while, but we quickly accustom ourselves to the dark as the cones of the retina sign off, the color receptors, and the rods that distinguish shapes grow acute. I like this kind of seeing: there is no place and no time in particular to look, and the peripheral vision picks up the falling star on the verge of going out. A satellite moves contrariwise to the celestial hemisphere, and once in a while a plane goes over with its landing lights bright for the airport. One after another, absolutely unpredictably, the bits of combustible iron meet the atmosphere, with an instant clash of temperaments. Sparks fly. After an hour sore necks drive us inside but I lie awake for a while knowing that the bright lights are still streaking the sky's black negative.

# Jack Anderson
## THE PARTY TRAIN

To bring joy and friendliness to the New York subway system, which is all too often bleak and indifferent, I propose that a special train be instituted to be known as The Party Train. Each day, this train would follow one or another of the city's existing routes, sometimes on the local, sometimes on the express tracks. No extra fare would be charged, the cars would be painted exactly the same as those of any other train, but inside there would be a perpetual party. The poles and straps would be festooned with streamers, and Japanese lanterns would hang from the ceiling. Food and drink would always be available, ranging from corned beef to caviar, from beer to champagne. Strolling musicians would roam from car to car. And the last car would be transformed into a gigantic bed where anyone could take a date, no questions asked.

The Party Train would not only be fun to ride, the very knowledge of its existence would be a source of cheer. For the route it would follow on any given day would never be announced in advance, but would always come as a fresh surprise. Thus any citizen waiting in any station could hope that the next train to pull in—accompanied by a shower of confetti and a whiff of pot smoke—would be The Party Train, so he could step aboard and glut himself on cashew nuts and kisses from the Battery to the Bronx. Or if he were in a local station and The Party Train happened to be an express that day, he could watch it rumble by, glimpsing paper hats and saxophones bouncing in the front cars and naked bodies flickering among the pillows at the back. Then he would chuckle to himself, glad that there was something interesting to look at while waiting for the subway, and wishing that tomorrow The Party Train might finally stop for him.

≈

RETURN TO WORK

I have returned to the job from which I was fired a whole decade ago. The funny thing is, no one recognizes me.

The same fat jolly bleached-blonde woman who was my department head then is my department head now. We get along well together. From the very first we share favorite jokes.

The same vice-president who fired me then is vice-president still. He is tall, skinny, nervous—he twitches. He doesn't like my looks, he keeps lecturing me about duty. Yet he has to approve my appointment. What a bastard he is.

And there at their desks are all my pals from the old days. Bill, Carolyn, Russ, Al, Serena, David, Monty, and Cliff. Just as before.

And not one of them recognizes me. I have begun anew, totally anew.

Sometimes I think my fat blonde department head recognizes me. She smiles at me as though she's guessed my secret. But I know that's a subject she'll never bring up. Best of all, the skinny bastard vice-president, though he may not like my looks, doesn't realize who I am.

So I sit at my desk as though I never sat there before. I sit there powerful in my secret knowledge. How wonderful.

I am a new man. How wonderful. How wonderful it is to return to work

⁓

## THE SOMNAMBULISTS' HOTEL

Only sleepwalkers stay there. When they get to town, something draws them to the place, even if they already have reservations somewhere else. Checking in, smiling shyly, they glance about the lobby. Yet they give no sign they are in any way special. And, like everyone else, they see the sights or do business by day and spend their evenings in restaurants or theatres.

But late at night all return to their rooms at the very same time and almost in unison switch off their lights and climb into bed. Their hearts beat faster in happy expectation, yet they cannot say why. Soon, sleep comes to them all.

Then in each room, as the moonlight pours in, a sudden wind lifts the sheets off the beds and sets them swirling. The guests rise up, too. Still deep in sleep, they step out of bed while the sheets drop behind them like swaddling bands or shrouds.

Some leap to the window ledges and teeter above the street. Others climb the fire escape to the roof where they race back and forth, holding their heads high and throwing their arms wide in the glimmering starlight.

Some—after opening their closets and finding strange apparel there—put on these garments and venture into the corridors. Clinging to the walls, some struggle in the wind that has now become a great gale. Yet in another corridor only a gentle breeze blows. Women in white nightgowns float through these halls, skimming along in toe shoes, lighted candles in their hands, their long hair streaming loose behind them.

Other guests take the elevator down to the lobby. Fluttering aigrette fans, women in century-old evening dress glide past the night clerk (who never looks up from his paperback novel) and waltz around the ballroom to music only they can hear. Whirling deliriously and breathing harder, they pelt each other with lilies, then stagger as if ready to fall in a swoon.

Yet when City Hall clock strikes the first hour of dawning and the garbage men come banging along, the guests quiet down and, after fumbling their way back to their rooms, lock the doors and sink into bed.

You can find them the next morning at breakfast in the coffee shop. They are quiet, all of them, and very reserved. Each sits alone. No one speaks. Yet each looks rested and curiously content.

All at that moment are trying to remember something that happened to them in the night, something their minds cannot quite piece together, but something they know was strangely nice. This hotel is distinctly nice, they decide. They smile their shy smiles and glance about at all the nice people. Surely there must be some secret they share. Buttered toast is chewed in meditation. And all vow to stay here should fate ever lead them this way again.

# Daniel Bachhuber
## FELL IN LOVE, GOT MARRIED

You step out of the car—your first blind date, ever. You've grilled your sister on this woman's looks and worry about the size of her nose. It's no secret, being thirty, you are looking for a permanent way out of your loneliness, a form of deductive reasoning that has led you through fourteen dates in three months with fourteen different women. She sits on a cement stoop, creamy soft complexion, lots of gray in her hair, a lavender sweater. She is four years older than you, but so what? As you walk closer you realize there is nothing wrong with her nose. You fall in love for the rest of your life.

You have dinner at your sister's house, imagine you are an amazingly charming guy and keep your hat on throughout dinner. She spends a lot of time talking to your sister. They met each other in a poetry class. Your brother-in-law passes you the salt. The next night she tries hard to say no, she doesn't want to go out. You get angry, claim you didn't drive three hundred and fifty miles for one date. It had to be two, and how could she justify breaking that promise, which she in fact never made? She finds something funny in all this, is intrigued by someone who could get angry at a total stranger. You end up at "Lyle's" in Minneapolis and she tells you the story of her life. You smoke seven cigarettes which causes her to take an asthma pill, but in the back of your mind you take it on faith the two of you can still live in the same apartment. As you listen, you fall in love with her courage. She falls in love with you because of the handwriting on the letter you send three days later, in which you say things about her intelligence and courage and how you have to see her again soon.

At the wedding, friends play a Mendelssohn trio that has you both crying at the altar. It is the perfect moment of placing two lives in the hands of yes, but you never could have guessed how much labor God would have to do, how hard and wrong the world would seem, for those two lives to work together.

≈

RASPBERRY PICKING

My son and I found them halfway up the abandoned road, dangerously juicy. We eased the berries gently from their white posts and thumped them into the bowl in his lap, and fingered some squishy berries into my mouth, the first burst of tart sweet juice giving way to tiny seeds pressed between the teeth. As we slowly gorged our appetites, I thought about bears. I wondered how a bear could feed itself eating berries. Did it take them off with its mouth or with its paw, eat the whole bush or neatly remove single berries? And how many berries would it take? And mightn't the expenditure of energy required to pick a single berry equal the caloric count of each, leaving the bear just as hungry as when he began? Or maybe they pick together, one bear lounging and eating while the other toils, and they trade off so that each bear gets fed every other day. Red juice stained our fingers, my son's mouth, my pants. We picked another bowlful. By this time we had berry vision. The road and forest hung with red lobes larger than coins.

～

## SHOE SALESMAN

He is like a psychic medium calling down shoes from the other world. He litters the floor with half-opened boxes, the appearance of living beings inside: a bunch of heels with leather jackets and big tongues. My feet can't decide whether they want to live in a ranch house on the plains or a rowhouse in Boston, with iron grillwork on the balcony. I can't believe he's being this patient with me. I know what he's thinking by the way he gazes out the window, an attitude of abstracted indifference cultivated for effect. He knows that one of those pairs of shoes is trying to communicate with me but he isn't sure which, and if he were to meet my eyes or speak, it might fuzz the message. He has only spoken once. His words, "People who think too much about the heel slipping usually end up with a pair of shoes that fit too tight," were precise. He knows that by my compulsive perfectionism I have made my whole life fit like a too tight shoe. He is as surprised as I am when I cradle the rowhouse in Boston and I am walking in them as I used to walk in the Italian Alps, and I am shopping in them as I used to shop at the fruttivendolo. Buddha-like, he upturns slightly the corners of his mouth, in satisfaction, not for money—he is deeper than money—but for love; the way, in Italy, good fruit and vegetables found their way into my plastic sack in spite of my italiano cattivo, a silent waterfall of incarnations tumbling from nonbeing into the flesh, and I say, "Yes I will yes I will yes."

# Michael Benedikt
## THE TOYMAKER GLOOMY BUT THEN AGAIN
## SOMETIMES HAPPY

(1) How can a person practically drowning in our usual, daily, dirty, di-
urnal dreck possibly attempt to engage, full-time, in the production of
Magical objects? That is a simple question which, I imagine, virtually
every person who prides himself on being both a serious craftsperson and
a good citizen of our ordinary, everyday world must, after all, ask him-
self or herself every now and then. Good heavens!—just try waking up
first thing in the morning with a few nice, clear Visions of Bliss in your
head, and then try perambulating just a few blocks beyond the relative
safety and calm of your own house or apartment—and see how long
your otherwise probably quite cheery, creative, early-morning attitude
survives even *that* little stroll into madness and disorder! Yes, if only as
a form of mental exercise, just try calculating the exact effect that even
your very first everyday encounters with the external world and the
people in it, exert upon you and your early-morning psyche and dispo-
sition   and see then whether *you* feel like going around all day long,
thinking playful, creative thoughts, chuckling pleasantly to yourself,
and generally smiling and laughing! (2) I don't know how you feel about
it, but for years and years, particularly from the point of view of a per-
son practicing our own, would-be benignly optimistic profession—that
of struggling Manufacturers of colorful and sometimes even relatively
amusing toys—I've felt that this constant placing of myself into bad
moods by the conventional world, practically amounts to theft! Theft
of my good moods, theft of my creative, inventive capacities—theft of
my peace-of-mind! Don't you, yourself, think that most of us spend a
whole lot more time than we should have to, defending ourselves against
the incursions of a virtual slew of tedious mentalities, intent on slipping
themselves into our mental or even actual billfolds? (3) Still, we press
on! As devoted Toymakers, of course, we must! The children, after all,
want to be entertained! The public is practically crying out for novelty!
(4) And besides, there is at least one additional reason to press on: It

must be admitted—must it not?—that we ourselves sometimes get miserably bored. . . . And so, occasionally (sometimes when we least expect it!), we feel the sudden need to try to produce, in counter-response, a pretty doll with eyes sharp and bright enough to light up the world; or, sometimes, a stuffed teddy-bear which sings whimsical tunes—and which, every now & then, sometimes even dances. . . .

∾

## THE VOYAGE OF SELF-DISCOVERY

It's the voyage of self-discovery: it started out with enormous sails, a drunken Captain, and a bosun going toot-toot. Now, when you think you hear them piping you to quarters, it usually turns out to be a reference to a heavy smoker who is about to receive interest at the bank. So now the ship sits upon this bank, fifteen feet above sea level, dripping ooze from all her portholes. It seems a pleasant enough little bay, however, and the Captain, who has just discovered after the disaster that he is still an incurable optimist, wonders if, given enough time and money, the old hulk might not be converted from a former four-masted schooner to a large barge for inland waterway travel; or even, just possibly, a houseboat.

# John Bennett
POSTAGE DUE

The magazine came back marked deceased and with 21¢ postage due. I paid the man and took the envelope out into the sunlight. When I got home, I made a cup of tea, then sat at my desk. I ripped open the envelope and took out the magazine. I placed it back into supply. I leaned back in my chair, twisted to the right, thumbed thru the three-by-five cards until I came to his name. I took out the three-by-five card with his name on it and tore it in two. I dropped it into the brown paper bag.

I sat with my elbows on the desk and my chin resting on the heels of my hands, staring out the window, my eyes focused on nothing in particular.

# Carol Bergé
## GREY, OR TURTLE, SONG

There are just so many ways a sea-turtle can show affection. Or, for that matter, emotion of any kind. On the assumption that sea-turtles have, or could show, emotions, as we use the term. Thousands of folks at Marine World every year, more all the time. Admiring the seals as they balance beach-balls and wave their flippers in what looks like applause. Considering it a distinct possibility that dolphins can "speak," or at any rate communicate to humans on their level. A certain patronizing attitude. A couple I know keeps a sea-turtle (actually, a turtle from the Amazon River region, so it's a river turtle) in a tank, in their apartment. It's been there and alive for some fifteen years now. There's no way to tell what kind of time-measurement works in the life of a turtle, since some of them live for 500 years, the idea of time as we see it must be relative. The turtle is made with fins rather than feet, and navigates the length and breadth of that tank in about half a minute. Or what must seem like no time at all. The other night, there was a party at that apartment, and, as usual, the turtle got a lot of attention, especially from those who'd never seen it, because it is "unusual-looking," that is, it doesn't much resemble what our conditioned and ordinary concept of a turtle would lead us to expect: it has no little feet, pointing inward to leave tracks on tropical sand, no round shell to paint palm trees &c. on . . . its very expression, if that is the word, begs for anthropomorphic metaphor. It is at that point that the question comes to mind, human mind that is: how does this sea-turtle or river turtle express itself, if indeed it does? It is limited by more than its environment. First, certainly, there is the ovoid shell, the shape of the aquarium, then the physiological construction of the head and facial structure. There was a woman at the party who looked very much like the turtle. She passed close by the tank and the turtle pivoted clumsily on one end of the tank, the left end as we saw it, and seemed to hurry toward the end where she stood, and moved to the top of the water, in fact got its head out of the water and veered on its long neck toward that woman. She, passing, stopped, and put out her hand toward the tank—the turtle. The head of the turtle, as it came out of the water, pierced the skin of the water crisply and came toward her in a direct gesture. How could the turtle make itself understood? What does it have available to communicate whatever it is—to that woman? "Woman," we call her, meaning the female of a certain species. Yet her nose is shaped very much like a snubby version of the turtle's snout. Neither of them has what the rest of us would call much of a chin. Her neck is long and viable, rising up from her grey, strong gown, her eyes are grey like its, and her basic overall coloration a silver grey like its. The turtle took her finger in its mouth. Catherine and the turtle stared at each other for that moment. They were in love. As much with the Self as with the Other—as is often the case. The moment passed, as all such moments pass. Some barriers are not meant to be breached, more's the pity. Out of synch, they were, in time—she, after all, is descended from the turtle. Nowhere is it written that love is relative to time. All of the dimensions have been explored except that— and the one across species.

～

## TIMEPIECE (MICHIGAN), OR, A MOEBIUS TRIP . . .

On Monday, she arrived at the airport, expecting to be met there by a friend. He did not show up; she called around, and another friend came to pick her up. When she arrived back in her city, she felt like going to a movie, consulted the local paper, chose one that sounded good and was playing at a convenient time, and went downtown to the theatre. The marquee indicated another movie was showing. Figuring perhaps they'd changed it for the next film that would go on tomorrow, she inquired at the box office, and was told it had never been scheduled. And that the movie actually playing was on at the wrong time. She had a cup of tea at the corner restaurant and went home.

On Tuesday, she had a 4:00 appointment for working with a part-time secretary. Four o'clock came and went and the man did not show up; she called his home and his office; no answer. The woman, beginning to be depressed, went to take a nap. The phone woke her around 9 P.M., a man intended to visit her the coming weekend; this call was to tell her he was not going to be able to be there. As long as she was up, she called the secretary again; no answer. She made another call to her shrink to confirm an appointment she'd made a couple of weeks earlier, before getting on the plane—fine, for Wednesday, at 2:30.

She arrived at the shrink's office at 2:40 because she knew he was usually ready to see her at that time. She talked to him for 75 minutes and was charged for "an hour," as usual. She left his office to go straight home, as she was expecting a delivery of books at 4:00. The shipment arrived, by UPS, at 5:05; there were five cartons, due four months earlier; she opened the cartons and discovered that they contained strange books, books she'd never ordered. She went into the bathroom and threw up. Then she wept, and slept.

The following morning, Thursday, the household helper, due at 9 A.M., did not show up. No call. The mailman did not show up as he usually did at 11 A.M. The phone finally rang. The phone rang at precisely noon. It was her husband, a man thought to be dead years ago, saying he was at the airport, and would she come to meet him? Sure, why not! When she got there, no one there looked like him, no one there had ever heard of him, no such plane had ever arrived. By now, it was 4:00 again. She arrived home in time to receive a phone call saying that the children were being taken away from her, would be placed in someone else's custody. The clock had stopped at noon.

# Cassia Berman
## NOUMENON

*—in memory of Uncle Lou*

It would snow so much in Russia, my uncle told me, that the roads would rise and pass over the houses and trees. The snow was about fifteen feet high, and summer continued, all filled in with whiteness, beneath the road you walked on.

The men would dig themselves out of their houses in the morning after their tea, and walk across the snowbanks carrying large sacks, greeting their neighbors, asking each other how life went, and why. It was so cold outside that your words would freeze as soon as they came out of your mouth and stay in the air, silently, waiting to be taken. The men would come home at the end of the day, as the snow was darkening, with bulging sacks slung over their shoulders, and shake the icicles out of their beards and mustaches, and remove their heavy coats, and unwrap the rags wrapped around their legs for warmth, and their wives would empty their sacks, and as they drank their tea they would hear the answers to their questions.

# Roger K. Blakely

## ICEBERGS

After a winter of cold nor'easters, summer halts at a threshold forty miles south. Like a giant tray of ice-cubes, Duluth's bay remains uneasily and noisily congealed all spring, sometimes into May. Floes large as tennis courts secede and reunite, occasionally turn belly-up, or stagger ashore piggyback to drip and melt under the same heat that buds lilacs and blooms crabapples elsewhere.

In due time the sun hangs overhead. Ice decays. Channels open between shrunken Antarcticas. A routed flotilla of gleaming flat-decked slabs rides low where waves slosh its hulls and swab its forecastles. Gulls perching out there in disciplined rows exactly one wing-span apart look for all the world like midshipmen on review.

And one morning vacant water reaches toward Canada or Cathay, and only a few honeycombs of ice, their prisms and glassy shards decomposing into wet sand, mark the shipwrecks.

As for the gulls: preferring wings to a sham solidity, they must have flown off the night before.

~

## PERFECTIONIST

Our tourist descends a switchback to lakeshore. Split Rock Lighthouse soars from its lofty cliff. Hot, hazy sunshine makes the head throb; a stench of herring persists; the waves glow pewter, not azure, on a day that Nature, to quote Emily Dickinson, is caught without her diadem. But a big, easygoing fellow in khaki shorts, bare-chested, slouches like Rodin's Thinker on top of a boulder huge as a refrigerator. His tripod supports a 4x5 Graphic with lens zeroed in on the lighthouse's bigger optics. Obviously this outmoded Ansel Adams gear does wonders in skilled hands.

The tanned photographer looks naive or else assimilated. Calmly he ignites a new cigar from the stump of an old one. Calmly he opens a beer and offers his audience its mate. Yes, he wants pictures but the light's wrong. See those shadows in ugly places?

The tourist nods sympathetically. They chat. The tourist finishes his Budweiser and ponders the empty can, hating to drop it in front of an initiate. The expert grins, catches it, tosses it into a duffelbag.

A day later our traveler's curiosity tempts him down the same steep path the same time of afternoon, and of course the cameraman waits in identical pose, a few hours more sun-browned, smoking a descendant of those first cigars. No, the light's still bad, although it looks pristine to the other. The light's not right, but it will be, today or tomorrow or eventually, so what's the rush?

In principle the traveler agrees; in practice he's due in Minneapolis by evening.

# Douglas Blazek
## THE TWO-NATURED MONSTER

A man sits cross-legged on the living room rug awaiting god's blood. This is what a fish must feel as it lies on dry gravel in an aquarium waiting for water.

When the room fills with blood the man effortlessly bobs to his feet. Slowly he floats toward the bedroom. He opens the door. There on the bed lies his body, the blood from the living room rushing to fill it like air into a deflated tire.

His body then sits up, grabs hammer and nails, climbs the wall and becomes an icon. The man leaves his body on the wall and slowly walks toward the kitchen. He prepares an omelet, adds honey to toast, pours a glass of orange juice. But before he eats he again meditates.

Slowly he folds his legs on the living room rug meditating upon an image. If the icon in the bedroom leaves the wall it will rush to fill only the meditation. More dry gravel.

If the man takes the hammer and shatters the icon, fragments of it will imbed in everything the eye beholds. His task then will be to fill each fragment as a way of devouring it.

He decides a good place to begin is breakfast.

# Robert Bly
## THE DEAD SEAL

1

Walking north toward the point, I come on a dead seal. From a few feet away, he looks like a brown log. The body is on its back, dead only a few hours. I stand and look at him. There's a quiver in the dead flesh: My God, he's still alive. And a shock goes through me, as if a wall of my room had fallen away.

His head is arched back, the small eyes closed; the whiskers sometimes rise and fall. He is dying. This is the oil. Here on its back is the oil that heats our houses so efficiently. Wind blows fine sand back toward the ocean. The flipper near me lies folded over the stomach, looking like an unfinished arm, lightly glazed with sand at the edges. The other flipper lies half underneath. And the seal's skin looks like an old overcoat, scratched here and there—by sharp mussel shells maybe.

I reach out and touch him. Suddenly he rears up, turns over. He gives three cries: Awaark! Awaark! Awaark!—like the cries from Christmas toys. He lunges toward me; I am terrified and leap back, though I know there can be no teeth in that jaw. He starts flopping toward the sea. But he falls over, on his face. He does not want to go back to the sea. He looks up at the sky, and he looks like an old lady who has lost her hair. He puts his chin back down on the sand, rearranges his flippers, and waits for me to go. I go.

2

The next day I go back to say goodbye. He's dead now. But he's not. He's a quarter mile farther up the shore. Today he is thinner, squatting on his stomach, head out. The ribs show more: each vertebra on the back under the coat is visible, shiny. He breathes in and out.

A wave comes in, touches his nose. He turns and looks at me—the eyes slanted; the crown of his head looks like a boy's leather jacket bending over some bicycle bars. He is taking a long time to die. The whiskers white as porcupine quills, the forehead slopes. . . . Goodbye, brother, die in the sound of the waves. Forgive us if we have killed you. Long live your race, your inner-tube race, so uncomfortable on land, so comfortable in the ocean. Be comfortable in death then, when the sand will be out of your nostrils, and you can swim in long loops through the pure death, ducking under as assassinations break above you. You don't want to be touched by me. I climb the cliff and go home the other way.

～

## SNOW FALLING ON SNOW

Snow has fallen on snow for two days behind the Keilen farmhouse . . . no one has walked through it, or looked at it. . . . It makes the sound the porgies hear near the ocean floor, the sound the racer hears before his death, the sound that lifts the buoyant swimmer in the channel.

Wind blows four pigeon-grass heads, scarce and fine, above the snow. They are heron legs in white morning fog, a musical thought that rises as the pianist sits down at her table, the body laboring before dawn to understand its dream. . . .

Everyone in the house still asleep. . . . In its dream thin feet come down the mountainside, hooves clatter over the wooden bridges, walk along the stone walls, and then pause, and look in at an orchard, where a fount of water is rising in the air. . . . Men are lying asleep all around its base, each with his sword lying under him. And the orchard-keeper, where is he?

～

## THE EXHAUSTED BUG

*—for my father*

Here is a tiny, hard-shelled thing. He is the length of a child's tooth, and clearly the fire of life is flickering out there. Its upper shell, the shape of a long seashell, wears its overlapping sidings, eight of them, all delicate brown, shaded as if it were some great cloth made for delicate wrists. The two antennae look bent and discouraged. When I turn it over with the tip of my Pilot ballpoint pen, the white legs move appealingly, even though my first response is confusion, as when we see the messy underside of any too-well-protected thing. It has twelve legs, six on each side, pale as tapioca. There are two pincers that come out to protect the head from hostile knights; or perhaps the pincers are meant to take hold of food. What else could they be?

I guess that it has exhausted itself, perhaps over weeks, trying to escape from this cloisonné dish on my desk. This dish is too little to hold a breakfast roll, and yet it is a walled Sahara to this creature, some courtyard in which the portcullis is always closed, and the knights, their ladies, their horse-drangers always, mysteriously, gone.

The sharp lamplight lit up the dish; it is odd that I did not see him before. I will take him outdoors in the still chill spring air and let him drink the melted snow of late afternoon on this day when I have written of my father stretched out in his coffin.

～

## WARNING TO THE READER

Sometimes farm granaries become especially beautiful when all the oats or wheat are gone, and wind has swept the rough floor clean. Standing inside, we see around us, coming in through the cracks between shrunken wall boards, bands or strips of sunlight. So in a poem about imprisonment, one sees a little light.

But how many birds have died trapped in these granaries. The bird, seeing the bands of light, flutters up the walls and falls back again and again. The way out is where the rats enter and leave; but the rat's hole is low to the floor. Writers, be careful then by showing the sunlight on the walls not to promise the anxious and panicky blackbirds a way out!

I say to the reader, beware. Readers who love poems of light may sit hunched in the corner with nothing in their gizzards for four days, light failing, the eyes glazed. . . . They may end as a mound of feathers and a skull on the open boardwood floor. . . .

# Michael Bowden
## CITIES OF GOLD

At an edge of sleep the sentences in a reporter's head begin to fracture
into words and phrases. Because it's dawn a lawn mower growls, sput-
ters, and stalls. A line of sound at the end of consciousness. Light
strengthens in the sky as clerks stock shelves for a grand opening and
songs of revolution scale ramparts of spaghettios. Far off a bell rings out
upon an empty schoolyard which borders the river valley Coronado tra-
versed 450 years ago seeking cities of gold. Bridles chiming in the dark
mouths of his horses. Now two sepia leaves blow over the bottom of a
drained fountain. Small yellow flowers roll along a blue patio as the sun
returns to fill the branches of the roses and time's impact makes itself
known. In the still house, meanwhile, a refrigerator repeats its mantra
behind the confused lead of a graveyard shift story involving gunshots
and sirens and a biker woman bent over the grill of a '59 Fury shouting
fuck you at the stars and her old man over and over.

SCRAPS

On a morning like any other the apple tree appears unbalanced now that its branches have been trimmed. But the apples are still the red of Japanese lanterns, glowing from the inside. Getting heavier. In time one limb bends slowly into blades of grass, carrying that sweetness, imitating the woman behind the garden window combing out a blond braid. Attaching the worn stocking to its garter. Meanwhile a forgotten inkwell and pens wait in the cupboard's darkness for someone who'll teach us how to make the beautiful letters again. Now, in the heart of the city, a janitor dusts behind the clock, gazing through the rust on Roman numerals. Pedestrians hurry past the statue of Justice toward a bridge they must cross. A neon sign's words burning out behind them where, not so many decades past, a peddler in a coat of scraps shouted Knives sharpened!

～

SONG

We have all the time in the world. We have no time. The bed's raft is kissing the banks of a life we recall in designs of sofa fabric, the wrinkled pattern of an art print behind glass. Because wind snaps flags over a bone orchard, the thrush alternately sits on her nest, then takes wing. We know how that feels too. Even so, the street gives up its newsgirl, her twin red braids knotted into a small tip worth more than all the petroleum fueling headlines. As your wife rises from blue sheets, and you, without shame, call the bird's three quick syllables song.

# Jane Brox
## APPLE BOXES

Some of our apple boxes come from a hundred miles away: "*Moose Hill Orchards*, Derry, New Hampshire" is stenciled onto the side of several of the boxes, and so is "*Badger Farms,* Wilton," and "*Bartlett and Sons,* Temple." Apple boxes are often bought second-hand, so the pine is weathered gray—the color of apple bark itself—and no longer smells of resin, but of old soil.

For most of the year these boxes are nested together and stored in a shed: more than a hundred stacks of them, each stack six or seven feet high. They come into use gradually around mid-August, when the summer apples—Astrakhans, Gravensteins, and Early Macs—begin to ripen. We have only a few trees of those varieties, and their fruit may seem incidental among the peaches, corn, and tomatoes. Nevertheless, it's their tight-hearted scent you pick up on a diminishing wind.

September drives down, the Macs are ready to drop, and apple boxes are hauled by the truckload to the orchards. Then the place is littered with pickers—some on the ground, some on ladders—all badged with apple buckets, which are slightly kidney-shaped so they'll fit snugly beneath the chest of a man. The canvas straps are worn low against the shoulders to prevent a sore neck, and I suppose it's those straps that make apple buckets look like collapsed marionettes when they are stowed away at the end of the year, waiting to be taken up by a human hand.

The galvanized buckets have a felt rim to keep the fruit from bruising, and they have a canvas bottom closed by a drawstring so the fruit can be lowered into boxes without being dumped or handled a second time. Eight or nine hours a day, one apple at a time twisted off its stem and placed into the bucket, the bucket filled and loosened into a box—this makes a gentle, clustery rumble—and then again. . . .

McIntoshes, Macouns, Cortlands, Baldwins, Northern Spies. So many apple boxes unnested, filled, stacked beneath the trees—three, sometimes four high. Here and there, one of those names speaks out from the stacks—*Moose Hill, Badger, Bartlett,* orchards now lost to neighborhoods and industrial parks. Or maybe they have simply been abandoned, the apple trees now rowed among saplings and wild grasses, their crowns still shaped by old prunings.

⁓

## PEACHES

The handful of varieties that grow in this part of the country have hardiness bred into them. Reliance. . . . Elberta. . . . Not names to dream on, though to grow peaches here, near the northern limit of their range, is something of a dream. My father was well over sixty when he planted the peach orchard in a long-time meadow. That was the last piece of land to be hayed—cut and cured and stored. I barely remember it, the rectangular bales spaced like footsteps across the land.

The peach trees—fifty or so of them—were no more than whips to start with, and it hardly seemed they'd survive a January. In truth, the trees don't always winter well—some years there is barely a crop, and once in awhile, no crop at all. The peach orchard blooms early and pink. It will never look as crabbed and thickened with the years as an apple orchard—the trees aren't long-lived and they are pruned in their own way—without a central leader—so the limbs curve out and up to embrace an open center. Each crown, a ballroom of its own.

I have never seen relic peach trees crowding a cellar-hole the way apple trees often do. Apples are old in these parts, a cash crop talked about endlessly. How many times have I heard about the Ben Davis, too bitter to eat, that would cling to the branches until spring. Or about Cortlands, developed by accident during the search for a McIntosh that would redden on the tree. Or the original Red Delicious, fenced and locked at Stark Nurseries. About cider years. Snow apples. Astrakhans.

Somewhere to the south there must be like stories about peaches. People traveling up from Georgia and the Carolinas will say our peaches just don't have the flavor of theirs. They'll name varieties I've never heard of that ripen right down the summer. Here the peach season doesn't last long—a few weeks in August and maybe the first of September when we have a fruit that isn't meant for storage, that doesn't smell sharp as the cold side of the mountain, and whose flavor isn't deepened by the frost. Reliance and Elberta are hardy names, but like all peaches, their fragrance blooms at the back of your throat as it passes.

~

## WHITE PINE

A given name. It has nothing to do with their blue-green needles or their branches, their cones or fissured bark. It isn't tied to their wintry scent. We call them white pines after the quality of their lumber—the dressed wood is the palest of all pines, close-grained, soft, and long-prized.

Always the stories tell how white pines reached over the Northeast—stands of them that neared two hundred feet in height, many so true they were felled for the masts of a foreign navy. The rest: squared off to exhaustion. What remains of those old forests are the stories only, and perhaps a mullion flecked with milkpaint or a floorboard scoured to a deep patina. In early homes I've seen wood panels that must be almost two feet wide, and still I can't comprehend the vanished size of those trees. The white pines I know, the ones I've always believed to be characteristic of these parts, are no more than a century's growth. People call them old-field pines because they took hold on abandoned farmland, thriving on thin soil and the bald heat of the days. Their wood is rarely as clear as that of the deliberate primeval growth—boxes, matches, pulp. Still, white pines are the most majestic tree I know.

There are four of them behind my house that have been full grown for as long as anyone can remember, and now they must be a hundred feet tall. They're so far above our accustomed sightline of berries, sheds, and fruit trees that my eye is drawn to them from wherever I am on the property. Even when I'm indoors they sometimes come to mind. During the strong night wind I might start thinking they'll go down, though they've withstood a handful of major hurricanes and all the squalls in between. In truth, they are shaped by such exposure: knotted, warty trunks that are too staunch to creak in rough weather, and crowns that lean in from the north as if they've kept the brunt of the wind in them.

In winter gales their boughs don't clatter like the birches. They don't work into your thoughts like the oaks, whose dry leaves rasp. White pine needles are sheathed and soft; their branches, supple as muslin. It's a steady, clear flame of a sound they make. I can hear it way above the roof—ash-throated and abiding.

# Anita Olachea Bucci
## IN PASSING

The bee man sells his honey down the road, where the sign says "Park here for Leonardo's house." The tourists leave the Mercedes in the lot and stroll back buzzing: "Is this it? Is this it?" Ready to slip into the reverence mode. Up a short incline and there it is: the house is stone, and bone bare, and swept. Now, they're thinking, we must use a little imagination. This is the door he touched; here is the hearth he sat on, close to the flames; he looked out these windows when it rained. They glance down and see the boy in the grass, watching the mill wheel as it turns; they look up and see the birds dipping over the field, so the boy below can feel the shape and inclination of their wings. These things will haunt him, even after he's been sent off to Florence.

A hill above the house is shifting. This happened: part of the hill slid, with quiet dignity, down down across the road and beyond into the ravine. An entire island, with its olive trees perkily upright the whole time. It engulfed a house of no particular historical importance, but of considerable sentimental value, as they say, to the family living there (they were out shopping at the time). No one seems to have heard it happen and yet, it was a great event. People spoke of it in the tone of voice reserved for emigrated relatives and stories of the war. It closed off the road for a year.

The tourists leave Leonardo's house with postcards in a fold of cellophane. They walk back to the car through the specific smell of mint and rosemary, and climb in. "What a marvel," they say as they drive away; "I wonder if anything's changed at all here in five hundred years."

∼

## JACK

"You and I have a lot in common," I tell him, as we bundle up on the brick wall overlooking the river; "we're both good listeners and we both have a fine imagination." His snoot and neck are elongated over the precipice, below which run various pipe lines, below which runs the river—in season. Out of season, which is now, shrubs and trees cover the river bed, sheep graze, corn grows, people run: up to the center of town, which is one bridge away, then back. We are there to spy on it all. The runners are beautifully dressed; they wear colored satin shorts that catch the light, and striped tops—yellow and blue, purple and green, red and silver. Their socks are a faultless white.

"We're very curious types," I go on, "but prudent." This is a warning. It is very daring to be there at all; one false move and the medieval brick could crumble away beneath our seats: we like to think this. He stretches his chest and lifts a paw, pointing above the abyss at something I can't see. Through the center of the river bed runs a mosaic of cracked mud; imagine flood tides, imagine crazed water slapping the bastions, like last November. Imagine men with fishing poles. He prods my arm with the raised paw: Jack—the name of champions! His coat is glinty, red, his parentage pure conjecture.

Our eyes are fingers picking at the years; he senses flight, the peeling off of past that my perceptors can't detect. The air rings and jingles with it, the bank is littered: cacophony of sighs and unexploded screams, visions of green-masked game cocking an eye. Across the river, the scent of time converging, banked up like big guns.

We shiver in the sun: who said there's nothing new beneath it?

# Michael Carey
## THE DARKENING HILLS

*—for Chuck Offenburger*

It went on longer than anyone thought possible. During full regulation play and three overtimes, the score was tied and tied and tied again. Other than that, it was Iowa small town high school football: everyone on both teams playing both ways, a total of four on either bench. At halftime the players marched with their respective bands, playing their flutes and piccolos and glockenspiels. Everyone was so tired, no one noticed the harvest moon, like a well-lit tunnel, gaping so wide in the east end zone, even though they kicked field goals, all night, into it.

After the game the coaches didn't shake hands but hugged at midfield, while their trembling players fell to their knees around them. Everyone had asked of themselves more than they had, and yet they gave. Now they didn't want to leave. Their legs wouldn't let them. Each player wanted to shout to the now-silent stands that tonight something important had happened. But after a while they, too, fell silent and forgot about the game as their fathers' combines shook and roared and shaved the earth, climbing slowly through the darkening hills.

~

## THE DEAD CENTER

*—for Will Keller*

He didn't know why he did it, he just did. There were seven tornadoes skipping and jumping through the fields. He would find out later how many. He'd know then who died, whose barns exploded from the inside because of the differential in air pressure, whose chickens were plucked but still breathing.

He didn't know why he opened the old wooden door, the family packed like summer's beans onto the shelves of the fruit cellar, he just did and saw then, between lightning flashes, the stalled twister hovering above him—the green sides of the gray mass three hundred feet apart, spinning at six hundred miles an hour, snapping and hissing at him.

He could see a mile up the dead center. He could see the sky beyond, but he couldn't breathe because there was nothing there, just a whiff of grass and a fading terror and the rush of blood in the urge to be lifted.

⁓

## HOW GRANDMA AND GRANDPA MET

*—for Winnie Gee*

She was quiet and a good student, so no boy, at first, warmed up to the shy stranger. No one did until the box social. He too was shy and had few friends, so there was no competition to bid him up during the auction. They sat together on the grass for two hours over fried chicken and pickled eggs and some of the sweetest candies he had ever tasted. Not a word was spoken during the meal, after the meal, nor during the auction. A nod of his head was all that was needed to purchase a meal with the girl he desired. On the way home, neither of them laughed when the old horse broke wind loudly, straining by their one-room schoolhouse and all the way up the mile-long incline. All three kept eyes to the ground—the two lovers, at least, thinking about their meal and the new sweet taste in their mouths. Sixty years later, Grandma let us know and Grandpa publicly laughed, for the first time, over their shy beginnings.

Now, all is quiet. Nothing remains—not the wagon, nor the horse, nor the schoolhouse, nor Grandpa's soft laughter: only this story and just as I've told it.

⁓

## TRANSLATIONS

We were at the bank, at the drive-in at the tube shoots to the tellers'
window. I don't remember if I was putting money in or taking it out. I
was doing one or the other like I always do, like I have to do once a
month for a lifetime. Every effort I've made in the past twelve years has
come down to this window. Whether the weeds got the best of me,
whether Walnut Creek rose over the corn on the old river bottom,
whether the cut-worms cut again into our theoretical profit and digested
it into real loss. The same old litany of sweat and prayer and sorrow is
translated here into a tongue the Board and bankers can understand.

This year, the corn is deep and green, its leaves have opened and
dropped to shade out the weeds naturally, cheaply, without chemicals.
There is sun enough and rain enough for both the corn and the beans
to shine. Just when I think I know what the future is saying, it speaks
again another language. When we finish our business, the van in the
row beside us stops, backs up and slides down its window. It is Wayne,
kind Wayne, sincere and sober, "Michael," he says, "I just wanted to tell
you, your bottom has never looked better!" He then closes the window
and drives away. My wife raises her eyebrows and stares quizzically at
me across the front seat of the old pickup. I stare back, blankly at first,
then, for once, all words dissolve into laughter.

# Siv Cedering
## IN THE MUSEUM OF NATURAL HISTORY

My getting locked in the Museum of Natural History was no accident. I was sure that all the words in the dictionary could be sifted out of dinosaur bones. So at night, when the guards were gone, I tapped the ancient remains, unfossiled, reconstructed, let a little bone dust fall, and printed a language already deciphered:

Air   Fire   Water.

But when I stepped out on Central Park West, the morning sun spilling coffee and doughnuts, I realized the only egg layers in my head were chickens and garter snakes. Alchemist, Almagest, I had to try again.

Locked in with stuffed birds and hard gems, I became schooled in the wind-flow across a wing and in the structures of crystals. In a small body, beauty is comprehensible, but the tail is so far from the dinosaur's head it must grow a brain of its own. Perfect. Body and soul, each has its tiny mentality, let that be my cybernetic duality. Morning comes: a soft rain of coffee and doughnuts on Central Park West, and the city is shrinking.

It isn't that the dinosaurs grew too big, it is the world that became too small, and it is growing smaller. Chickens and garter snakes are properly proportioned. Comic Strip. Tidbit. The hum of the gnat I write.

~

## THE JUGGLER

I had practiced for years. Whenever I had a chance, I juggled with oranges, plates, pine cones, pennies. My uncle encouraged me, though my mother said: The boy should do something better. He should read. He should learn to make a living. She said: If your father was alive, he would show you. But I didn't stop. How could I stop? There was always some space above my hands calling me. Behind a tree, behind a tent, behind a truck, on the other side of the field, there was always this space where I could be God throwing the planets, or the wind commanding the leaves.

On the night of the first kiss, the air touched my hands in some new way. I juggled with soft skin, Lena's lips, not quite open, her lapel, my own chin, the two pimples by my ear. My hands were clumsy. I almost dropped something, but caught it, just in time. I juggled No, Well, Maybe, Yes. The director saw me. The boy is not so bad, he said. Give him some time in the third ring. I juggled lights. I juggled time. I juggled sound.

On the night I first entered a woman, the lights danced out of my hands. I juggled hair and lips and breasts and vulvas. I juggled small wet spaces that could suck me into some sweet oblivion I mastered, I juggled a soft curtain, a blood stain, my own large penis swelling. The music lifted me. I juggled applause and more applause. I juggled a soft voice calling me.

On the night my son was born, there was nothing to throw. My hands were empty, waiting. There was a strange fear inside me. The music was building, the lights were on me, but nothing happened. Until out of all that waiting, something came. I could reach my hand up into that waiting space, and suddenly there was a small shape, settling to the shape of my hand. My hand fell, rose, lifted high, fell again, and all things in the world were attached to my hand, rising, falling, holding, protecting.

On the night the girl died, my hands were some independent objects moving without me. A broken leg, a cut thigh, some blood stained clothing, a sequined ribbon, all tore out of my hands, pulling at the skin, exposing the bone, catapulting with a small scream out of my hands, to fall back to the space of my palms without a moan. The lights were on me, but I didn't juggle them, they juggled me. In the dark space of the tent, I bounced up and down, while the music of my own voice came from some strange distance, a slow heartbeat of sound repeating. No. No. No. No.

# Maxine Chernoff
## A VEGETABLE EMERGENCY

There is something new among the vegetables in my garden this morning; a sinister weed, with brown, hair-like filaments. I start tugging, but find it surprisingly resilient. Bracing myself like a sailor hoisting anchor in a gale, I nearly fall over backwards. The ground gives way to the head of a man, attractive, about forty, with brown wavy hair. A small white butterfly, straying from the cabbage patch, has landed above his ear. I picture Gauguin arriving in Tahiti in much the same way, a startled islander pulling him from the rhubarb-colored sand. But a head seems to be all that exists of this man. I wonder what he's doing in my garden, a city plot smaller and less enticing than even the Paradise Lounge down the street. I ask him this, but he stares off at the white fence, stony and mute.

I wonder if the head, like a hangnail, is a little-discussed but nevertheless common occurrence. I consult manuals, finding only parasites, fungi, and frost among vegetable emergencies. No mention of a head, obtrusive as a fireplug in a desert. I call up a few neighbors for advice. They are sympathetic, but noncommittal.

That night I sit in bed, watching the fireflies circling the jar-like head. I wonder what will happen when fall comes and I've eaten or canned all the crops. I imagine plowing up the garden, burying the head under a mound of earth, and hoping for an early blizzard. But what if the head resurfaced each year, perhaps doubled in size, edging the other vegetables far from the sunlight? One blow from my spade might dispatch it abruptly as it arrived. But what if it screamed? A head so obstinately silent, given the right situation, might be absolutely vociferous. Unable to sleep, I listen to the crickets as if to canned laughter.

Over my morning coffee, I distractedly read the newspaper. Outside the window, the head, like a silent Mafia don, dominates the garden. A sale at the greenhouse resolves the problems for me: by 9 A.M. I've purchased a dozen geranium plants. Like an expert milliner, I artfully cover the head with pink and orange flowers. Green fuzzy leaves

101

patch closed the relentless eyes. I hang the "For Sale" sign in front of the house and wait for a prospective buyer. I hope, in its cloister of leaves, the head has vowed silence.

～

## HIGH RISE

The man next door has extended a long, wooden plank out of his window. Twenty-six floors above the city, I watch him every night. It is with the certainty of a commuter train that he arrives at eight o'clock. He always dresses in the same orange trunks and black flippers. A white towel drags majestically behind him. He bends at the waist, extends his long arms, swan-like, and springs up and down three times. He never loses his footing.

Later in the evening, he and his wife enjoy a stroll to the edge of the plank. They sit facing each other, hand in hand. Then like hungry birds they open their mouths cavernously and look straight up at the sky. Often they sit there for hours, still as a bowl of fruit on a table.

When the woman leaves around midnight, the man performs his nightly ritual. He braces himself on the board and throws his head back with such force that the plank moans hideously. He closes his eyes and howls once in the voice of some strange animal. The stars turn over in their graves of sky.

～

## AN ABRIDGED BESTIARY

—for Peter Kostakis

As the story goes, Noah took animals of every variety aboard his famed ark. This, however, was not the case. The aardvark and the zebra were the only animals that the concise Noah allowed to join him. "Bears to yaks be damned," he shouted, when his wife asked permission for her pet monkey to board. Not recognizing in his single-mindedness the very quality that had endeared Noah to God, she smuggled the monkey onto the ship. This feat was easily accomplished, since Noah was extremely busy the forty days that the ship labored on the swollen sea. He was revising all known bestiaries, tearing out pages and tossing them overboard with the abandon of a crazed housewife cleaning out her refrigerator. By the end of the voyage he had written what he called *Noah's Book of Animals,* a two-page pamphlet praising the grace of the aardvark and the wit of the zebra.

Contrary to popular myth, it was the stowaway monkey, and not the fabled dove, who announced the sighting of land. A strong swimmer, the monkey had followed the boat, collecting the pictures that Noah discarded. On the last day of the flood, Noah saw the pictures drying on a line suspended between two palm trees in the receding water. Amazed, Noah asked God what it could mean. God admonished Noah for his excessive frugality and blessed the intrepid monkey. The next morning all the animals were recreated, according to the discarded pictures that the monkey had saved for God.

~

## SAILING

Benjamin Franklin used to lie naked on the water, attach a kite to his leg, and let the wind gently carry him around the pond like a sailboat. On days when the weather was especially pleasant, you could hear him talking to himself above the jabber of various pond creatures. It was in this liquid medium that he wrote his clever epigrams. He explained that the water actually spoke to him in sentences, thus inventing the concept of "onomatopoeia."

One rainy day he met with near disaster when lightning struck the tail of his kite. The electric current traveled through his body, setting his wooden teeth aflame. For a week he lay unconscious, a Jack-o-lantern grin behind his badly blistered gums.

# Rick Christman
## ASYLUM

The asylum was in the most hotly contested area of Bien-Hoa Province, near the tiny hamlet of Tam-Hiep—a few, dusty isolated weed huts along the muddy banks of the Bien-Hoa River. The asylum was three hundred yards away from the village, surrounded by a high cement fence topped with embedded broken glass, to keep the insane in and the evil spirits from drifting over to contaminate the village. The Vietnamese traditionally considered insanity catching.

Since the insane were locked in and no one wished to be contaminated, the patients were left to fend for themselves. There were no attendants. The courtyard of the asylum was piled with bones, discarded paper, feces, and busy rats.

Once a day, in the early morning, their food was brought in by an old man from the village in a creaky water buffalo cart. He placed the day's rations on a squat table just inside the gate, and left again until the next morning. There would be a cauldron of rice, a pot of meat, ten large French loaves, three packs of Park Lane cigarettes, and two small boxes of matches.

When the Fifth Infantry broke through to the village and entered the asylum grounds, they were appalled by what they saw. They stared with dropping mouths at the incredible filth. They couldn't believe it.

Then something drew them to it. They dropped their weapons and other gear at their sides and went to work. They didn't hesitate; they dug right in.

They opened the doors and windows and drove out all the rats. They buried and burned all the garbage. They brought out paint, boards, and nails, and all the other equipment they had lugged along for the pacification of the village.

All the villagers from Tam-Hiep came out and looked on, amazed once again at the strange things appearing before their eyes. They watched the men work all day and on into the evening. They took a spontaneous holiday. They watched as the infantrymen fed those who had difficulty feeding themselves. They watched giant, battle-hardened soldiers take grown Vietnamese men and women onto their laps and delicately feed them with their messkit spoons. They watched them fix and paint and clean. They watched them and smiled. They shook their heads.

Once it grew dark, the men set up camp on the asylum courtyard grounds. They pitched tents, cut trenches, and ate C-Rations and leftovers. The villagers returned to their weed huts for their own meals. As they squatted around their rice pots and shoveled in from their bowls, they chatted noisily. They grinned and smiled and laughed often. These Americans. They shook their heads over and over. Strange people, these Americans.

Later, after the men of the Fifth Infantry finished eating and smoking, for a little relaxation and amusement, and to relieve the tension they had been under, they raped and killed all the villagers. Then they burned the village down.

At dawn, they broke camp and left. The insane waved goodbye from the courtyard gate, and the men waved back. The village still smoldered as the men fanned out into the black-green jungle and disappeared. The insane ambled happily back into the asylum and went about the business of being insane.

～

## WHITEOUT, BOONDOCKS, IOWA

The cold saps the world of breath and the snow surrounds us, closes in. We have come to this place, this truck stop in central Iowa off Interstate Thirty-Five, huddled together in two small rooms, gathered like prisoners, forced off the highway to become more than we are.

We gather chairs and stools into a tight ring and smoke. One of the drivers relates casually losing his truck, panic stricken, on harrowing mountain roads. Once you're committed, he says, you have to go through with it. You have no choice. You ever hear a truck go by whoosh, you know. He grins and drops his eyes, then opens them wide suddenly and stares at us, from one to the other. We scrape our chairs, our stools, closer.

Another driver, one without long underwear peeking through his shirt front, without even a tee shirt, circulates, refuses to join us. As he paces the room, he relates loudly the intimate details of his life. He punches holes into the air with his cigarette fist. The heat in here is enough to suffocate you, he says, again and again. Damn it, don't they know there is never enough cool air?

A blonde, high-school-aged waitress rushes through the room, the hem of her tan and brown checked uniform rising and falling, rising and falling, like hours passing, twelve, twenty-four, thirty-six. Food is running out in the restaurant, she shouts to us, to the cashier across the room, to anyone who will listen. Her eyes, too, are wide, large light brown, but she turns quickly away from us and heads back into the restaurant. Food is running out, she calls one last time on her way out.

A man who looks like Hemingway comes in out of the night, his full gray beard frozen like crystal. He walks directly to the corner of the room and stares at the brown wall and talks. My God, he says, he has just come in off the road. The snow swirled around his lost vehicle for two hours, and now all he can do is look at the dark wall and talk. He was driving straight into the air, he says. And the white. So *white* everywhere. Before he joins us, he touches the wall finally, the brown of his fingers caressing it like it is skin.

There are even blacks here in central Iowa, in off the road from Des Moines, on the way to St. Paul and Minneapolis. They cluster together among this Midwestern prairie white, in the midst of all this incredible white snow. They move together about the filled rooms, caroming enclaves of black. But as the hours pass, they stop moving about and look from one to the other. They grab chairs and stools and slide easily into the circle, into the spaces we provide for them.

Cigarette-fist man crowds in among us, too, finally, and admits, whispers softly, his breath, his words almost visible, how in Viet-Nam helicopter blades swirled in the jungle, vibrated the jungle, moved the grass like snow on his feet, his legs, to his waist. It was like life there, he says, but it was the heat, waves of substantial air trapping his breath in his throat. And now, since, he can't get cool enough. He will never again be cool enough. He strips his shirt then, there in front of us, to his naked, sweat-beaded skin. Cool, he says, and then tells about actually punching holes into the walls of his house for cool, cool air. As he talks, we hear sounds in the night, snow sanding the windows, tapping like fingers, as it swirls around us, then over toward Thirty-Five.

But the wind and the snow die suddenly, as if they had never been. At once we rise and step lightly, nearly jaunting, out to our vehicles, as if nothing ever happened, as if the world remained the same the whole time. The drivers move on to their jobs without thinking, blowing down mountain roads whoosh. And the blacks move back out into the white world.

I wait, lag behind, then head to my own vehicle, alone, last, after all are gone. Halfway there I stop and feel the world, dark as death out in the night. And it cracks suddenly—I can hear it crack—splits us apart, hard, complete, sundered, like logs between the axe.

# Kirby Congdon

## THE MOTORCYCLE SOCIAL CLUB

After a run, we all meet at the Club—those of us who haven't broken down, dropped their bikes, or gotten hurt, injured, or killed. We play pool and drink, and move in even strides about the room, showing off the thick backs of our curving thighs, gleaming where the black leather stretches tight. We spend the evening sending messages—flowers, emergency telegrams and time-bombs—with our eyes. When we pair off, we are casual and conceal the excitement we feel at our public but silent commitment to destruction. The veteran members disappear one by one to recover in hometowns, or to wait in hospitals or graves. But the membership grows, though the initiations become more stringent. The local people laugh nervously at our public image, or they ask, Where will it all end? But the game, underneath, is serious and there is no end. In the land of plenty, death grows, fertilized and lush. And we get drunk on the habit-forming perfumes of its secret and majestic, its black and addicting blooms, and each flower broken off sheds a glittering shower of hard new seeds. There's the fascination. To join the Club is difficult; to be a member is final and permanent. Meanwhile, as we wait for our own last night, we drink and play pool.

# Olga Costopoulos
## CLUB SANDWICHES

### Faculty Club Saturday Afternoon

I don't trust the double glazing of the wall of window in the bar this frozen afternoon. Waiting my turn to read poems, I order a hot buttered rum, on the principle of warming from the inside. I hold it closely, sipping slowly. I watch the paper birches in the courtyard, their bark wind-whipped into hoary tatters. Two frail emeriti near the glass wall sit holding time like the grail in their hands, sipping it (mixed with pale lager) slowly, as if to draw it out upon the tongue without disturbing it. I catch bits of their conversation: "February is still suicide month." "Yes. The bottom of the icy slope of January. The valley of the shadow of debt." "From Christmas past." I hesitate to read. The birch trees are already growing new bark. But men. . . .

### Faculty Club Saturday Evening

Upstairs now, in the formal dining room. This is the night of the week ties are required. We are greeted by the waiter. He's an Alberta boy but tonight he is Kreshta, affecting a limp and Hungarian accent. (Sometimes he's Jeeves, replete with silver salver, napkin adrape over one arm, the other arm behind him.) He drinks club vodka by the tumbler. It looks like water, so he drinks it like water. But he never stumbles or slurs his words. Across the room, in their usual corner, the husband-and-wife psychiatrists are having their regularly scheduled fight. When the pasta arrives, as if on cue, or perhaps from some subliminal suggestion from Kreshta, they ceremoniously exchange dishes of linguine alle vongole and tagliatelle al salmone—over each other's heads. But they never raise their voices. It will be dessert and coffee before the ancient countess in the other corner bares her breasts and declaims to the whole room that "it was these breasts, these beautiful breasts, that saved me in the Revolution."

109

# Lorna Crozier
## HOME CARE

The woman from Home Care is late. She apologizes, but she had a hel-
luva day yesterday. She was supposed to go fishing with her boyfriend
in LaRonge, packed the sleeping bags in his truck, found the Coleman
stove and fishing rods, made a big pot of chili while he was supposed to
be at work, poured it into coffee tins, then drove to her friend's to pick
up a cooler. This woman's the same age as her mother, but guess what?
There he was fishin' already, she says, but in her friend's bed, get my drift?
So, she goes back to her place and waits, gets all dressed up as if she's
going out, puts on her new shirt and cowboy boots. When he gets there,
sits at the kitchen table, all sorry, blubbering *never again*, she takes the
boots to him and she means what she says, she kicks him right in the face.
Boy, did he look stunned, like a big one when the hook bites in, too
stunned to lift a finger, blood spattering his shirt. And he deserves it. His
first wife said he used to beat on her but who wanted to believe it? *Fishin'
good?* she says. Now he's gone, she means for *ever,* but he'll never be rid
of her. She opened him right above the cheek—there'll be a scar there
three inches long saying *howdee-do* every time he looks in the mirror
and he's the kind of guy has to shave twice a day for the rest of his life
so that's a lot of lookin'.

≈

## QUITTING SMOKING

The phone says smoke when it rings, the radio says smoke, the TV smokes its own images until they are dead butts at three A.M. Three A.M. and the *dépanneurs* are open just for you. White cartons, silver cartons that mirror your face. Behind the counters, the young men who work the night-shift unwrap the cellophane as lovingly as you undo the buttons of a silk shirt, your fingers burning.

Your cat is grey. When he comes in from the muddy lane, his paws leave ashes on the floor. The dirty burner on the stove smokes, the kettle smokes, your first, your last cup of coffee demands a smoke. The snow on the step is a long Vogue paper waiting to be rolled. Above the chimneys stars light up and smoke the whole night through.

In Montreal there are stores where you can buy one cigarette. Cars parked outside, idle, exhaust pipes smoking. Women you could fall in love with approach you from the shadows and offer a light. The sound of a match struck on the black ribbon of a matchbox is the sound of a new beginning. In every dark room across the city, the fireflies of cigarettes are dancing, their small bodies burning out.

Dawn and the neon cross on the mountains melts in the pale light. Another day. Blindfolded and one last wish. Electric, your fingers ignite everything they touch—the curtains, the rug, the sleeping cat. The air around your body crackles and sparks, your hair a halo of fire.

Breathe in, breathe out. Your lungs are animals pacing their cages of bone, eyes burning holes through your chest. The shape of your mouth around an imaginary cigarette is an absence you can taste. Your lips acetylene, desire begins and ends on the tip of your tongue.

The grey of morning—smoke from the sun settling on the roofs, the snow, the bare branches of maple trees. Every cell in your body is a mouth, crying to be heard: *O Black Cat; O ageless Sailor, where have you gone? O Craven A, first letter of the alphabet, so beautiful to say, O Cameo. . . .*

# Philip Dacey
## THE ELEPHANT

I said it was an elephant's turd, but Fay, six, didn't believe me. She wanted to see for herself. I walked her out to County 75, the gravel road a few blocks from our house at the edge of town, where the thing lay, a gray and wrinkled dinner plate. Bending close to study it, she said, "I think it's tar." She had reason on her side, but I stuck to my story. At my age, I had had enough of reason, but she, at hers, was still coming into it. Nevertheless, I could tell that Fay wished she was wrong and I was right. She wanted that elephant turd to be there, in that most unlikely place. She wanted an elephant to have been walking near her house. She wanted to live in the kind of house near which, at any time, an elephant might walk. But her skeptical, rational self made her ask, "How did it get here?" I speculated that when the vans from the circus we had seen in Marshall the previous week drove past on the nearby highway, the back doors of the last one, the one containing the elephant, swung open—someone had forgotten to fasten them—and the elephant tumbled out, rolling surprised but unhurt into the ditch by the side of the road. We saw him then, if it was a him, after a minute or so push himself up and leave the highway to wander down the road leading into our town, a parade of firs on one side, a field of wheat on the other. It was night; the moon bathed his hide in milky light. We talked about how he'd feel, perhaps a little frightened, but glad, too, released from the truck, wandering at his own pace along the inviting gravel road and lifting his great head now and then to observe the domed and cloudless sky. We figured the stars would look to him like appreciative eyes shining through a darkened tent during one of his performances. This night's performance, however, would be his best because here he could act according to his own truest impulses. Tonight he took orders only from himself, listened only to internal cues. The wind was blowing, and he spread his ears out to catch more of it. The silky air must have said something to him about love as elephants know it. As he walked, he swayed, and his tail waved behind him, shyly conducting the moon and the busy stalks of grain bent over themselves like cellists. And then we saw him stop and tense a little, just where we were standing, and make himself happier than he already was.

∼

## THE OPERATION

They take all the parts marked X. You watch this in a mirror above the operating table. You never knew you had so many parts marked X. You ask the doctor what the X means. He says, "Negligible." You worry about this, how your insides are rapidly growing hollow, how a heap of yourself is accumulating in a white pan. A nurse says something about all this going to feed stray dogs. She means well, to comfort you, but you cannot help thinking of the old days, how you posed for pictures in magazines, modeling swimming trunks. You were rich then. The first sign of trouble came when a woman put her hand up inside you, up through the hole you did not know you had. She grimaced, as if she had discovered something damp and maggoty, something luridly and obscenely alive. When she removed her hand, you both saw how it had already begun to turn black. Now the doctor is staring down at you. His face is goggled like a pilot's. You are so light now, so unballasted, you have begun to fly.

# Karen Dale

INVISIBLE

For a time I am invisible, it seems, swathed in thin blankets, waiting in a wheelchair outside the x-ray department. The pain medicine is wearing off; I'm cold and tense, worried I've been forgotten. Twenty feet in front of me a beefy, suntanned doctor dressed in greens, mask dangling at the ready should he be called back into surgery, glances past me, then over his shoulder. Arm extended near his side, his best covert delivery, he brushes hands with a uniformed girl approaching him. She palms the packet, eyes darting in all directions. They are right about me. I am too sick to care about anybody's addictions. He whispers near her hair. Ah! the thrill of secrecy, the intimacy that will sustain him this afternoon, her slight genuflection as she turns back the way she came, assuring him he is needed, worshiped, loved.

~

## BIRTHDAY PARTY

Complications, months of setbacks. I never feel well enough or happy enough to celebrate a clean second-look surgery, certainly not like Patricia Wettig on *Thirtysomething* which I will watch with disdain in reruns. All I can manage are short phone calls, gratuitous smiles. Every word sounds like a cliché. I cannot summon the joy I should feel.

I expected my marriage to improve, that my husband, thinking me precious, would want to change. But his way is to forget the worst, put it behind us, return to normal. Life resumes routine, except that part of me remains apart. I don't fit and I don't want to.

I plan a birthday party for myself in January, invite friends to brunch at Las Brisas and say I am five years younger than I am. It gets a laugh. For hours we stuff ourselves with Belgian waffles, garish fruit-and-whipped-cream castles we build at the buffet. The coffee is brisk and good. We wait for the clouds to lift off the Pacific's pearl gray surface, but this morning they do not lift. A few of us linger, walk the path down through the hundreds of roses, their palette outstanding this dull day. A couple sits on a bench on the bluff, his arm around back, supporting her head. They have been here all morning. She is dying of cancer.

# Julie Dearborn
## COMMUTING

Get back on the Muni. Don't forget your umbrella, it looks like rain. If people stand still and crowd around the door, give them your best "What an asshole" look and gently prod them with the tip of your umbrella. This usually works and they will grudgingly make room for you to push through. If they refuse to move, ask them politely, but with as much scorn as possible, to "please make room for everyone." This almost never fails, unless they are obviously deranged, muttering to themselves or quoting passages from the Bible. In this case, ignore them and let them have their way. Quickly scan the bus for empty seats. Since it's rush hour, there probably won't be any. Pick your spot to stand carefully. Look for a seated passenger whom you think will get off soon. There are lots of telltale signs: the gathering of briefcases, the adjusting of collars and scarves, the quick glances at the door. Soon, you will develop a psychic ability to stand next to people getting off at the next stop. Position yourself with care so that when they rise you can slide gracefully into the vacated seat. Gracefully and with an air of inevitability, as if this seat belonged to you all the time and you were just being nice and letting them use it. Of course, if there are any really old people, or pregnant women, or women holding babies, you must offer them the seat. Otherwise assume it is yours. Once seated, stare vacantly into space or out the window into the black tunnel. Don't meet anyone's gaze. You have probably made some standing passengers envious of your superior ability to obtain a seat. It is a talent like dancing or painting or figure skating. But you must not flaunt this talent, you must take great care not to be arrogant. This is very immature and will offend less-gifted passengers. Carry yourself with an air of aloof yet pained dignity, as if you feel burdened by your genius. If anyone gives you a dirty look, simply stare at them with eyes full of empathy. I understand, your eyes must say, we're all in this together, I know what you're going through. It is best not to speak. After your eyes have won them over, turn your head gently back towards the window.

～

116

## THE SATURDAY PLUMBER

His name is Gil. He smiles as he stares into the sink filled with greenish water, bits of onion and celery. "Did you put celery in the disposal?" he asks. His voice sounds like dirty pipes clanging together. "Uh, I might have," I answer. "Celery doesn't work in a disposal, it gets stringy," he says as he stoops down and unscrews the pipes from under the sink. "Oh yeah," he sighs, "look at this." He pulls mounds of sludgy refuse from the opened pipe, displays it triumphantly. "Oh yeah," he repeats, pulling more and more sludge from the pipe, "it's impacted." "Did you have spaghetti?" he asks as he holds up a bit of unrecognizable goo. "Uh yeah, a few days ago," I mutter, silently vowing never to eat spaghetti again. I stare at his drooping jeans, at the crevice of flesh they reveal, covered with bristly dark hairs, many more than are on his head. He grunts as he works: low, guttural noises. The water, onion, celery mixture pours out of the sink, through the pipe, into a sparkling white plastic bucket. "How much water is left in the sink?" he asks. I peer in, watch it drain. "Not too much." "Okay, I need another tool, be right back." He goes to his truck. I wait by the sink. He is probably not really a plumber at all. He isn't the regular plumber, he is only third string, it is Saturday, all the real plumbers are busy. He is probably a member of a highly sophisticated gang of criminals. He will come back and use his shiny tools as weapons, abduct me into white slavery or leave me bleeding and unconscious on the kitchen floor; I will become an urban statistic. Paralyzed with fear, I listen as he climbs back up the stairs with a stone-age plod, comes back to the kitchen and chuckles as he looks into the opened pipe. "Still clogged." I smile feebly. "I was worried at first," he says, "but I think I'll be able to fix this in no time." He pokes, prods, grunts. "Okay, lady," he grins at me, "let me show you a few things," he says while screwing the pipes back together. "Sure." "Got any bleach," he asks. I go to the cabinet for Clorox, place it carefully on the counter, watch him grasp it with eager hands. "I'll teach you a trick," he says, winking at me conspiratorially. I remain silent. "Let me tell you something about cleaning grease," he holds up blackened hands, gleefully pours bleach onto them, rubs them together vigorously. "Plumbing products are usually nothing but scented bleach," he says, leaning toward me, holding up his hands, now faded gray. "See," his voice is proud, "bleach cuts grease." "Wow, that's great," I say. He pours some Clorox into the sink. "Now, I'm gonna need your help," he squats down to pipe level, his pants droop, I avert my gaze. "You bet," I answer. "What I need, lady, is for you to turn on the water and fill up the sink." I follow his orders and watch the sink fill with water as he rubs his gray hands over the pipes. "How we doin' up there?" "It's almost full." "Okay, let's test it out, let her rip," he commands. I release the stopper, water swirls into the unclogged pipes. "Oh yeah, it's working, it's working," he rubs his hands together as he turns to me. I take a step back. "Now," he says, taking a step toward me. I stand perfectly still, curse myself for having put celery in the chicken soup. He looks at me intently, pauses, raises his hands. "Never," he says, making a fierce negative gesture, "put crystal drain products down the sink, it'll ruin the pipes." "I won't," I promise. He grunts, leans down for his box. "Well, this is it," he says, "my job is done." "I'm so glad," I say. He gathers his tools together. "I love being a plumber," he says, "it's great making people so happy." He snaps his tool box shut with a satisfied flourish. I try for a hearty tone. "May I walk you to the door?" I ask.

～

## SIGNS

My ex-wife's in the trunk, 3-hour service, no extra charge. Custom bookcases computer furniture orthopedic appliances. No nukes no irradiation no nerds no jerks no fat chicks. Divisadero meat market. Ribs chicken beef cocktails dancing. Self-serve. Come dine in our garden. Just say Yes. Ask us about our wedding gown certificate program. Why rough it in a dirty sleeping bag? Compare our prices. Now, I know better. No parking day or night. The touchless car wash is here. Hand picked for freshness. Quality tune-up smog center. Unleaded unleaded unleaded. The sauce of the future. The Kennel Club Little Chapel Church of God in Christ. A birthday celebration in honor of Malcolm X. The Warriors applaud. Move up to the freshest new packs. Battery charges wheel covers recycled gourmets coin-op laundromats leased drivers. All sizes. Bake until golden brown. Give your decorating problems the brush. Honk if you're horny. It works every time.

# Diane di Prima
## WISTERIA LIGHT

In the early days of eternity when none of us was naked as yet, and a good thing too, I opted to plaster the back stairs. Not that the stairs wanted to be plastered, but I was certain that was the only way the billiard table would fit. Workmen dropped hammers here & there. You were vacuuming, by god, though the plaster wasn't dry, as if you were going to get an A for neatness. There were two slots in this greeting card, a kind of microchip it was, with Franz Kline wiring, not that we thought then that black & white would be a problem even for the moon. Our returning to the same haven as uncertain as coming out each time in a different one. No one distinguished between the blessed & unblessed, no immortals had immigrated here for some time. I wanted to order wisteria, something to mitigate the light in those canyons. When you wisely pointed out it wouldn't grow there, I thought to murder you with the pail with which you were mopping the windows. I clearly saw brick walls, the red mellowing to yellow, or brown shingle shadowed with the ancient vines. I wanted none of those we had invited, whoever they were. Or the flat light they loved. I saw that clearly. Return to the present was an unhappy business, saturated as it was with murdered swallows. *I Vesperi Siciliani* slid into one slot, and I was afraid *Pagliacci* would find the other. And there we would be, like the king who drives his chariot around & around in that tiny courtyard, circles of paving stones without even a pear tree. Stuck as a crow on a telephone pole, once you've seen it, the pole is never again empty, there's always a crow, black in your mind's eye in front of the white sky before sunrise.

# Joseph Duemer
## A THEORY OF LANGUAGE

His office phone chirps twice, & then falls silent. They had agreed to break off, but she was signaling. They had agreed to decide on their own what to do about their marriages, that the lust flickering between them created too much static. He punched out her area code, then her number, *Hello?* Her kids in school, or at the neighbors'. Husband at his church, working, counseling someone about their flat or cracked or violent marriage.

They were in the same line of work, & had been meeting in hotels—Atlanta, Minneapolis, San Francisco, Chicago, New York, Phoenix. He didn't know what her living room looked like, nor she his, though there were moments talking to her when he thought he lived there too, an extra member of the family, some weird cousin.

A hotel room is an erotically charged space—complete privacy. Once, in the Southwest, a line of dusty trees wavering far below them in the heat, air conditioning cold from the ceiling, she had asked him to tie her up, wrists & ankles, before making love. He used a couple of his ties, gifts. In a hotel room, as on a stage, you can use any language you can imagine. They used the words they couldn't use at home. The most public language in the world became for them a code, as mysterious as the clicks & whistles of dolphins, or electrical storms echoing through telephone lines. *Yes, hello,* he says, the air of his office still, silent, private.

~

## BLUE DOGS

Singing tonelessly, a blues if only because the phrases keep repeating. Stomping around the room in a kind of dance he doesn't understand. Couldn't understand in an evolutionary—a geological—stretch of time. Her smell on his hands & in his beard. Blue curtains, ceiling flecked with gold. Oh, no stars anywhere. A bunch of dried flowers stutter in the light from a wobbly lamp on the dresser & the room vibrates as the mirror responds to the rhythm of his awkward dance, strange even to himself. Naturally, he stands outside himself. Outside his marriage, which is chugging along without him some hundreds of miles of jet flight away. Where a house & garden sit placidly in sunlight, a child's perfect drawing. He hears a distant hissing & coughing, muted. Rain. Trucks. Cold air seeps into the room around the edges of the loose panes. There's the leading edge of winter sliding into town & soon there will be snow. Some stray dogs raise their muzzles into the air, a tragic music only they know. Music comes from the chintzy radio—a Brahms trio that reminds him of twittering birds gathering on limbs outside the window as the weather changes. Like something of Goya's kept in the Prado basement. He must be drunk. He knows how the dogs talk to each other. The tongue is everything. He looks out his upstairs window at the bloody tail lights of cars rolling down Elm & wants to be going where they're going, with dogs in the car, their smelly breath fogging the windows. A pair of traffic lights casts oily streaks of green/amber/red across the intersection & the rain drives nails into the black parking lot. He remembers Paris! Under the loading docks across from the hotel a couple of dutiful mongrels gnaw something that missed the hotel dumpster, then settle down against each other, sleepy & alert.

# Stephen Dunning

YOU MIGHT SAY . . .

## This is the story of my life

### i.

The dark bruise of the August storm touches down near Blue Earth, snaps power lines and throws Laverne's cousin up against Ed Loeffler's barn. Later the boy will say the plangent wind "grabbed me like a giant, flung me halfway up the barn." Laverne and I are safe in Faribault. We meet at uncut fields, romp bare-ass in the wheat. We wonder where in the entire universe could there be two such lovers as us. Early fall we sign off, take our pay to party in Mankato in motels with TV and indoor pools. We hear the feds are hunting Inez, Black Kettle's great niece. We put out word we'll take her in. Quick as fire she finds us, stays two nights, and splits without a goodbye, taking Laverne's blue cotton blouse. Through the blinds we see the FBI pull out for St. Paul. We buy six bottles of Yoerg's, chug-a-lug to the failure of the fuzz.

### ii.

Earlier, at home after a gig one Sunday in Faribault, my old man's band drinking beer. Arn Bower says, "Man, we don't even got us a name." Les Bruch says, "Well, we're only six fat Dutchmen." "Oh yass," the old man says, holding out his Yoerg's. "That's us, Six Fat Dutchmen, for sure!" He leans to me and says so everyone can hear, "Don't never drink water, son. Fish fuck in it." I'm embarrassed but never forget.

### iii.

I take the job in Blue Earth, raking cans. At the Christmas party, Green Giant 2, Arn Junior puts his hand on Laverne's ass and pulls her in for a kiss. Laverne just flirts, a real sweet girl but dumb. Truly, though, she's A-OK with me, we've had great times. Yet that night my arms are filigreed with cuts from raking cans. I got me two weeks' pay. I got Arn Junior's map to Scarback Lake, a lake I never fished, supposed to be walleyes big as sharks. My Plymouth's running smooth, I'm feeling care-free and wild. On Christmas Eve I call Ma and take off, never even kiss Laverne goodbye. I wonder is she still in Blue Earth, scared and alone? did she parlay her smile and flirty eyes into more than what her parents had for thirty years? did she keep her derring-do? find herself another sweet man like me—a wanderer, pockets hot with cash?

iv.

It ends up Maria and me in Grand Forks, where the wind lives west of town near Malt-O-Meal and smells at night like fresh-baked bread. We learn we cannot hear the siren's wail—our son says whale—when great winds wrap around the town and topple silos and trees. Maria says, "Our crew's OK, but this town lost its mast." Maria's Filipino, says she won't stay and hear that Mayor speak on the Fourth of July.

v.

So off we go, heading west. We hear Doris Day sing "Que Será Será" maybe one thousand times. Past San Juan Capistrano we buy dishes and a red dragon kite from a tall man on the beach and drive to where we will live but never leave unscarred, where our chickens finally hurl themselves into the scarf of traffic on Camino Real. "The dishes are so beautiful," Maria says. "Will it last, do you think?" "Talk right," I say. "People here care what you say."

# Stuart Dybek

## BELLY BUTTON

What was it about the belly button that connected it to the Old Country?

Perhaps, Busha's concern for its cleanliness. Those winter bath nights, windows and mirrors steamed as if we were simmering soup, my hands "wrinkled as prunes," the slippery water sloshing as I stepped from the tub into her terrycloth embrace.

Outside, night billowed like the habits of nuns through vigil lights of snow. Krakow was only blocks away, just past Goldblatt's darkened sign. Bells tolled from the steeple of St. Kasmir's, over the watertowers and smokestacks, over the huddled villages and ghettos of Chicago.

And at the center of my body, Busha's rosary-pinched fingers picked at that knotted opening that promised to lead inward, but never did.

~

## CONFESSION

Father Boguslaw was the priest I waited for, the one whose breath through the thin partition of the confessional reminded me of the ventilator behind Vic's Tap. He huffed and smacked as if in response to my dull litany of sins, and I pictured him slouched in his cubicle, draped in vestments, the way he sat slumped in the back entrance to the sacristy before saying morning mass—hung over, sucking an unlit Pall Mall, exhaling smoke.

Once, his head thudded against the wooden box.

"Father," I whispered, "Father," but he was out, snoring. I knelt, wondering what to do, until he finally groaned and hacked himself awake.

As usual, I'd saved the deadly sins for last: the lies and copied homework, snitching drinks, ditching school, hitch-hiking, which I'd been convinced was an offense against the Fifth Commandment, which prohibited suicide. Before I reached the dirty snapshots of Korean girls, stolen from the dresser of my war hero uncle, Uncle Al, and still unrepentantly cached behind the oil shed, he knocked and said I was forgiven.

As for Penance: "Go in peace, my son, I'm suffering enough today for both of us."

～

## HOMETOWN

Not everyone still has a place from where they've come, so you try to describe it to a city girl one summer evening, strolling together past heroic statues and the homeless camped out like picnickers on the grass of a park that's on the verge of turning bronze. The shouts of Spanish kids from the baseball diamond beyond the park lagoon remind you of playing outfield for the hometown team by the floodlights of tractors and combines, and an enormous, rising moon. At twilight you could see the seams of the moon more clearly than the seams of the ball. You can remember a home run sailing over your head into a cornfield, sending up a cloudburst of crows. . . .

Later, heading back with her to your dingy flat past open bars, the smell of sweat and spilled beer dissolves into a childhood odor of fermentation: the sour, abandoned granaries by the railroad tracks where the single spark from a match might still explode. A gang of boys would go there to smoke the pungent, impotent, home-grown dope and sometimes, they said, to meet a certain girl. They never knew when she'd be there. Just before she appeared the whine of locusts became deafening and grasshoppers whirred through the shimmering air. The daylight moon suddenly grew near enough for them to see that it was filled with the reflection of their little fragment of the world, and then the gliding shadow of a hawk ignited an explosion of pigeons from the granary silos. They said a crazy bum lived back there too, but you never got a look at him.

# Russell Edson
## THE BREAKFAST THAT CAME TO DINNER

A sailor who was actually a bathtub merchant; or should I say a baker who was actually a fur trapper. . . . No no, I shall say a lunch that was actually a delayed breakfast, came to our house for dinner.

It was explained that while making its way in the streets it suddenly became confused and knocked on the first door, the one seen most prominently, though vaguely, at the height of its confusion.

We quite understand. No need to explain. Just in time for dinner. Here, let us hang up your pea jacket. We'll just put those bathtubs in our bathroom, they won't seem so out of place there. Your muffin hat, here, we'll put it on this hook. The animal skins and traps, we'll hang them in the hall closet.

Did you say you were lunch? Oh, I see, a delayed breakfast, sort of a brunch. Well, what's the difference, it's already suppertime. If we're not careful it'll be getting on to midnight snack time. Time is always running out. Then it becomes breakfast time again; then brunch, and so on. No wonder you were so confused.

You must get away someday early in the morning before the traffic, as it were, before the hunger, before we rise from our murdered sleep. . . .

Find yourself a nice kitchen table in a good normal home. Arrive just at breakfast time. The birds full at song. Lay out your pretty things, your dowry of bathtubs and traps—Yes, lay out your pretty things, your grapefruit juice and toast; pretend you are a bride—Pretend the kitchen is the bed of consummation.

~

## THE EXPLOSION AT THE CLUB

The ape is accepted, and sits quietly smoking a cigar and reading a newspaper, which he holds upside down.

This is all after the commotion. . . .

And so the ape begins a career at the club of sipping scotch and flicking ashes from his cigars.

Someone says, he does seem a decent chap. . . .

And yes, the ape is blending quite nicely with the paneled walls and leather chairs. One has to look quite carefully to pick out the six hundred pounds of animal flesh.

And many club evenings pass, the ape lost in a moth landscape of newspapers poised at the financial news. . . .

Someone says of the ape, he's really not a bad fellow, he minds his own business. . . .

Then one evening the ape's head explodes like a small cannon going off.

All the gentlemen turn to see what the great beast has been up to.

Out of the place where its head should start are uncoiled clock springs exploded out of its neck like a battered rooster's tail.

Someone says, I never did like him, always had a feeling there was something funny about him. . . .

～

## THE FAMILY MONKEY

We bought an electric monkey, experimenting rather recklessly with funds carefully gathered since grandfather's time for the purchase of a steam monkey.

We had either, by this time, the choice of an electric or gas monkey.

The steam monkey is no longer being made, said the monkey merchant.

But the family always planned on a steam monkey.

Well, said the monkey merchant, just as the wind-up monkey gave way to the steam monkey, the steam monkey has given way to the gas and electric monkeys.

Is that like the grandfather clock being replaced by the grandchild clock?

Sort of, said the monkey merchant.

So we bought the electric monkey, and plugged its umbilical cord into the wall.

The smoke coming out of its fur told us something was wrong.

We had electrocuted the family monkey.

⁓

## MR. & MRS. DUCK DINNER

An old woman with a duck under her arm is let into a house and asked, whom shall I say is calling?

Mr. and Mrs. Duck Dinner.

If you don't mind my asking, which is which?

Pointing to the duck the old woman says, this here's my husband.

A little time passes and the butler reappears, yes come right in, you're expected, the kitchen's just this way.

In the kitchen there's a huge stove. The butler says, I'm sorry, we don't have a pot big enough for you; so we're using an old cast-iron bathtub. I hope you don't mind? We have a regular duck pot for your husband.

No no, this is fine, I'll make pretend I'm having a bath.—Oh, by the way, do you have enough duck sauce? says the old woman.

Yes, plenty, and the cook's made up a nice stuffing, too.

My husband'll need plucking; I can undress myself, says the old woman.

Fine, that'll be a great help; we'll have the kitchen girl defeather your husband.—By the way, what would you suggest with duck? asks the butler.

Wild rice, but not too wild, we wouldn't want any trouble in the dining room; and perhaps asparagus spears. . . . But make sure they're not too sharp, they can be quite dangerous; best to dull them on a grinding wheel before serving. . . .

Very good, Madam.—By the way, do you think that having the kitchen girl defeather your husband might be a little awkward, if you know what I mean? She is rather pretty; wouldn't want to start any difficulties between you and your husband, says the butler.

No worry, says the old woman, we're professional duck dinners; if we started fooling around with the kitchen help we'd soon be out of business.—If you don't mind I'd like to get into the oven as soon as possible. I'm not as young as I used to be, not that I'm that old, but it does take me a little longer these days. . . .

⁓

## THE SECRET GRAVEYARD

Elephants like burlap underwear. It wears better than silk, and has more style.

They're shy about this appetite. Underwear embarrasses them.

When the desire overtakes them they head for the secret graveyard of elephants. No one know where that is. They feel safe there.

Surrounded by the bleached bones of their ancestors they shyly submit themselves to the delicious feel of burlap. They feel even more naked wearing it. They don't know why. And then they giggle.

Of course they cannot reenter the forest wearing underwear. A hyena might laugh. Tarzan is another thought. . . .

Sadly they must leave their underwear in the bones of their ancestors. They remember to murmur brief prayers as they leave. . . .

⁓

## UNDER GREAT LIGHT FLOODED CLOUDS

The horse is sticky. If you touch it, it sticks to your hands like chewing gum. The moon is all over the place.

A small village in the distance; dark brooding turtles with faint yellow eyes.

The horse, touching against its stall, leaves most of its rump. I scrape it off and pat it back, and start the horse out toward the moonlight.

One of its hooves sticks to the floor, and becomes a long dark thread.

The moon is falling all over the place. In the sky great light flooded clouds are torn like bread.

I mount, and am away. . . .

# Heid Erdrich

## BOYFRIEND

He was ugly as a troll and sturdy as a troll. His stubby arms and legs bunched with muscles, his chest was barrel-wide and hairless. His grin half looped up his cheeks like a happy face. Though not a simpleton, he smiled most of the time. And yet no woman would have him.

When called Pumpkin Head or Pie Face, he stamped with fury, growled like the Tasmanian Devil and turned the deadly ray of his piggly gray eyes upon the name-caller. He shut whole restaurants up. Men twice his size wouldn't mess with him. And yet no woman would have him.

With his father always on their couch pickled and curled like a fetus, and his mom with her pug-dog face, with her punched-in face of a drunk's wife—what did he have to be beautiful for?

Greasy to his elbows, monkey in a car engine, handy with tools— you wouldn't want him with your daughter but let him slide beneath your junk cars, slide into that dark and private world of parts—He charmed cars, or cursed them with his boot tips screaming Work you Dog Fucker! Dog Fucker! I could kick a dog to death!

And yet no woman would love him, but I did. I was a girl. Think of how beautiful we all were once and how we learned to love the beast.

# Dave Etter

## BASEBALL

We stand for "The Star-Spangled Banner." The home-plate umpire shouts "Play ball!" The leadoff batter spits tobacco juice through his teeth. The pitcher spits. The catcher spits. The first baseman spits into his glove and rubs it in with the heel of his hand. The second baseman spits on the infield dirt, and so does the rookie shortstop, who, being a bit nervous, just called up from the Iowa farm club, dribbles some spit on his chin. The third baseman spits. The pitcher spits again and checks the outfielders, who all spit at the same time. The first pitch of the game is a fastball strike, right over the outside corner of the plate. The batter turns his head and says a few angry words to the home-plate umpire, and spits. "Have an eye, ump," shouts the visiting team's manager from the dugout, and he spits a brown stream of Beech-Nut halfway to the third-base foul line.

~

## GRAIN ELEVATOR

It was one of those sunny, shiny penny, slicked-back mornings in the middle of May. The purple and white lilacs were in full bloom and the soft breeze smelled like homemade bread and just-ironed clothes. "What are you doing today?" Doreen said, when I came out of Butterfield's Bakery carrying a sack of still-warm jelly doughnuts. "Well," I said, "I'm going down to see the new grain elevator by the Chicago and North Western tracks and ask somebody how tall it is, and how many bushels of corn it holds, and could I see if there's anything stored there now?" She gave me her best Doreen smile—the one she used to get an A in English from old man Engstrom—and squeezed my arm. I spread my right hand over her blue-jeaned left buttock and rubbed it gently. "Does that mean you want me to come along?" she said. "I wouldn't have it any other way, lover," I said, reaching for a jelly doughnut.

132

# Roland Flint
PAINT


He's twenty-two and left everything to come here and paint and this morning he thinks he wants to paint the sunrise again, so he must get up at four-thirty to gather and ready his gear: canvas, portable easel, a paint box with many paints and brushes, because he can't anticipate exactly the colors and textures of sunrise, and he knows that, and that is part of what he likes about painting it.

He knows the best place in this frozen town for watching the winter sunrise: it is the top floor of a girl's dormitory on the campus of a formerly all-women's college.

He looks like a student himself, and he knows it, and knows he will have no trouble getting in, and anyhow he is carrying all that unrefusable zeal and equipment and has those bright sunhungering eyes, slightly crazed.

The guard mistakes him for an ordinary part of the bright cold ordinary morning: "Jesus, these kids are sonthin'—I mean they *never* sleep, ehnn? and they're screwin' *all* the time—I had a kid come up 'ere at five in the mornin', says he ain't got a girl here, says he's a *painter*—are you ready for this?—says he's gonna paint the *sunrise—bull*shit."

But he is, and he is all set up in time and he is ready when the sun begins, bright-eyed and nuts in his clarity, everything ready, very happy about what he thinks he is, which happens this time to be exactly what he is, ten stories of beautifully sleeping girls he has ascended through to find himself right here, on this perfect scaffolding of drowsing arms and legs, the lovely heads turned this way, or turning, light and dark, shiny and tousled, all sighs and shapes of hollows and color, resting and waiting too, and he is ready for the sunrise, all his brushes and colors ready.

~

## SABBATICAL

What am I sleeping to on these days, a sabbatical in the second year of my fifth decade—*fifth* is what I mean to write, but I almost write *last*.

I've never slept so much, so well, so long and dreamless as now, the last two weeks.

I've come north from a February spring in Georgia to this March winter and the reverse has spun me back to something, a phase of infancy or some new prenatal term, some getting ready again.

I roll to the crook of my sleep and stay, in the dark comfort of some innocent change I'm turning to.

This could be the last great sleep of youth, a menopausal sleep, the last innocence and separation to the final wakefulness of age, the drifting snow to the rickety laths of a fence I'll never see—that is, if it is a sleep at all and not the permanent insomnia in the corner of an eye—whose eye?

I think of Grandma Dvorak reading from her Czech Bible all night long, rocking back and forth, moaning, davening, telling the air around her, "I'm ready for Jesus, unhhh, I'm ready for Jesus."

No: I sleep because I can. It has taken me almost three months to feel no deadlines, no deadlines, the lumped failure in my neck when the daily bread is chewing.

The last dream I remember, before the Sabbath rest came down, I was running scared to give a talk I'd never heard of, something heavy pulling the left side.

But after three months I have found my drowsy holiday, my first three months without a job since the fifth or sixth grade.

After how many years on the stones of that scent—a dampness on copper, must of clarinets, the spit-metal smells of fear—after all these years I have found the boy to sleep. So soundly and full and soft I don't get up at all until morning and then I have to hurry and almost do that adolescent handstand to make my water.

In the five hour sleeps of my other life, I'm up almost every hour to worry and dribble.

Yesterday I had a long walk, and a nap, and I slept nine hours last night.

This morning I had oatmeal for breakfast, the snow is so deep.

∾

## HIS OYSTER

He lives in Washington, D.C., and he goes all the way to Georgia by car, passing through Virginia, North Carolina, South Carolina, then through part of Georgia on his way down to Savannah, then he goes by bus through Savannah to Vernon View, then he goes by boat across bays and inlets and sounds of the Atlantic to Ossabaw Island, then he goes by station wagon to the main house, then he goes by pickup truck with Mr. Jimmie Willard Perkins (nicknamed Middleton) to a tidal river to fish two hours for trout, with no luck, then he goes by foot, with Middleton, one mile downriver through the woods to an oyster bed Middleton knows about, and there he finds an oyster—or a hard, gray-brown shell, covered with little stones and carbuncles that looks like it could be an oyster. He knows there is something in it he wants. He takes a razor-sharp knife that has come from Sweden for this (via Sears in D.C., trips to Maine, Vermont) and he tries to open this thing which has the brave, angry face of a petrified knish. It will not open. He takes a stone and taps easy, then hard, on the base of the handle, trying to drive it into the oyster—it doesn't work, the oyster slips away, sideways, he tries again and fails again, and then he blows up and puts it on a big flat rock and pounds it with a stone, just trying to smash it, and that doesn't work, and he picks the sonofabitch up and throws it down as hard as he can and he thinks well now would be a god-damned good time for a miracle, for it to roll over and just open slowly and teach him something about the futility of violence, the shame of pride, the pride of anger, the surprise of faith where not to knock by Christ is open wide. Instead it stays tighter than a bull's ass in fly-time, teaching the horseshit of inwit, the agenbite and fuck you of fantasy, and the true kryptonite hardness of an oyster you can't have even if you're Clark Kent and have driven six hundred miles to get it. Middleton spits some Honey-cut and says, "ats fuckin oyrsters."

# Jennifer Footman
## DALLAS

Here she is in this tin box thing about to fly from Dallas to Reno. God, give her air, hands full, sweating like a pig about to be stuck, she examines her ticket and it says 13A. 13B and 13C are empty but someone is in 13A—the window seat. It's been one of those days. The hell plane from Toronto to Dallas. Sturmbahnfuehrer stewards, and stewardesses who must practice S & M for Sunday School picnics. Then four hours in this white, so white terminal in Dallas. She went out with a doctor called Dallas once. Not once, in fact, she went out with him for two years starting when she was fourteen and he was forty and he told her his family, way back mind, was in the slave trade and that, kind of, put her off—just a bit, you know, because at the same time she was going out with Ibrahim from Ghana, as black as Dallas was white, and it wasn't as if she was fucking either of them, not her. The man she finally fucked, halfway through her fourteenth year, while she was still seeing Dallas and Ibrahim, was Gordon the fish filleter who stank of haddock and sometimes cod and he had purple hands and chewed nails and smelly feet and breath and . . . oh . . . gray underpants. The gray underpants did it for her and she dumped him after the first two fucks. Back to Dallas. He was the one to teach her the slick, fine art of masturbation and how to drink just like a man. Yes, at fifteen she could hold her beer just like a laborer. But here she is on this dumb plane and this, Oh, So-Perfect-Gentleman sitting in her window seat. He asks if he can help her with her bag though she is managing just fine. She shakes her head and thanks him. He tells her she's standing at the correct place and she should sit down. She sits. Later, during the three-hour flight, he chats about how he had always wanted to see the Sierras in daylight. Well, so had she. She had ached for mountains after her home of sea-flat Southern Ontario. That was why she had booked the window seat a good month ago. Her mouth full of bile, she thinks her teeth are dissolving and her tongue tanning into a whip. To add insult to injury they charge for drinks on this American plane! He offers to buy her a drink. She orders a double scotch and smiles sweetly as she sits in his seat and he sits in hers and he knows it and she knows he knows and she says nothing.

∾

## DELIRIUM TREMENS:
## TRAIN FROM GLASGOW TO EDINBURGH

My sister—the one who was an alcoholic—had a vision of angels: three of them were perched on the corner of her ceiling, calling to her. They said *don't worry, be happy, don't worry.* This was before the time of the song of the same name so she couldn't have got this from the song. Don't worry. When she told people about the vision they said she had finally developed D.T.s. Angels are such silly things. It would be most inconvenient to have angels popping up all over the place and it's not as if they are any practical use. There, and not there. You can't pin them down. Not exactly. Gone like the seeds of a dandelion. Gone and still there. A bit like those phantom limbs. When a limb is cut off in the middle of pointing it points forever and forever. The leg which had cancer and used to get cramps at night will still get cramps at night. It's the same with shitty angels popping up all over the house. She argued that they are there all the time and we don't see them, not even a poet like me. Just for a moment they do appear and become as real as the amputated finger.

Our cousin Harry, who looked very like my sister, liked to stick his head out of trains. He did it once too many times when he was twenty. Another train passed and neatly de-skulled him. His mother told my mother it was as if a boiled egg had been shelled. So neat. Hardly any blood and the brain glistening as clean as an eye. He died before they could get him to hospital. She had tried to put his head back but it didn't fit once it was off. She said she hadn't known what to do, holding him, his brain blinking at her and the vessels pumping all the time. As if there was nothing wrong with her being able to see right into his head.

# Carolyn Forché
ANCAPAGARI

In the morning of the tribe this name Ancapagari was given to these mountains. The name, then alive, spread into the world and never returned. Ancapagari: no footstep ever spoken, no mule deer killed from its foothold, left for dead. Ancapagari opened the stones. Pine roots gripped peak rock with their claws. Water dug into the earth and vanished, boiling up again in another place. The water was bitten by aspen, generations of aspen shot their light-colored trunks into space. Ancapagari. At that time, if the whisper was in your mouth, you were lighted.

Now these people are buried. The root-taking, finished. Buried in everything, thousands taken root. The roots swell, nesting. Openings widen for the roots to surface.

They sway within you in steady wind of your breath. You are forever swinging between this being and another, one being and another. There is a word for it crawling in your mouth each night. Speak it.

Ancapagari has circled, returned to these highlands. The yellow pines deathless, the sparrow hawks scull, the waters are going numb. Ancapagari longs to be spoken in each tongue. It is the name of the god who has come from among us.

~

## THE COLONEL

What you have heard is true. I was in his house. His wife carried a tray of coffee and sugar. His daughter filed her nails, his son went out for the night. There were daily papers, pet dogs, a pistol on the cushion beside him. The moon swung bare on its black cord over the house. On television was a cop show. It was in English. Broken bottles were embedded in the walls around the house to scoop the kneecaps from a man's legs or cut his hands to lace. On the windows there were gratings like those in liquor stores. We had dinner, rack of lamb, good wine, a gold bell was on the table for calling the maid. The maid brought green mangoes, salt, a type of bread. I was asked how I enjoyed the country. There was a brief commercial in Spanish. His wife took everything away. There was some talk then of how difficult it had become to govern. The parrot said hello on the terrace. The colonel told it to shut up, and pushed himself from the table. My friend said to me with his eyes: say nothing. The colonel returned with a sack used to bring groceries home. He spilled many human ears on the table. They were like dried peach halves. There is no other way to say this. He took one of them in his hands, shook it in our faces, dropped it into a water glass. It came alive there. I am tired of fooling around he said. As for the rights of anyone, tell your people they can go fuck themselves. He swept the ears to the floor with his arm and held the last of his wine in the air. Something for your poetry, no? he said. Some of the ears on the floor caught this scrap of his voice. Some of the ears on the floor were pressed to the ground.

## Sesshu Foster

Five kids slept in the car on the long highway to L.A. Their mother, the woman who had been beaten, drove the grapevine down into the smoggy basin. When the little ones cried, she told the older ones to pick them up in the hot, sticky confines of the car hurtling, they say, through a stream of traffic into a city smeltering like an immense parking lot. They drove the freeway for a long time; perhaps the woman made a mistake and took the long way or traffic was bad at points or perhaps there was no direct route by freeway. They were a long time negotiating side streets, boulevards and avenues. The city looked big and hot, ugly, strange. This was their new home (the bruise of her broken cheekbone a black line almost invisible now, the stiff knuckles of fingers on her left hand swollen as if from arthritis). Finally, she pulled into a gas station to buy more gas. The kids looked out the windows; their mother made a phone call. The older kids noticed how people looked at the battered station wagon full of dusty kids, how their mom, too, looked more like them in her drab, threadbare blouse than she looked like the people staring on the street. She drove out onto the boulevard, with the kids whining, thirsty, tired. She pulled over to change the baby's diaper again. She rushed into a liquor store and bought three popsicles to share. She drove to a drive-in movie theater. There was a field next to it full of cars and she parked in heat waves dancing from cabs and hoods, coupes and cartops. She lined the kids up outside the creaking, sighing car, spit into a paper napkin and wiped snot, chocolate, and dirt off of their faces. She combed the girls' hair while they complained, and the oldest girl wiped sweaty dirt from her palms onto her dress. Their mother led them all through the crowd to a fat man sitting under a tarp selling used car parts and tools. When he saw them he looked them over as the woman lined her family up before him, and told the kids, "This is your uncle. We will be staying with him for now." The man spit onto the ground beside his folding chair, shifted his immense bulk and snarled, "Send 'em to go fetch me a beer from the snack bar. It's hotter than shit today."

∼

Sometimes I'm dragged. Sometimes I'm very dragged. The sun hits me like a hot glacier. And I'm transfixed like a traffic light. Sometimes you can see the mountains from here, sometimes you can't. Sometimes you can breathe this air, sometimes you can't. When it gets too rough, I go walk up around the hill. I go to see Nestor's Mom. Lupe's getting into her late sixties, and if it's a sunny day I'll find her someplace on the steep side of the hill she planted with an orchard. A solid, nicely-dressed woman who favors bright color, she'll be busy up there, pruning her trees, or maybe harvesting fruit: oranges, plums, avocados, lemons. She cultivates enough for a fruit stand. Lupe'll have her hair—just starting to gray now—tied back in a kerchief. She'll take a minute, finish what she's doing and come down off the ladder, wiping the dust off her face or neck. Taking off her gloves and handing them to me, calling my name and smiling as if she had just noticed me. "You get the rest of the ones on top, the ones I can't reach," Lupe'll say. "You got here just on time!" I'll put on the gloves, if they are the pair that fit, and work up on the ladder for awhile, as Lupe goes down the hill and drags up the hose, or does something else. As we work, and Lupe's telling me what to do next, she'll complain about her son, my friend Nestor, how he drinks too much and hurts her daughter-in-law, how they fight and make up, how they make her feel old with their fighting all the time. And I'll say, yeah, that's how Nestor is, but at least he's kept his last job for almost five years now and hasn't gone crazy yet. And we talk about everybody. She knows more people around here than I do, generations that came before I lived on this street. And Lupe will tell me when to quit. I will bundle the branches or haul sacks of litter to her screened-off back porch. And it will feel to me like I'm back in the thirties or forties, when the Japanese side of my family used to work the fields. There is the purity of green things, the warm calendar of earth they abide, the dusty smell of moldy sacks and boxes of glassware and flats of shoots or bulbs on the porch, things I imagine my relatives knew in their lives before the concentration camps of World War Two took that away forever. And Lupe will take my gloves, hand me a clean towel, and tell me to go wash up. And she'll insist I sit in the kitchen for something hot off the stove, or ice-cold juice. We will gossip and laugh. And as I leave, telling her to have Nestor call me soon, she'll press on me as much fruit as I can carry away. And I will laugh, thinking about the things she says, and walk away down the street, having stolen as much as l can of sunshine from Lupe's side of the hill, her orange blossoms and warm kitchen scents, of her laughing eyes and her smile. She will never know how grateful I am for half-moons of dirt left under my fingernails, for the jasmine-sharp tang of crushed leaves, for the cool shade of the porch as you come up out of her yard. For a time I will be fooled into believing that I, too, show some of the grace of strong hands able to make things grow, of laughter that survives the years. I will pour the fruit in a bowl at the center of the table, and for a time, I will have it to remind me.

# Richard Frost

## A BIRD OF SOME KIND

There, through my new glass door, the moon heads to the trees. For now, it's bright, the frost sharp, my dog curled by his post, everything settled. What's left of the cabbage, the heads half-formed, creaks on its fat stems. Next year I am not planting a garden. I think I will go get the six-pack.

From the creek, probably the swamp willow, something calling, same as last night. A bird of some kind. If I were out there, the twigs would slap me. I'd be no warm ball of feathers. I'd see the moon pasted on my door. If I put my tongue against the window, it would freeze. I'd have to break out the glass, carry the piece against my face, lean over the stove. I should drive somewhere.

I could kill myself, but I know this bird, who moaned to my ancestors in this house and to deer scratching in the snow for grass before there was a house—this bird would have my tongue.

The trees cover the moon. The bird hides his face, if he is there. I could be his dream. I'm losing the lines of the trees, the barn, my car in its place, my dog. There's nothing to do.

～

## BURRO

Posing beside the huge rattlesnake head at the Mexican pyramid are my mother and father, my brother and his wife, and myself at nineteen. My mother leans against the pyramid, ecstatic with travel. My father glares at the guide, who is taking the picture. My brother and his wife stand tightly together, still in love. I sneer gallantly in my new prescription sunglasses. We have named Arturo, our guide, Arturo the Burro. Once last year I laughed on the telephone with my sister-in-law about it. Now whom could I tell?

Arturo, I would like to talk with you about my fine trip with my family. I apologize for the name we gave you, and for my arrogance the

143

night you brought me to that hotel bar with the fat little Indian whores around their table. Now I would nod politely and quietly drink my beer. And if one of them came to our table, I would ask her name and buy her a drink. Now I would not be afraid, for I am much older, and all my family are dead.

～

## THE ROOF

You go up there with your wife, with flashing cement and Old Reliable tar paper. You go up there with brushes and hammers and nails and a roll of membrane and a can of tar. Then your wife, less afraid of heights than you, works all around the edge, cutting out the cracked sections and replacing them with new paper and cement. You yourself work similarly all over the center. You cut away the bad paper and fit under a new piece and cement and nail it down, and you do this dozens of times until the roof looks good. Then you and your wife open the can of tar and take up the brushes as far as you can and come down the ladder to the porch roof and climb in the window and track tar all through the house and throw away your clothes and take a can of gasoline and some rags and clean off as much of the tar as possible and then take a shower together and open a bottle of Scotch and get drunk while the storm gathers and the sky opens with more water than you've ever seen. The ceilings leak, the brown stains grow, the plaster comes down, the beams rot. The room you've just remodeled warps and wrinkles. You set pans in the attic. The water crawls on the ceiling and falls where it wants. It comes downstairs. It all wants in from the storm. You fight with it and pour it into the drain, but it comes back, crying to meet itself in the cellar. You carry all your tar and caulk and flashing and brushes and plugs and everything you have heard of for roofs, and you set it ready by the ladder. And next time, next time, in the good clean sun, you will get the whole thing right.

# Maureen Gibbon
## TRAINS CARRYING SLEEPERS

The dolphins made me stay in that town. The first time I saw them I could not believe they swam so close to shore. The water darkened and blistered above the places they swam and the strange blister of the sea moved, ignoring the current. When the dolphins broke the surface I could see their fins above the roiling water. On sunny mornings the dolphins' bodies looked gray-blue against the silver surface of the ocean but on cloudy days or in the evenings the dolphins were black arcs. When they left the shore, they headed toward the southern horizon, the coast of Africa. If I did not see them on a certain day I imagined that they stayed in some brighter water to feed.

I had a cheap room in the town, far from the water in a pension near the train station. The coming and going of trains broke my sleep but comforted me, too. I liked to wake and think of all the people sleeping in their compartments, going further along the coast or north, and then I would sleep again. I didn't care that my room was small and that my sheets weren't changed very often—I was there for the sea. I walked to the beach each morning and did not go back to my room until night, and, in a week, my skin was brown and accustomed to the sun. I believe I could have stayed all day in the light but always I left the beach at noon to buy fruit for my lunch and to find a quiet place to sleep in a park that overlooked the city. No one bothered my sleep, though they might have—a woman alone. My reddish-brown skin and tangled hair, my cheap clothes—even my smell, since I bathed only in the sink in my room and at the showers on the beach—something protected me in my sleep. When I woke up, I went back down through the vielle ville to the beach for the evening.

I lived like that for a month, then another month. I was too poor to go anywhere except the water but I didn't care. At night I walked home along the avenue, my skin brown and tight, and watched people promenading in the night air. I could have had lovers—the owner of the pension knocked on my door with magazines in English and asked me not to call him *vous,* but I didn't want him. I didn't want the young Swedes who threw francs in my window when I forgot to close a shutter and they saw me bathing, and I didn't want the young Arab workers on vacation from the industrial cities who hissed at my white hair when they saw me walking on the boardwalk.

They were all handsome but I did not want a man. I wanted to sleep on my dusty sheets which smelled of my hair and skin, of baby oil, and the strange sea-sweet smell I carried between my legs. I lay in bed each night listening to the trains carrying their sleepers and thought of the dolphins. I longed to touch their blue-gray skin and I wished for a tail strong enough to carry me through the dark sea. I wanted a body that did not split at the hip, that did not open and open.

～

## UN BRUIT QUI COURT

On the island, women are moored like boats.

In late summer the grass and ground vines of the island have dried. Crickets rub their wings together and all day long the brush on the side of the road ticks and scratches in the heat. Men have returned from the morning catch to sit at their dinners. Voices and the sound of knives and forks on the plates come through the closed shutters of the island houses.

In the harbor the women wait. They are tied to logs sunken in the shore-bottom or to metal rings along the stone seawall of the port. The paint on the boats is scorched, hot to the touch. It peels away in layers. These are small boats, skiffs, only large enough for two or three men. Fish swim beneath the boats in the cool shadows.

The men do not understand that their women are moored boats. One side bakes and dries in the sun and the men know it is for carrying and ferrying, but the underside is a blue world they do not know how to see or harvest. Sometimes a plank of wood splits in one of the boats because of the heat. The sound is sharp, like a hand clap, but has a small cry or screech in it, too. And there is the plank, split in two. The men can do that with their heat, make a woman cry out. She may also split silently so that you would never know.

# Reginald Gibbons
## ON BELMONT

Watch it! brother, he said, who had come up beside me without my even noticing it as I was walking on crowded Belmont late one summer night. He had already dropped into a squat, half-leaning against the building wall, a brown-bagged bottle in one hand. Get down, he warned me.

Ragged, stoned, looking full of fear. I stopped near him.

I don't think I had heard even a backfire.

Machine guns, he said. I know, I was *there,* he said, turning his head from side to side.

Not machine guns, I said, to be helpful. Then I had what I thought was a good idea. I said, And even if it is, they're a long way from here. (They'd *have* to be, suppose it *was* possible, they were still blocks away from here, at least, off down the busy late-hour streets lit too bright. We had plenty of time.)

Oh, he said; meaning, Is that what you think? With a quick glance. His gaze sidelong, but strong. It would take too long to teach me. But he explained: That's when they're really bad, that's when they get you, when they're far away.

He stayed low, one knee half up, squatting on the other thigh, protecting the bottle held half behind him. He looked up and down the street. I waited as long as I could, maybe half a minute, but all this was over now, that was about as far as we could take it, now that we had had our moment of contact in this world, after the accumulated years when separately we had wandered other streets and other countries. We had happened to be momentarily side by side at the sound of whatever it had been, maybe a gun. I started on down Belmont, and got back my pace, I was heading for the train.

Maybe to him, still squatting and leaning there, not yet ready to stand up, or able, it seemed like he was the one who would get to where things made sense and were safe, and I was walking foolishly in a place of danger. How could he explain it to me, it was way too late for me and everybody like me.

147

# Allen Ginsberg
## A SUPERMARKET IN CALIFORNIA

What thoughts I have of you tonight, Walt Whitman, for I walked down the sidestreets under the trees with a headache self-conscious looking at the full moon.

In my hungry fatigue, and shopping for images, I went into the neon fruit supermarket, dreaming of your enumerations!

What peaches and what penumbras! Whole families shopping at night! Aisles full of husbands! Wives in the avocados, babies in the tomatoes!—and you, Garcia Lorca, what were you doing down by the watermelons?

I saw you, Walt Whitman, childless, lonely old grubber, poking among the meats in the refrigerator and eyeing the grocery boys.

I heard you asking questions of each: Who killed the pork chops? What price bananas? Are you my Angel?

I wandered in and out of the brilliant stacks of cans following you, and followed in my imagination by the store detective.

We strode down the open corridors together in our solitary fancy tasting artichokes, possessing every frozen delicacy, and never passing the cashier.

Where are we going, Walt Whitman? The doors close in an hour. Which way does your beard point tonight?

(I touch your book and dream of our odyssey in the supermarket and feel absurd.)

Will we walk all night through solitary streets? The trees add shade to shade, lights out in the houses, we'll both be lonely.

Will we stroll dreaming of the lost America of love past blue automobiles in the driveways, home to our silent cottage?

Ah, dear father, graybeard, lonely old courage-teacher, what America did you have when Charon quit poling his ferry and you got out on a smoking bank and stood watching the boat disappear on the black waters of Lethe?

~

## THE BRICKLAYER'S LUNCH HOUR

Two bricklayers are setting the walls of a cellar in a new dug-out patch of dirt behind an old house of wood grown over with ivy on a shady street in Denver. It is noon and one of them wanders off. The young subordinate bricklayer sits idly for a few minutes after eating a sandwich and throwing away the paper bag. He has on dungarees and is bare above the waist; he has yellow hair and wears a smudged but still bright red cap on his head. He sits idly on top of the wall on a ladder that is leaned up between his spread thighs, his head bent down, gazing uninterestedly at the paper bag on the ground. He draws his hand across his breast, and then slowly rubs his knuckles across the side of his chin and rocks to and fro on the wall. A small cat walks to him along the top of the wall. He picks it up, takes off his cap, and puts it over the kitten's body for a moment to try it out. Meanwhile it is darkening as if to rain.

# Diane Glancy
## IF NOT ALL THESE

What's it like to pass from this world? Is it a tunnel with a light at the end? A field in which your father waits and you talk to him again? Is it a drop into a well? A step you forgot was there jarring your teeth? Possibly death is a long trail to the far corner of the prairie. Sometimes wolves still howl. Maybe death is a structure of language outside the voice. A getting-out of the body like the chores you never wanted to do. Here comes death wearing a khaki raincoat—an acquaintance whose name you can't remember when it's time to introduce him. A mother who finally picks you up after school when everyone has gone. Maybe death is riding a horse for the first time and not getting thrown. A burst of gladiolas from an amphora. Could death be the laundry chute in the old house where you sent your overalls? Even the cat. Maybe it's the dust-bowl. Or lunar desolation. The edge of the highway from which you can't step back. Maybe death is a morning when you wake and remember it's your birthday. No—the first day of school you dreaded but find it's not so bad. And soon you get into it. You put on your pinwheel skirt, your halo like an old propeller hat. You flap your teflon wings and soon you're far above the Rio Grande.

~

## WAR HORSE II

The next time I see my old car is in the movies. Yes. You won't believe it. But there's this film. This documentary. *Without Reservations*. And my old car is in it. Showing up like a big shot. Next to the moose hanging on the scaffolding after hunting season. The Indian friend, who has my car now, starting to dress the moose. And the car there as if it took part in the hunt. As if maybe it held the bow and arrow. Just like when you go to the Hunting Grounds you are new again and the old way of life returns as if you'd never had to do without it. Yes. I know someday I'll see the car again on the highway. We'll pass as if old friends. Did not our heart burn within us? the disciples asked when Christ passed them on the road after the resurrection. They were going somewhere talking with their friends. And he just passed. Yes, sometime I'll be going somewhere and my old car will come up from behind and pass me the way I know sometimes my father has been beside me. Only I didn't know it until the moment he left.

# Paula Goldman
## IN THE LOCKER ROOM

Undressing I look down, see my belly and hate myself. Don't other women? I think of the Venus of Willendorf, her tiny arms over her breasts, her stomach a voluminous pouch. My book says, "she exudes pride and contentment." I see roundness and softness where I want to be hard as Lady MacBeth's gallstones.

Rosa, the Argentine health director, passes and says, "Ah, Paula, suck it in." Here in the locker room, we're all bellyachers. In Ingres' *The Turkish Bath, 1862,* "a scene forbidden to the male gaze," the women are enjoying themselves, one clasping another's breast, one playing a lute, another dancing. They look a little dazed, like they've been smoking hashish.

And they all have soft bellies as round as their instruments. They seem at home in their bodies while I'm always out visiting. It's a circular composition. In the inner sanctum of the locker room, the whirlpool, a turbanned woman dries herself, applies lotion. The slit of her backside is a gorge between snow peaks, or a dark slice of moon. She lifts one leg to the bench and a shock of black hair blooms into a rain forest. Old *women* ought to be explorers.

It's a matter of topography, I once explained to my young daughter who'd asked, "Why do painters paint naked women?" I said the body was beautiful without really believing it. She thought it was funny that I should be looking at other women, but my mother's large, shapeless body loomed over me like a white tornado; her thunderous breasts falling to her waist like boulders I was pinned under.

Philip Pearlstein maintains the languorous nudes he paints are the same to him as boulders. Some boulders, I think, as a Fellini-esque woman steps into the whirlpool. I turn my back to the jets, my body spread like a rippled table. I think of Bonnard's paintings, his wife, Marthe, floating in the bathtub. Almost necrophilous, he made her blue and purple. She was always taking baths, suffering from a mysterious illness she pedaled from doctor to doctor; her only relief was underwater.

I don't want to get out. I feel like a shelled shrimp, pink and simple. There's a picture of Imogen Cunningham, the old photographer, and Twinka, the young model, peering at one another next to a tree, its bark crenelated like elephant skin. I remember my *bubba,* her belly, an apron over her sparse pubic hair or was that my mother? Where am I in this picture?

~

## TRUE LIFE STORIES

I'm going berserk, running up and down the aisles looking for a bald head decorated with one gold earring, that smug kisser. "What's the matter?" a friend shouts down the aisle. "I'm looking for Mr. Clean," I yell and we start laughing, block the aisle with our carts and howl.

Mother calls me to the television set. She wants me to see this, a dog howling "hamburger" on one of those contest shows she lives for. She believes you can get something for nothing. Married fifty years to a man who never took her anywhere, she goes on a cruise with him, pops a free seasick pill and passes out. They put her off the boat at Freeport. My father continues on to New York. He doesn't want to leave his car.

Once we had a dog named Lucky, a brown mutt my little brother adored. Every day I came home from school, I found a pool of Lucky's pee in front of my dresser and yelled. I never had an animal I loved. Lucky bit strangers at the door so my father took him away in the car.

My husband insisted on black and white tiles in our kitchen. I agreed on one condition: he'd clean it every other weekend. On Sundays he pulls the shades down, gets on his hands and knees in a white undershirt like Mr. Clean's and enjoys himself. My mother says I'm lucky.

# Miriam Goodman
## THE RECIPE

I wanted something with no salt, no fat, for you, so I started with a little olive oil and made it up. That's the kind on your diet, the kind you like, the oil without cholesterol. I cut up an onion, listening to a program on obsessive compulsives: you know, these people who are never sure, they get no feedback, they have no biology of certainty, so they do something and have to do it again. They work up soothing rituals to substitute so they can take the obsessive thought and go on. So I chopped the onion, but I used the wrong kind, absolutely; it was a Bermuda; it perfumed the sauce; I'm sorry—I hope you still like it. I threw in chopped tomatoes—you have to peel them first, plunge them from boiling to cold; when they're skinned, you can juice them. Then I threw them in with the onions. Once the stewing starts, the frying is over. I threw in some slices of ginger after the Indonesian dish we ate at that Protestant Inn. I seared the chicken breast in a little more oil—you know how that yellow, unpleasant blob of a breast turns firm and opaque in a moment— while the radio told the story of a nice Jewish boy with homicidal thoughts who played the violin, sure he'd committed a crime, so he'd stop himself—no literally—check his walk, his speech; and of the girl who's afraid to touch anyone, who fears contamination and must always wash her hands. Then I worried it didn't taste good so I put in some curry, tasted, put in some more, added the vegetables, a little Balsamic vinegar, a little wine; a soupçon of bouillon, the low-salt kind—actually I didn't use that kind this time, though that's the kind you want—and *voilà*. Here we have it: a perfectly tasty, low fat, almost low-salt dish. Perfectly Pritikin. Eat. I feel good when you say it's delicious.

∾

154

## SHOPPING TRIP

I try on clothes with you and fifty other women in a mirrored room. Down to my panty hose and bra, I step into a dress and hold my breath. The moment I know my body fails to fit, an apparition of my mother comes and warns me not to get involved with you. You're fat and sad, my mother says, wearing her half-sized navy crepe, a window of lace at her breast. She also shopped for bargains.

I'm seeking our reflections in the mirrors, heavy, unsexual, trying a skin for the world. You look for slacks they can't see through. I look for skirts that hide me, yet push forward to be noticed. The stockgirls in the center of the room rehang the garments we discard like piles of novels taken back to shelve. I don't know how to dress the role you'd have me play: a woman who loves sex with women. It seems to me that I look bad in everything.

I ask if your grown daughters love you. "They'd better," you say, "since I don't love myself." We are alike in this as in less hidden things and yet we look for love to make us new. So let's get out of here and go pick up a turkey. We could slide our hands inside the carcass, roll them in the slippery juices, thinking of each other, of delight. "Look, there's the moon," I could tell you. And I could write you from the future: "Remember when?" I have nostalgia for this chance, and for my mother. And though I can't make love to you, I could make a turkey with her watching.

∾

## TWO PHOTOGRAPHS BY ROBERT FRANK

### (1) Office Workers, Fast Food

What were they looking at, this quintet of secretaries perched on stools at the White Tower, glancing at the street? They warm on gossip while white mugs steam on the counter, napkins in dispensers framed by black. Behind, dark-coated men, their faces hidden; countermen with cardboard hats.

They could be actresses contriving an effect before the next performance: black hair piled and pinned in pompadours. A row behind a window, watching back. "PIE 15¢" and "SOUP" parade from posters pasted to the glass above their heads; they've all the time in the world to smoke, be ogled by their old mistakes, nothing to do that wouldn't keep if Handsome came along.

### (2) Manhattan

A moment in a vast and empty square: a man under a slanting hat crossing in the foreground, scowling. Six scaffolds span a billboard wide as a city block. Taxis queue in the approaching street. Another man, with a short shadow, walks away from us toward the "Haircut 50¢" sign, and the "Havana Cigars" and the Pipe Shop, and Package Store, and Menswear. It's afternoon in Astor Place, 1947, no woman in sight.

Steam rises whitely from subway grates; the sunlit asphalt turns expressionless, and a city slips off balance. What can happen to us here? The scowling man will stride out of the frame, the stopped clock start, the scaffolding come down, ropes on the pulleys, loose ends, rise.

# Keith Gunderson
## NUMBER ONE MAN ON THE SIT-DOWN POWER MOWERS AT LAKEWOOD CEMETERY

and McKinley was number one man on the sit-down power mowers at
Lakewood Cemetery because he'd been there a long time and cared
about mowing and knew more than modern science about his machine
which was red and cared about mowing and was skilled at it and some-
times Emil would ask him if he knew how to adjust his own blades and
McKinley would always take him up on it shaking his head what a guy
that Emil and two or three others mowed with McKinley and they were
McKinley's Boys and even Ernie who'd been there twelve years was one
of McKinley's Boys instead of being Ernie because he didn't think that
much about grass and once he said he wasn't for competition and McKin-
ley's Boys never lagged on their sections and sometimes got a rain or two
ahead and might have taken extra rests but instead had their blades set
high so they couldn't cut much and everyone kept mowing as if usual
because McKinley thought it better to keep in action and one year I got
to be one of McKinley's Boys so he had to teach me to do things like not
taking extra rests and keeping the blades even to the shape of the ground
and not hitting gravestones but I wasn't good at it and got stuck in the
rows and chipped MYRA P. SVENSON 1847–1912 and embarrassed
McKinley so he farmed me out to the just flat sections where the tomb-
stones weren't yet and Wittgenstein used to complain about his students
and say they didn't know much philosophy and didn't care enough
about everything but just to have heard him lecture is still a good call-
ing card and when I revisited Lakewood and met the new guys I casu-
ally mentioned I'd mowed with McKinley and even Barney 'Oldfield'
so-called because of his race-track speed with a stand-up was small pota-
toes compared to McKinley.

# S. C. Hahn
## CUTOVER COUNTRY

Southwest of town, where the Montreal River rushes black and cold
from the Gile Flowage, the slag-heaps rise from abandoned iron mines.
The Italians, Poles, and Finns who worked the mines are again deep
within the earth but for them there is no five o'clock whistle, no pay-
day: no more will they ride the cage up into this hurtful light. Their
grandchildren have moved to the cities or they clear trees for plywood
or they change motel sheets for holiday skiers. They dance to C & W and
drink and fornicate sometimes without pleasure but always with vio-
lent need.

Here in the north, the autumn sun knocks off early in the day, dis-
appearing into the tunnel of sky. When the plywood mill shuts down,
the taverns fill with noise and light. Along each vein of street, the town's
mercury vapor lights keep the night crouching behind trees on the far
hills: night with its grimy face, its soiled wet clothes, its hands smelling
of earth and darkness and death.

~

## THE DESK

It is flat and cluttered as a Kansas town I once drove through but whose
name I forget. A white Frigidaire lay by the WELCOME sign like a
Charolais steer dead from thirst before it reached the slaughterhouse.

It has a magnifying glass. Whatever I look at through the glass sees
one of my eyes as an obsidian stone in a blue pool.

It has piles of paper waiting for something to be written on them. Be-
fore the paper came into being, it was a pine tree in Vilas County, Wis-
consin, and it was waiting for nothing.

It has books. It has a dictionary with leather binding faded and
cracked like the back seat upholstery of a 1953 Chevrolet. In the dic-
tionary's back pages appear all the mottoes of the states. I want to be like
Idaho, I want to Exist Forever.

# Donald Hall

## FLIES

*—for Kate Wells 1878–1975*

A fly sleeps on the field of a green curtain. I sit by my grandmother's side, and rub her head as if I could comfort her. Ninety-seven years. Her eyes stay closed, her mouth open, and she gasps in her blue nightgown—pale blue, washed a thousand times. Now her face goes white, and her breath slows until I think it has stopped; then she gasps again, and pink returns to her face.

Between the roof of her mouth and her tongue, strands of spittle waver as she breathes. Now a nurse shakes her head over my grandmother's sore mouth, and goes to get a glass of water, a spoon, and a fly-swatter. My grandmother chokes on a spoonful of water and the nurse swats the fly.

In the Connecticut suburbs where I grew up, and in Ann Arbor, there were houses with small leaded panes, where Formica shone in the kitchens, and hardwood in closets under paired leather boots. Carpets lay thick underfoot in every bedroom, bright, clean, with no dust or hair in them. Nothing looked used, in these houses. Forty dollars worth of cut flowers leaned from Waterford vases for the Saturday dinner party.

Even in houses like these, the housefly wandered and paused—and I listened for the buzz of its wings and its tiny feet, as it struggled among cut flowers and bumped into leaded panes.

In the afternoon my mother takes over at my grandmother's side in the Peabody Home, while I go back to the farm. I nap in the room my mother and my grandmother were born in.

At night we assemble beside her. Her shallow, rapid breath rasps, and her eyes jerk, and the nurse can find no pulse, as her small strength concentrates wholly on half an inch of lung space, and she coughs faintly— quick coughs like fingertips on a ledge. Her daughters stand by the bed, solemn in the slow evening, in the shallows of after-supper— Caroline, Nan, and Lucy, her eldest daughter, seventy-two, who holds her hand to help her die, as twenty years past she did the same thing for my father.

Then her breath slows again, as it has done all day. Pink vanishes from cheeks we have kissed so often, and her nostrils quiver. She breathes one more quick breath. Her mouth twitches sharply, as if she speaks a word we cannot hear. Her face is fixed, white, her eyes half-closed, and the next breath never comes.

She lies in a casket covered with gray linen, which my mother and her sisters picked. This is Chadwick's Funeral Parlor in New London, on the ground floor under the I.O.O.F. Her fine hair lies combed on the pillow. Her teeth in, her mouth closed, she looks the way she used to, except that her face is tinted, tanned as if she worked in the fields.

This air is so still it has bars. Because I have been thinking about flies, I realize that there are no flies in this room. I imagine a fly wandering in, through these dark-curtained windows, to land on my grandmother's nose.

At the Andover graveyard, Astroturf covers the dirt beside the shaft dug for her. Mr. Jones says a prayer beside the open hole. He preached at the South Danbury Church when my grandmother still played the organ. He raises his narrow voice, that gives itself over to August and blue air, and tells us that Kate in heaven "will keep on growing . . . and growing . . . and growing . . ."—and he stops abruptly, as if the sky had abandoned him, and chose to speak elsewhere through someone else.

After the burial I walk by myself in the barn where I spent summers next to my grandfather. I think of them talking in heaven. Her first word is the word her mouth was making when she died.

In this tie-up a chaff of flies roiled in the leather air, as my grandfather milked his Holsteins morning and night, his bald head pressed sweating into their sides, fat female Harlequins, while their black and white tails swept back and forth, stirring the flies up. His voice spoke pieces he learned for the Lyceum, and I listened crouched on a three-legged stool, as his hands kept time *strp strp* with alternate streams of hot milk, the sound softer as milk foamed to the pail's top.

In the tie-up the spiders feasted like emperors. Each April he broomed the webs out and whitewashed the wood, but spiders and flies came back, generation on generation—like the cattle, mothers and daughters, for a hundred and fifty years, until my grandfather's heart flapped in his chest. One by one the slow Holsteins climbed the ramp into a cattle truck.

In the kitchen with its bare hardwood floor, my grandmother stood by the clock's mirror to braid her hair every morning. She looked out the window towards Kearsarge, and said, "Mountain's pretty today," or, "Can't see the mountain too good today."

She fought the flies all summer. She shut the screen door quickly, but flies gathered on canisters, on the clockface, on the range when the fire was out, on set-tubs, tables, curtains, chairs. Flies buzzed on cooling lard, when my grandmother made doughnuts. Flies lit on a drip of jam before she could wipe it up. Flies whirled over simmering beans, in the steam of maple syrup.

My grandmother fretted, and took good aim with the flyswatter, and hung strips of flypaper behind the range where nobody would tangle her hair in it.

She gave me a penny for every ten I killed. All day with my mesh flyswatter I patrolled the kitchen and diningroom, livingroom, even the dead air of the parlor. Though I killed every fly in the house by bedtime, when my grandmother washed the hardwood floor, by morning their sons and cousins assembled in the kitchen, like the woodchucks my grandfather shot in the vegetable garden, that doubled and returned; or like the deer that watched for a hundred and fifty years from the brush on Ragged Mountain, and when my grandfather died stalked down the mountainside to graze among peas and corn.

We live in their house with our books and pictures, writing poems under Ragged Mountain, gazing each morning at blue Kearsarge.

I dream one night that we live here together, four of us, Jane and I with Kate and Wesley. He milks the cows, she tends sheep and chickens. When we wake one morning the two old people are gone, and their animals gone also. In my dream I know they are dead. All morning we look for their bodies in tall grass around barn and chickencoop, until at noon we look up and see them walking the dirt road from West Andover, waving their arms to catch our attention, laughing with pleasure at our surprise, leading a column of giraffes and zebras, ostriches, lions, parrots, gorillas, and tigers up to the house and to the barn.

We live in the house left behind; we sleep in the bed where they whispered together at night. One morning I wake hearing a voice from sleep: "The blow of the axe resides in the acorn."

I get out of bed and drink cold water in the dark morning from the sink's dipper at the window under the sparse oak, and a fly wakes buzzing beside me, cold, and sweeps over set-tubs and range, one of the hundred-thousandth generation.

I planned long ago I would live here, somebody's grandfather.

# Katherine Harer

## FRIDA KAHLO & DIEGO RIVERA

The oil of frying onions hung in the air. When she woke up the next morning she could taste it on her fingers. When he was there he made the bed sink. She circled his back with her arms and sank with him. When he wouldn't talk to her she touched him all over with questions. A dozen moths loose in his closet. He liked to watch her in the bath. She made a halter of lace out of bubbles, her nipples slipping through the holes. He wanted her next to him but not too close. He wanted her nearby with room between. He sweat cheap liquor, cigarettes, and other women. She checked her face in every mirror, a small one pinned to her pillow. They built a bridge between their rooms. Separate entrances. He told her he was fragile. She laughed, and you such a big man.

∾

## FRIDA KAHLO & NICK MURAY

Her long hands his body bright and loose as a shawl rebozo he liked the sound of her lips together her tongue free in her mouth she found every-where in him color under his lean skin inside his thighs and there in the palm of her hand she took his roundness his weight and held him her thick black hair the length of her back when she undid it bent over him swaying he couldn't talk or think then she was both of them folding herself into his chest pigeon dove smell of mud straw cactus lemon they kissed under street signs at every traffic light in New York touch the fire signal in the corridor touch it everyday she said and followed with her fingers taking the key and making him whisper dirty secret words through the keyhole you're my fucking wonder he whispered holding the tiny cushion she gave him when she left

∾

163

TUNNELS

American tourists are looking for new ways to spend their dollars. They are flocking to Vietnam to see the tunnels, the ones used by the Vietcong in their long and clever victory. The Americans want to go down under the ground. They want to crawl on their bellies dragging their jogging suits across the earth. They want to sit in the small intestines of the tunnels and talk to each other. They want to imagine what it was like.

But they are frustrated in their desire. They cannot fit in the narrow passages. Their Western bodies are too large, too well-fed, to wedge inside and come out the other end. The solution is to dig out the tunnels, enlarge them, renovate history. This will be done.

*[The information in this poem comes from a talk given by Vietnamese journalist, Nguyen Qui Duc, in San Francisco, November 1993.]*

# Marie Harris
AIRBORNE

In the racetrack parking lot, just a few spaces down from "The Tent: where brotherhood is more than just a word!" where Christian bikers (beautiful bellies, glowing tattoos, vests embroidered with "Riding for the Son") man a table of free apples, homemade chocolate chip cookies, and hand-lettered pamphlets about Jesus, a group of clean-cut young men are filling helium balloons one by one to make a single enormous balloon which is being tied to bound wrists of a naked inflated woman-doll with a hank of synthetic yellow on her head, legs spread at a cartoon angle and orifices that are painted a stunning pink. She seems to be saying "O!" in wonder and anticipation as the boys fill the last balloon and pull her into the open where the crowd in the stands, alerted, turns as one man, astounded into clapping and laughter while the inflated woman tugs at her tether, spins, rises above the hot gleaming bikes, moves into cooler air, ascending more rapidly now into a blue background pillowed with clouds. They cut the string! She banks over Turn #8 and heads out. Her heart is pounding so loudly that she cannot hear the applause or the whistles or the screaming engines.

～

Louis Antoine de Bougainville, Who Circumnavigated the Globe (1766–69), Encountering Noble Savages, Cannibals, Adventure, Starvation, etc., in His Quest for Unknown Isles and Continents, Discovers Longboat Key in the Off-Season.

*—23 May 1993*

*We anchored in a bay and put ashore in several boats, approaching the settlement by one of the many man-made canals. Red-throated, long-beaked birds hung on the trunks of banyan trees. All manner of shore birds flew and fished in the shallows; some of our number were well-occupied recording their shapes and cries while others busied themselves at the listing of flowers which ran from whites to deep purples and seemed to have been cultivated for some purpose we could not readily discern. Grasses of blue-green hue had been cropped around shallow sandy pits in what appeared to be large gaming fields. At intervals, thin sprays of fresh water erupted unbidden from the ground. Enormous white houses of phantasmagoric design, each with a long blue pool shimmering under a delicate opaque structure, occupied every meter of dry land from the verges of the canals to the wide avenues to the raked beaches. We could discern no human activity within. There is evidence that the entire populace left hurriedly. What rumor? What disastrous news? They must have gone overland. How else to explain the powerful boats abandoned at docks?*

～

## PASSING TIME

> *If I had a boat,*
> *I'd go out on the ocean.*
> *If I had a pony,*
> *I'd ride him on my boat. . . .*
> *—Lyle Lovett*

. . . and in this manner confront the accumulated terrors of half a century while still having fun—an admirable pursuit that is, perforce, always limned by fear and colored in exigencies particular to the piloted vehicle (e.g., boat: in a microburst, otherwise called a "white gale" for its sudden disruption of an unstormy sea, back the jib, reef the main and keep it close-hauled while running before the wind until the craft is released; horse: try to intuit the cause of her momentary panic, idle her powerful engines of muscle and quiet the pounding of the blood). How I prefer a chosen end: *me upon my pony on my boat.*

～

## TENT CIRCUS

The cop clown is out back sitting on a hitch, nursing his sciatica while the Puerto Rican balancer shares a ring with his juggling son. Jana is changing out of her jungle queen cat tamer outfit into her trapeze rig. She still hasn't got the neck spins right. The ringmaster announces himself, then eats fire. Tonight the old man with the dancing poodles fills in for the chimp trainer who has allergies. Nostalgia hangs in the multicolored air. Lumbering behind their aging aunties, the last baby African elephants in captivity turn circles. They roll on their backs for the shrieking children. They remember nothing. They are post-modern elephants, the final orphans.

∼

## BEGINNING AND END

Every June her family retreated from Brooklyn to Southampton, where their houses and barns and cottages sat like dowagers above the Atlantic. The sun was served up daily as though the best specimen of fruit in season had been delivered from Herbert's Market on a Spode plate. Breezes bent the dunegrass, sowed salt and sand onto striped summer slipcovers, into drawers of summer towels and summer silver. Seersucker nannies fussed past shirtsleeved gardeners and grooms. Linen cooks and laundresses tended to clergy in sportshirts. Weekend uncles came by rail, loosening ties. Aunts arranged zinnias by day and read stories at twilight to little cousins in cotton pyjamas who turned brown as the rotogravure.

She rode horseback in the fields. She played tennis and golf. She dreamed romantic dreams, fixed her hair, and danced the foxtrot with young men called *beaux*. She said her prayers and sometimes she prayed for someone.

I want to remember her before I was there to remember, before she would turn to the handsome man on her left and realize he was the one who would usher her into her next life where there would be no doting father to order cut flowers be planted in the cooling September soil, one by one, down to the swimming pool, for her debutante party of which, on principle, he disapproved.

Before she became our mother, when she was simply her father's joy, she *"received the guests gowned in a bouffant evening frock of white tulle. She carried orchids and 600 guests were present for dinner and 200 more came in for dancing. . . . Fireworks climaxed the evening, ending with Miss Murray's picture and name done in lights."*

# Jim Harrison
## RETURN TO YESENIN

*For only in praising is my heart still mine,*
*so violently do I know the world*
                                        *—Rilke*


I forgot to say that at the moment of death Yesenin stood there like a
misty-eyed pioneer woman trying to figure out what happened. Were
the children still in the burning barn with the bawling cows? He was
too sensitive for words, and the idea of a rope was a wound he couldn't
stop picking at. To step back from this swinging man twisting clockwise
is to see how we mine ourselves too deeply, that way down there we can
break through the soul's rock into a black underground river that sweeps
us away. To be frank, I'd rather live to feed my dogs knowing the world
says *no* in ten thousand ways and *yes* in only a few. The dogs don't need
another weeping Jesus on the cross of Art, strumming the scars to keep
them alive, tending them in a private garden as if our night-blooming
tumors were fruit. I let you go for twenty years and am now only check-
ing if you're really dead. There was an urge to put a few bullets through
Nixon's coffin or a big, sharp wooden stake, and a girl told me she just
saw Jimmy Hendrix at an AIDS benefit in Santa Monica. How could I
disbelieve her when her nipples were rosebuds though you had to avoid
the snakes in her hair. If you had hung yourself in Argentina you would
have twisted counter-clockwise. We can't ask if it was worth it, can we?
Anymore than we can ask a whale its mother's name. Too bad we couldn't
go to Mexico together and croak a few small gods back to life. I've
entered my third act and am still following my songs on that thin line
between woods and field, well short of the mouth of your hell.

# Penny Harter
## HER BEDROOM WINDOW

Her bedroom window faces a brick wall. The wall is so close that when she opens the window and bends out over the sill she can stroke the dirty bricks with her fingers. The window is on her side of the bed. When her husband enters the bed she turns to lie on her right side, facing away from him. She looks out the window, studying the slant of moonlight, the streaks of rain. She imagines taking a kitchen knife and chipping away the crumbling mortar until the bricks are loose and she can pull one out.

Once, when it was snowing, she got up in the night to open the window and brush the snow away from the bricks as far as she could reach. Her flannel-covered shoulders and bare head were wet with flakes by the time she was done. When she got back into bed her numb hands were cold as the snow. She turned toward her husband and brushed his sleeping face with the stiff fingertips of her right hand. He did not wake up.

〰

## THE OLD MAN WHO LOVED BICYCLES

The old man who loves bicycles lives alone in a small gray bungalow. He spends hours polishing his family of seven bicycles: two tiny, four of various middle size (one with balloon tires), and one built-for-two. Daily he takes them outside, turns them upside down, and spins their wheels in the sunlight. Summertime, he eats all his meals with them at his homemade picnic table. Each evening when it is time to sleep he brings them inside his double-length garage and tenderly covers their wheels with old towels—for warmth, for company, and to keep the spiders from starting webs among their spokes. Then he counts them and says good-night.

The local paper decides to feature him. He has offered to repair neighborhood children's bicycles free, and has even given away some bicycles he's rebuilt from old parts. "Why do you love bicycles so?" the young reporter asks him one bright autumn morning out in the back yard as he runs around following the man from bicycle to bicycle, watching him spin their wheels.

"Because of the light," the old man explains, waving an arthritic hand toward the circus of flashing spokes. "And because we go places. We go places!" And he smiles at the reporter and spins around on one foot in the withering grass.

# Peter Harvey
## LIQUID DOMINOES

The days are all like one another. They're warm and the sun shines, showing that the earth is just slightly cracked and a touch more brittle as the days pass. The cracks manifest in the strangest places: in sidewalks, along pre-mesozaic faults, in telephone calls. And they come at the strangest times. Like right now, for instance. Right now the sun has just set and the sky has taken on that eerie royal blue. There is a plane that might be a star and it is trailing a little leader of iridescence that coats the eyes like sweet-sweet honey. And like every other night it is warm. And it has taken on the same characteristic cracks of the day but a little more gracefully. Gradations less forcefully. The cracks manifest in stratified clouds drifting and tugging the eyes out along the horizon. They sit and whisper to the ocean. The days pass and they are all alike; falling, liquid dominoes.

~

SALOME

I am still startled by the pale revolution of the mornings. Startled that the light is less violent than nightfall. Startled that I am still awake with the coming of each day and that each is different, the sun rising and reflecting off the night. The pale oranges and green spreading like the liquidest brush-strokes on canvas. The delicate snap of dawn air on the lips not unlike the cool rush of death. I would live a hundred more years to watch the night ease away just one more time.

I have lumbered through the last hundred years with savage grace if there is such a thing. I have killed. I have colored the night the most metallic crimson. I have settled some thousands of heartbeats and laid minds to rest. But lately she has come to haunt me like a waking dream. I taste her in everything. I feel her thin arms around me when I feed. I watch the delicateness of her fingers drawing my eyes to hers. Sometimes I hear her name. It is muffled as if it were a seashell or a teacup talking—Salome . . . Salome. . . .

I remember waking trapped inside another's body like a second skin. It was like a flesh cocoon, this waking. Like being smothered from the inside out. I remember the tearing through her. Pushing my fingers through hers. Gnawing my mouth out through hers. Wrenching my head through hers. But I did not burst out a butterfly. My appetites were not so simple. Whatever left me at my inception saw to that. They simply left me there.

# Jim Hazard

*from* The Snow Crazy Copybook

Lying in the dark, breathing slow, my chest growing with every breath....

The light was like moonlight inside the shack, but there was no moon only the snow light. I could see my table at a distance, across the shack. The fire was out and breathing was like bringing cold snow light into my chest on every breath.

I was bigger and bigger with every breath.

I was clearer and clearer with every breath in the cold light, I was like the great glacier growing and growing in the still snow light.

~

Towards sundown the storm broke and I went out for the first time in two days. Snowshoeing in the wood I thought of a poem by Emily Dickinson they had taught us in school. The light, how it was coming across the tips of the pine trees made me think of it.

Well, not the whole poem, just one line was all I called to mind. It was a beaut though, so I "read" that line last night, read it over and over and over. The more I'd read it the more that line would mean.

So after that comes my dream last night. Emily Dickinson and me were (it was one of those dream informations you know without it being said).... Emily and me were married. We were living right here in the shack. Emily is cooking our dinner and I am fixing a snowshoe. My left snowshoe.

She says very casually without looking away from the stove, "You got any plans for this evening, sweetheart?" She just keeps on looking at what she is cooking.

I keep working on the snowshoe. "Now you know," I say very gently, "we just stay here in the shack. We live in the shack all the time, honey."

Emily Dickinson turns to me from the stove. She has been cooking liver and onions (our favorite). I can smell it. I put down the snowshoe. We look at each other real soft. Any peeping tom at the window would see, just that quick, it is True Love between us.

"I was kinda hoping to snow shoe into town," my wife says—not naggy or whiny, but just saying the fact—"and maybe sit in the saloon and watch folks play bar dice, you and me have a shot and a beer." Emily Dickinson is so pretty when she's wistful like that she could break your heart.

But I have to say to her: "You *know* I'd like that too but we live in the shack here, Emily." She turns back to the liver and onions, and she's not being sulky or anything. The liver and onions now smell so fine turned brown and golden by Emily Dickinson's small hand. The smell is coming across the room at me, it's coming at me sort of sad and beautiful like afternoon light. It comes to me—and makes me so hungry I am speechless.

"O shoot," Emily Dickinson says, "I know you're right, sweetheart. But you know how it is, just sitting in a saloon with a shot and a beer. Oh come on now, and eat your liver and onions." She dishes it out, still wistful . . . "on a winter afternoon, I do love a saloon . . . you know how it is, hon, it just has that certain slant of—"

I woke up right there. I almost could smell the liver and onions. I had been sleeping on my back. My seeds were still warm in a puddle low on my belly. . . .

∼

It is snow on snow up here and that's a fact.

All day today watching the snow makes me think, the snowflakes dance on the wind as they fall and they bring their dance to the slow shift of snowdrifts.

When it melts there is water and its dance. When it does not melt, there is the Glacier and its slow dance across the landscape.

Watching the big flakes fall all day I know snow crazy is to love the slow dance. I think: nothing in this life it is too slow for me, my kind of show would be to sit in the good seats and watch the Glacier dance its way up and down the middlewest.

It would be so slow no one would watch it with me. It comes to that, I know. All day I watch the snowfall and all day I think just one thought: Nothing in this life is too slow for me.

# Tom Hennen
## CRAWLING OUT THE WINDOW

When water starts to run winds come to the sky carrying parts of Canada and the house is filled with the scent of dead grass thawing. When spring comes on the continental divide the snowbanks are broken in two, and half fall south and half fall north. It's the Gulf of Mexico or Hudson Bay, one or the other, for the snow, the dirt, the grass, the animals, and me. The Minnesota prairie has never heard of free will. It asks you, quietly at first, to accept and even love your fate. You find out that if you fall south life will be easy, like warm rain. You wake up with an outgoing personality and a knack for business. The river carries you. You float easily and are a good swimmer. But if you fall north while daydreaming you never quite get your footing back again. You will spend most of your time looking toward yourself and see nothing but holes. There will be gaps in your memory and you won't be able to earn a living. You always point north like a compass. You always have to travel on foot against the wind. You always think things might get better. You watch the geese and are sure you can fly.

## SHEEP IN THE WINTER NIGHT

Inside the barn the sheep were standing, pushed close to one another. Some were dozing, some had eyes wide open, listening in the dark. Some had no doubt heard of wolves. They looked weary with all the burdens they had to carry, like being thought of as stupid and cowardly, disliked by cowboys for the way they eat grass about an inch into the dirt, the silly look they have just after shearing, being one of the symbols of the Christian religion. In the darkness of the barn their woolly backs were full of light gathered on the summer pastures. Above them their white breath was suspended like the souls each one surely had, while far off in the pine woods night was deep in silence, the owl and rabbit were wondering, along with the trees, if the air would soon fill with snowflakes, but the power that moves through the universe and makes our hair stand on end was keeping the answer to itself.

∾

## WALKING THROUGH A NARROW STRIP OF WOODS

Pines, as always, pried at the sky with their tips, ignoring the wind making noise around their trunks. I dodged the stinging underbrush as it was snapped off. Sometimes a branch would hit my cheek. I would think for an instant how ungrateful nature is. I noticed how my boots crunched the new thin snow, pushing the flakes together. I remembered the last time I was in the city. How the grass was growing in the sidewalk. How the spruce tree was still standing in the morning next to the parked car. How the singing coming from within the tree might not have been birds, that the thread nature uses to connect all things together is joy. When I thought of this in a narrow woods, I was filled with shame for all the cruel things I've said about cities, for they too, will dissolve, as bones dissolve, as the rain is broken by the ground, and because we are allowed to pity everything, except ourselves.

# Michael Hettich

## MY BODY

The first time I met her she was swimming out and couldn't hear me as I yelled many names, trying to find her. Behind me, in the hot sand, children were burying their parents—leaving only heads, which chattered and sputtered and sneezed. Far beyond them, on the boardwalk, dark groups of people seemed to be dancing, while old men in wheelchairs sat lined up, looking out. The water was deep but I waded in anyway, after her. I hadn't yet learned how to swim, but somehow I knew how to float, and somehow my gestures propelled me. Then suddenly the ocean grew shallow. I stepped out onto a sandbar and glistened. There seemed to be hundreds of us there, pink children in the mica-colored sun, touching each other gently as though to convince ourselves we were really there. And the woman I'd followed was sailing by, singing a song whose melody fit me like nerves fit a body or a lifeline fits a hand. I grabbed her ankle as she sailed by, hearing wind through her hair, through her white dress, through the sail. On her ankle a bracelet sang like a tiny wind chime as I pulled myself aboard. As we passed the other children they dove down. We watched, squinting, but never saw them rise again. She turned to me then and I saw she was very old, was growing older as I watched. I was just a little boy. When she opened her mouth as if she would say something, sing something, I realized I could crawl in there, cover myself with her tongue, with her breath, slide down inside her. And she welcomed me there. I listened to her blood. Hours later, when I came ashore, my parents were still buried; otherwise the beach was empty, raked clean. It was dark and I felt moths beating at my body. My parents called my name. I was surprised for a moment that they knew who I was. As I dug their bodies from the sand they giggled and asked almost shyly if I minded if they danced on the boardwalk for just one song. They asked if I would sing their song.

∼

## TRUE STORY

As he walked, each house he passed grew smaller. At first this surprised him; later it seemed almost natural. When he'd walked so far the houses were small enough to carry, he leaned as though over the first crocus of spring, took firm hold of a beautiful gingerbread, pulled it from the ground and slipped it into his overcoat. By the time he got home, his wife was inside. He scrunched up one eye and looked in through the downstairs livingroom window. Although he couldn't see her, he could see her clothes strewn around the tiny room. The book he'd been reading that morning lay on the floor by the comfortable-looking sofa; he could faintly smell his smells and hers. He shook the house gently, still looking in through the window. Nothing moved, not book, not clothes, not utensils on the table. Glued down. His wife, though, from the upstairs bedroom, cried out as she was thrown to the floor and against walls and ceiling. Her door was glued closed too. Her voice, from such a tiny body, behind a glued door, was too small to hear.

# Jim Heynen
## THE MAN WHO KEPT CIGARS IN HIS CAP

One man kept cigars in his cap. When the boys sneaked up behind him during threshing and tipped it off, the cigars fell on the ground. This was very funny to everyone, until one day the man put a rat in his cap. It was a rat the man had fed with eggs so it was friendly to him.

When the boys tipped off his cap this time, the rat jumped to the ground and frightened them so that they screamed and looked foolish.

The boys said, He can't do this to us! We're boys from Welcome #3! Which was their township and schoolhouse number.

So they found a big tom cat that liked to kill rats. They took a striped engineer's cap like the cigar man wore and put a rubber rat under it and taught the tom cat to find the rat.

After a while they went walking toward the threshing machine where the man was working. One of the boys carried the tom cat on his shoulder, and no one paid attention when they walked behind the man. The tom cat saw the engineers cap and jumped at it as the boys had taught him to do.

But instead of a rat, the man had put a skunk under the cap. It was an orphan skunk the man had fed milk when it was a baby, so the skunk was friendly to the man.

When the tom cat landed on the man's hat, the skunk let go its spray in the cat's eyes and on the heads of the boys. Everybody laughed at the boys as they ran away to the stock tank screaming and crying.

When the boys had cleaned themselves, the biggest one said, He has made us look like fools again. Let's do something to keep him from making everyone laugh at us.

So they started practicing with their sling shots and practiced until they could hit a tin can from 30 yards. They crawled behind a fence where no one could see them.

The man had put an owl under his hat, thinking that the boys would have a weasel this time. It was an owl he had helped in the winter when its eyes were frozen shut so the owl was friendly to him.

When the man was not expecting it, the boys shot their stones at his cap. The stones hit the cap, some going through the cloth and through the feathers of the owl, killing it.

No one scolded the boys for killing the owl. Everyone agreed that the man had been asking for trouble right from the start when he put cigars in his cap.

# Gordon Hickey
## JEAN HARLOW


From the window King Kong is staring at his bed. It is a big bed, king size, with purple sheets and pillow cases, and a green spread. The tall headboard and frame are very old and were probably once beautiful. But they are painted white. King Kong thinks the whole thing is ugly.

He is standing very still with his back toward the window, looking at the bed. He is afraid to move. The old mattress is high on both sides and sags toward the middle where Martha is sleeping. She is lovely. King Kong thinks she is beautiful and says so. "Beauty," he whispers. He doesn't want to break the spell. He thinks now, as she sleeps peacefully, that she is even better than she really is. He remembers her voice and the way she walks. Her voice is high and sharp like Fay Wray's, but he remembers only the high part and thinks she sounds like Jean Harlow talking to Clark Gable, all soft and fading away in Malaysia. King Kong also thinks she glides level when she walks, though she shifts side to side, powerful.

King Kong does not exaggerate her beauty. Martha used to have short brown hair, very straight, but now she is letting it grow. Martha's hair is going toward blackness and it curls all over the purple sheets and pillow cases. Beneath the top sheet Martha is naked and small. King Kong knows every space on her body and can hardly believe she is before him now. By the window King Kong barely breathes as Martha moves just a little and Jean Harlow floats slowly away.

King Kong takes a small step toward the bed.

≈

## SPEAKING TOURS

Kong, at his kitchen table, peers around himself, and sees linoleum; formica countertops; a jar of petroleum jelly, open; a fly against the dirty window; and he knows that behind the cabinet door, hanging from a white plastic peg, is a fly swatter, the guts of some poor bug stuck in the plastic web. He closes his eyes, pulls at his ear, and remembers the jungle.

"Jack," he says, "Jack, why did you take me away from all that?"

He can see the ocean, the fog bank always just offshore. The giant wooden wall is comical, a three-pigs barrier. The natives' drums echo off his mountain, the foliage sways, the tree trunks and vines snap at his approach, the glorious woman dangles in his trap. King Kong wants it all back—he wants the linoleum gone.

Jack Armstrong, at one end of the kitchen table, is drinking Coors. King Kong, at the other, lifts his giant shiny face, opens his eyes, and says, "So how the hell are you?"

Jack sags. His pot belly, silly mustache, his awful khakis—Jack looks sad.

"I'm OK," says Jack. The room is yellow. "What are you doing with yourself these days? What's a big ape like you do for a living?"

"Speaking tours," says King Kong. "Still the same. Aren't as many though, now, and they don't pay so much anymore. They heard it all."

King Kong hates Jack Armstrong, just for a second.

Jack Armstrong drinks his beer, puts the can back on the kitchen table, looks at his old friend, and begins to cry. The tears well up in his red eyes and drop onto the table top. They lie there in small shining pools. Jack Armstrong sobs quietly and slowly with a pain he doesn't understand. He cries and tries to smile, and fails, and cries again.

King Kong looks quizzical, hangs his head, looks up, and says, "Come on, Jack, come on. It's OK here. It really is. I like it here with Martha. Really."

Jack Armstrong cries and cries.

King Kong wants to go back home. Wants it all to go away.

# Michael Hogan
## THE MESSAGE OF ONAN

In the Galapagos is a sea turtle who falls in love with a rock. Early in the morning he rises from the froth of the sea and mounts the rock as it lies damp and cool in the sand. He bites the igneous skin, moving his feet curiously in the air. He climaxes, then slides softly to the sand beside it.

Scientists at the Charles Darwin Institute name him Onan because he casts his seed without hope of procreation. But they are lost in the mechanics of things. For Onan the rock is Other and unity possible. For Onan his seed is not cast away but toward. His bites, the movement of his feet in the air, are yearning toward wholeness, driving for form.

At the Charles Darwin Institute they think they have it figured out. But the universe is flowing like a neap tide and they merely observe one departure. To leap before the movement, to see galaxies sleek and cool as pubescent maidens is the message of Onan, ironically named.

∾

## A NURSING MOTHER ON THE DORCHESTER–
## HARVARD TRAIN

It's good to leave the South End if only for a day. Good to trust where the tracks lead as your child does that dark areole. To forget there's not nearly enough nectar for the rich combs of honey his dreaming takes.

At the Park Street Station you offer the other breast. You guide it like Soyuz into Apollo. Above you the sign says: *Double your Freshness. Double Your Fun.*

You are going to the clinic, perhaps? There is little else for you this side of the river. Each time you arrive you discover you have none of the tokens to linger here.

I imagine the child screaming over the high-pitched steel as the subway returns to Dorchester . . . Roxbury. What will you offer him then? Your breasts pleated like empty wineskins. A finger soaked in amber liquid? Your dreams? Listen. A chewing gum jingle? The rhythmic rocking of the train?

# Bill Holm

## BRAHMS' CAPRICCIO IN C MAJOR, OPUS 76, NO. 8

*—for Marcy*

All this lonesome fall I practice Brahms, mooning over a faraway woman, while my fingers twist around this constipated soulful counterpoint. Day after day of gray drizzle, both in October and inside the piano. I don't even like this music and haven't touched a note of it for years.

Tonight, I remember when I played it last; it was the melanoma ward of a huge gray hospital, a hallway chock full of the doomed. An old upright piano sat in the sun room, where I waited day after gray drizzly spring day for news I had already gotten inside. I had only Brahms along, and he seemed all right, so I practiced playing and grieving together, conscious of the one, avoiding the other.

Up and down the hall walked glucose bottles attached to bodies. All over those bodies, black holes in the skin sucked up life and energy, burrowing inside from eye, back, hand, cheek, slow black bullets whose trajectory stopped only when they found a brain or liver to explode.

"A nasty disease," the Chinese neurosurgeon said. "We don't know what causes it. Perhaps the sun. . . . Probably the sun. . . ."

Without much hope for either music or survival down this hall, I practice Capriccios and Intermezzos that old Brahms probably composed while his own black holes ate at his liver. One day, I sit bungling through something in C Major when a young boy with freckles, red hair, and a glucose bottle slides noiselessly into the sun room and listens. He claps weakly when I finish, and I turn around. The glucose bottle still wobbles on its iron stand, the plastic tube trembling.

He is my color, could be my brother, but he is thin, pale, dying, and I am fat, flushed, full of angry life. "I always wanted to play the piano," he said.

"Do it!" I said. "It's a great joy to play."

"Did it take you long to play so well?" he asked.

"Oh, not long at all!" I said. "Just practice all you can."

186

Then with a weak excuse, I left the sun room, went and sat next to my mother's bed and wept, because I had lied, and because I knew what happened in this world as inexorably as Brahms' ruthless logical contrapuntal knots tied and untied themselves around the human ear.

For twelve years, I forgot those Capriccios and Intermezzos, and neither lied nor wept too much. But all this lonesome fall, I practice Brahms again, mooning over a faraway woman I love—no, over two women, one gone out, and the other just come in, the old grief and this new joy so alike inside this music. One brave melody in C, clear and full of leaping rhythm, rears up against a minor tune as if to say: Let everything sing together inside you, lose nothing.

～

## GIRL EATING RICE

Dinner on a dusty February night in a teacher's cramped cement flat. After cooking, she comes in to eat leftovers, carrying a bowl of rice. Rice steam curls up around her black hair. Her face is like an ancient Chinese painting trying to explain to the future what it meant to be beautiful in an old, long gone dynasty. That could be a pippa in her hands instead of a bowl of rice; her black chopsticks could be plectra. She plays the rice as much as eats it, each mouthful perfect as an old poem, sung slowly, a little tinkling laughter and a wrinkling of the eyes between bites, like sighs of pleasure at how the tune goes.

I sit there, neither listening to nor understanding the hum of Chinese talk around the table. I can't keep my eyes either off her rice or her opera hands moving from bowl to lips to a cold morsel of pepper or pork.

She is not an old painting of music at all but a lovely young girl in a lavender sweater who has cooked a long time for her husband's old teacher. Yet she is the other thing too, thousands of years old, a girl from the mountains of such beauty and grace that the emperor sees her eating rice in the palace kitchen, and weeps for his passing life and the misery of his country.

～

## JOHN CLARE'S LAST LETTER

*—in memory of Alec Bond*

Browsing one day in the college library, I find on the shelf the letters of
mad John Clare, a gay pink book. I wonder what old Clare said in his
last letter after all those years in the loony bin? He wrote on March 8,
1860 to James Hipkins, an "unknown inquirer from the outside world."
Clare was sixty-seven years old, twenty-three years locked up, four to
go until the end. The editor says in his neat brackets, this letter was
[sent]. Most asylum letters never make it to the post. The letter says:

> *Dear sir:*
>
> *I am in a Madhouse and quite forget your name or who you are you must excuse
> me for I have nothing to communicate or tell of and why I am shut up I don't
> know I have nothing to say so I conclude*
>
> *Yours respectfully*
> *John Clare*

Who was Hipkins? Why did he write? Had he fallen in love with
those poems full of wrens, mice, badgers, larks, flies, crows, fish, snipes,
owls, moles, and imaginary wives? Did he weep when Clare's little note
came back to him in the "outside" world?

I leaf through the other last madhouse letters. Clare wrote to a son,
long dead, inquiring if the boy ever saw his sister, even longer dead.
Had life and death ceased to make any difference to him? Was that his
madness— that he couldn't tell the difference between one world and
the next, between the quick and the dead? Had the walls between the
worlds fallen down inside him, so that angels, devils, ghosts, specters,
moved calmly back and forth between them?

The gay pink book falls open to the flyleaf. There's a name—Alec
Bond—in neat red pen—long dead Alec who loved mad John Clare
and gay pink books and owls and badgers and sometimes even his old
friend—me!

Sometimes those walls fall down for a while inside me too, and I
catch myself asking questions that will have to wait a long time to be

answered. Sometimes I think I'm shut up too and can't tell why and ought to respectfully conclude.

But sometimes, in empty libraries on muggy September days in Minnesota, all the letters arrive with my name, written in a language I can read. News passes jauntily between worlds as if that required only a stamp.

When this happens, what need does a man have to make anything up? The world is enough—either or both together—if you can say plainly what happens. If you say it plain enough, like mad John Clare, sometimes they shut you up, though what difference that makes no one can tell yet.

# Brooke Horvath

ABRASION

In the photograph, grandfather hammers risers. They are both perfectly fit. At the business end of his intensity, teeth clench upon a mouthful of finishing nails and the dark, chewed mass of a cigar stub, eyes bright with expertise and grandfatherhood. We are two and I am two and beside him, eyes closed against the pounding, small arm raised authoritatively in a gesture of command. He always liked to tell how I helped him build that house through all those long nuisance hours, evenings and Saturdays, how I never left his side, learned the names of tools—molly bolts, caulking gun, putty knife; sander, rasp, Phillips screws—holding, handing them to him, steadying the boards he sawed, sawdust on both our knees. Now, thirty-three years later, it is my fate, and his, to direct him once again, something like sawdust obscuring his finish. And I think how age and illness have left us without the tools we need, have rubbed me softly raw.

~

THE WOMAN IN THE PETER PAN COLLAR

It is 1953, and my mother stands, so young, slim, in a calf-length woolen skirt, red cardigan, white cotton blouse, smiling down at her blue-blanketed one-month-old. Behind her lies a stack of lumber piled on dirt that will stay dirt four years before becoming grass, and behind that, a cement-block foundation above which rises a roughed-in frame—the house my father, grandfather, their friends and neighbors are building for her, for me. The sun is bright; she squints toward the camera, trying to smile, not knowing how long it will take to raise a house (that once finished will be too small too soon) or a son, who once grown will betray his immigrant roots to run away and hardly ever write, forgetting even the names of relations, yet who will come to waste his time obsessively fingering Ektachrome clues to what once was and what, once once, can never be again.

190

# David Ignatow

## AN ACCOUNT IN THE PRESENT TENSE
## OF HOW IT ALL HAPPENED

I am about to close the refrigerator after removing a package of meat when I hear my door lock turning and a crew of men, without so much as first knocking, walk in. They stride directly over to the refrigerator, tie rope around it, hoist it upon a dolly, and ride it out the door. Who are these people and why are they taking my refrigerator when there is nothing wrong with it? They are making some kind of mistake. Stop, I cry. You are in the wrong apartment. Not one turns his head to look at me or to listen. At that moment, three men, a second crew almost on the heels of the first, stride in and lift up my television set between them and walk out with it. I scream for help. I pound their shoulders but get no response, as if they were made of wood. I scream and scream, and another crew is right behind the second, this time to remove my bed. I am going to be left with nothing, nothing. I am about to get on the phone to call the police when I notice that they have cut the wires and taken the phone with them.

They remove dishes, cutlery, rugs, books, lamps, screw out the bulbs. They leave me an empty apartment and begin to tear down the apartment walls. They knock out the walls of the building itself. I flee into the street, just barely in time before they begin to attack the stairs and the elevator. Out in the street I see that it's happening to each apartment building on the block and all the tenants are milling around, with the few clothes on their backs they managed to grab, and are shouting at each other in panic and wild rage. We are totally stranded, there are no police and no emergency crews in sight. The streets are beginning to resemble a bombed-out area, and we see that we will have to fend for ourselves with our bare hands. There is a park nearby and we begin to converge upon it. It has large, open spaces where we will be able to lie down and rest and perhaps make our beds there for the night with what linen and bed clothes we were able to rescue from inhuman hands. It's all over, it seems, that which gave us our comforts and pleasures. It's back to the woods and fields, and did anybody bring a knife or a gun with

191

which to hunt a rabbit or a bird? We look at each other in the dawn of an understanding.

～

I am standing on the soft, spongy surface of my brain and looking down into the space between the halves, expecting the surface to give way under my weight and hurl me down. The surface caves in suddenly and I fall. I am an object in space flying downwards, head over heels, shrieking my terror though I am falling without harm to me physically, but lost, lost without foothold, without hope of foothold. I have done this to myself, I say as I fall, and since this is what I did in all consciousness then I cannot blame myself either. It could not save me, it is no rescue, and I accept myself falling and sing out my terror like a song.

～

I sink back upon the ground, expecting to die. A voice speaks out of my ear, You are not going to die, you are being changed into a zebra. You will have black and white stripes up and down your back and you will love people as you do now. That is why you will be changed into a zebra that people will tame and exhibit in a zoo. You will be a favorite among children and you will love the children in return whom you do not love now. Zoo keepers will make a pet of you because of your round, sad eyes and musical bray, and you will love your keeper as you do not now. All is well, then, I tell myself silently, listening to the voice in my ear speak to me of my future. And what will happen to you, voice in my ear, I ask silently, and the answer comes at once: I will be your gentle, musical bray that will help you as a zebra all your days. I will mediate between the world and you, and I will learn to love you as a zebra whom I did not love as human being.

～

COCKROACHES

I have become friendly with baby cockroaches that dare to come out in the daylight to see what I am cooking or peeling. They're like little children curious about their elders and would like to know. I watch them scurry about on their invisible legs, they are so gentle and enquiring and frightened. When I raise my hand or lower a spoon they race off to a crack in the stove fixtures. Occasionally I crush one with my thumb on an impulse and go back to my cooking or peeling potatoes.

As for their parents, long as the first joint of my thumb, when I turn on the light at night I watch them in anger. I begin to spray with a poison. That their deaths will diminish the birth rate of their children does not bother me. It's the horror of their aggressive search for food that I react to viciously.

I leave the kitchen with its noxious poisonous smell and forget about their struggling death to listen to my radio, to read my book, to do my schoolwork, to think of how empty is my apartment with just myself in it, sick of being alone, always alone and not knowing how to change it to a life of friends.

～

## WITH QUESTIONS FOREVER

I do know that birds continue to live and procreate, as long as the weather is amenable, and the food is there, as if it were a deal between them, the weather and the crops. No questions asked. And the birds are in earnest about it, as I am in earnest about finding a reason for their lives, for what reason I myself do not understand. So in my way I too am ignorant of my self, my purpose, to perform simply the role of questioner.

If I were to say that it is because I want to know, I will again surely be carrying on my function of questioner, as the birds carry out theirs of eating and procreating.

I must call it good, because to deny it is not one of my functions, or is it? And here I am asking a question once again, carrying out the function I have been assigned.

Meditation is its name, to meditate on the practically nothing and to find something to say about it, this that I have written, its own purpose in being, for the sake of the living, with questions forever.

# Louis Jenkins

## BASKETBALL

A huge summer afternoon with no sign of rain . . . elm trees in the farm-yard bend and creak in the wind. The leaves are dry and gray. In the driveway a boy shoots a basketball at a hoop above the garage door. Wind makes shooting difficult and time after time he chases the loose ball. He shoots, rebounds, turns, shoots . . . on into the afternoon. In the silence between the gusts of wind the only sounds are the thump of the ball on the ground and the rattle of the bare steel rim of the goal. The gate bangs in the wind, the dog in the yard yawns, stretches and goes back to sleep. A film of dust covers the water in the trough. Great clouds of dust rise from open fields that stretch a thousand miles beyond the horizon.

## FROST FLOWERS

In the morning people go off to work all wrapped and bundled, through frozen doors, over cracking snow, huffing and puffing, each fueled by some simmering private indignation: low pay, something that was said at break. . . . The sun is far away on the southern horizon, a vague hope, more distant than the Caribbean. Eight below zero at eleven o'clock. The coffee boils and grows bitter. All afternoon the same old thing, knuck-lebone of mastodon, stews on the stove. The radiator hisses at the long shadows which finally engulf the winter day. Lights come on for a time in the houses and go out one by one. We breathe deeply of the dark. We exhale great plumes and fronds that form on the windows. Intricate icy blossoms open around us all night.

194

LIBRARY

I sit down at a table and open a book of poems and move slowly into the shadow of tall trees. They are white pines, I think. The ground is covered with soft brown needles and there are signs that animals have come here silently and vanished before I could catch sight of them. But here the trail edges into a cedar swamp: wet ground, deadfall and rotting leaves. I move carefully but rapidly, pleased with myself. Someone else comes and sits down at the table, a serious-looking young man with a large stack of books. He takes a book from the top of the stack and opens it. The book is called *How to Get a High-Paying Job*. He flips through it and lays it down and picks up another and pages through it quickly. It is titled *Moving Ahead*. We are moving ahead more rapidly now, through a second growth of popple and birch, our faces scratched and our clothes torn by the underbrush. We are moving even faster, marking the trail, followed closely by bulldozers and crews from the paper company.

# Jim Johnson
DESCRIPTION OF THE LAND

Nothing but sea bottom until the drought. Then what we now know as Sections 7–18, Lots 4, 12, and 34, Township 4 South, Range 20 East, Carbon County, the state of Montana, the United States of America, was carved by running water, buffalo hooves, and wind. The Crows watched over it until Gust Johnson signed with an X and did what a thousand years of buffalo hooves and hundreds of thousands of years of water and wind couldn't. He turned the land inside out. His family divided it further between cattle, oil, wheat, depression, corporations, suburbs, and the Conservation Reserve Program until now it is part of a movie star's 225,000 acres. He lives in Australia. And the drought continues.

≈

## SQUARE

Bales, boxcars, red barns, white farmhouses, grain elevators, summer fallowed land, wheat land, 640-acre sections of land, steers, trees in winter, real butter, blue-black prairie ponds, drought, eroded land, more drought, all the reasons why, a slip of paper, a signature, the price of wheat rising and the price of wheat falling but always posted in the lobby of the Yellowstone Bank, and the bank itself, Mondays, hogs, silos, more sections, more Mondays, another slip of paper, then the same old life again, a good meal, a short woman.

# Peter Johnson

## BEDTIME STORY

When I was twelve, a horse appeared. It carried King Richard disguised as a policeman. All night long, my street glimmered. Car doors opened and closed. The owner of the steel plant wanted to know the secret, wanted to stroke my mother's perfect breasts. The secret was to be in the presence of a horse, or surrounded by red and green flowers that never grew in my neighborhood. There were dandelions. And tulips coated with metallic flakes. In the suburbs, privileged armies faced off displaying their silken banners. I could hear the clash of armor when I closed my eyes.

～

## NIGHT CRAWLER

The last automobile of night passes. I exit, drop to knees on a wet blanket of dull blades—an advance accompanied by thick silence, except for the give and take of flesh and hole, opening and closing of tiny dark doors.

Flashlight in my right hand, night crawlers scatter at its bulbous eye. Or I'm quick, with steady left hand catch them coupling, half out of holes, or damp noses barely breaking the surface.

Strange creatures, rooted to ground yet aspiring upward, anonymous, soft-bellied fragments, night's dark, dismembered fingers, I gladly suffer wet indignities of dirt for a handful of them.

# Sybil Kollar

## THE BOOKSTORE

In the bookstore I walk quietly as if barefoot. There is the smell of dust on the last Sunday of this cold month. A bearded man looks at me. I hesitate to look directly at him. I pick up a tiny book with pictures of birds. They look painted and ready to drown.

The bearded man's hand touches a photograph in a book. It is of a girl standing near a tree holding a hat and smiling at nothing. I am hatless and there is no tree but I see a photograph of a bearded man standing in an old bookstore looking at a woman who is smiling into a book of dead, painted birds.

~

## SNAPSHOT

A yellowed snapshot of four faces blinded by the sun. A mid-winter moment, its light spread on the frozen lake like butter. In the background, an iced fire hydrant, thickly glazed, stands fancy as a wedding cake. My eye rests on its crystalline stalactites. My four Russian uncles don't smile. Are they being detained in Siberia, the taste of pears and vodka a memory stuck on their tongues? This is what I imagine—no matter the heavy scrawl on the back, Prospect Park, Chanukah, 1920.

# Mary A. Koncel
## COME BACK, ELVIS, COME BACK TO HOLYOKE

They still love you, Elvis. They want your hair, stories about your Harley ripping up pavement between Nashville and Memphis, your sequined gaze, your big-breasted women in too-tight bikinis. "Teacher," they ask me, "make us walk and talk like Elvis."

I tell them you're dead, fat, bloated, overweight and dead. But Juan Carlos insists that you live below him, that you stir steaming pots of black beans while singing "Maria Encantadora" on the radio every Tuesday. And Clarence calls you Father.

These boys need you, Elvis. Every day they sit, shaping their lips and grinding their hips beneath the desks. Across the room, I watch them, see little birds, baby roosters, dull-voiced peacocks with bare chests and tender white throats.

Elvis, I'm only a woman. I can't do it all. I'm only a woman, and they're asking more questions. When I stand up, they point at me, stare at the split of my skirt, the breasts beneath my blouse.

Next time, Elvis, forget the supermarkets in Denver, the trailer park in Lafayette. Come back to Holyoke. Teach these boys to be men, great manly men, men that love women, red meat, and '58 Buicks. Elvis, like the streets of Holyoke, my arms open to you, wait for you, your low lean rumble.

~

## THE YEAR OF THE MAN

My friends aren't hungry anymore. When they walk down streets, they belch and rub their fat, slick bellies. "You, you, and you," they say, pointing their fingers as if sorting Buicks from Fords, left feet from right ones.

Yep, these men are looking pretty good. And it's not even spring. It's the year of the man. Before it was a drought, a drought on top of a drought. Now they're dropping from trees, sprouting through cracks, littering parks and alleys like empty bottles or dented cans.

And my poor, poor husband! Every night he dreams he's a windswept virgin stranded on a ragged cliff in some dark, undeclared country. "What does it mean?" he asks me. "What does it mean?" I tell him about the sad old days, about big vacant beds and the song of the drought, that long, long drought. And always, of course, I tell him, "Sure, I want you, I need you," over and over.

Last week even Peggy called me. She said, "It smells a little fleshy today," then abruptly hung up. I stepped out on my porch and breathed, letting beads of sweat and full ripe muscles fill my lungs. "Yes," I wrote back three days later, "the sweet still scent of thigh."

～

## THE SECOND SONG OF INSOMNIA

A stranger is humming outside my window. He looks like my dead uncle or a drunk angel in rubber boots and a baggy wool overcoat. I'm just not sure. I'm easily confused by that black spot of mustache that shimmers in the half moon air.

But every night this stranger follows me home. He leans against the tree, taking for granted my grass, the staggered line of streetlights, this curtain that separates me from a deep husky sleep. Now he's rolled up his sleeves. I watch his lips, but he's too clever, his mute breath lingering inside my head like a dream, like a bad dream running over and over.

It's not right for a stranger to be humming outside my window. He should go home. He should read books, thick red books, and let me close my eyes. But I know he's there.

Listen. I need words, even simple words. I won't apologize. I want a song, a really nice song, with words that grab my heart and swing it dizzily around this room, then drop me into some midnight abyss. Instead I find myself pressed between these sheets, throat aching in my hands, waiting for the first howl of a hungry dog, the rise of footsteps, something that brings night closer to day.

# Ellen Kort
## SEA TURTLE

Tonight she lumbers up from the sea as though she knows I am wait-
ing. Up through snarls of seaweed and plankton. Her front flippers pull
hard against wet sand, like an old woman gone heavy. Water spreads
out around her into white sea hair, braided silver by the moon. She claws
her way up the beach, stopping now and then to bury her nose, the way
a dog sniffs at first snow. She goes into the grains of sand, feels how they
rub and grind against one another in the night. I can see the big green
darkness of her, the humped shell that looks like the earth-spattered,
rusted dipper that hung for years on a nail outside my grandfather's
barn. Her front flippers are flying now, beating some ancient rhythm
that sends showers of sand over her, whirls it into streaks and sparks,
voicing it wordless from belly to mouth to sky. Head bowed, slow breath-
ing, gusts fuse sand and sea and moon. She is completely covered. Ex-
cept for her eyes, which are cleansed by a continuous flow of tears. There
is singing. A humming sound. At first I think it's wind strumming the
casaurinas, until I feel it rumble inside me. A memory song, bone deep,
as familiar as my grandmother's melody for sick children and babies. I
hear it . . . this calling song from my dreams. Is it what brought me here
tonight along this lonely stretch of beach? And does the turtle hear it,
too? Maybe it's true that we all scatter trails of words and music that are
embedded in our footprints. That dream-tracks cover the land, are
woven through waves like a map to find our way home. And maybe
there's nothing: no tiny grain of sand, no rock, leaf or the smallest trickle
of water that can't be sung. Maybe it's the same music the swan makes
before she dies, how she finds her true voice just that once. No barking
to call her young. No blaring like a bugle or the snort and hiss of anger
or fear. Just the plaintive, melodious song as it falls from the sky. All those
notes stitched from air, riding the wind. The moon passes through a
cloud and the turtle and I are in the black hole she is digging. I am pat-
ting the sides while she goes deeper. Sinking front flippers into the sand
at the edge of the pit, she lowers the back of her body to the bottom of

the hole in the same way my daughter gripped the bed when the baby came ripping through her. The turtle eggs are round and white and she brushes sand over them little by little with her hind flipper until they are covered. I help her fill in the rest. To disguise the location, we churn the sand all around the nest, moving further and further out. I look at the sharp jaw, hooked nose and it is my face, but older. She is tired. I brush sand from the dark map of her shell, wishing I had some of Marianne's wild geranium tea. We sit side by side listening to deep water echo in the distance. I can hear my heart talking inside my head, words that work slowly, pulling the warm starquilt of night close in around us. Words that will store this image on the back of my mind. She moves then. Slowly, into the widening waves. I breathe time as she breathes water . . . water we are buried in and rise from . . . until there is only her dark shadow after-image. I try to get beyond aloneness into the greening light that brushes over the beach. It's as though I'm sitting somewhere else, watching the night play itself out against a watercolor of sky and water. I bed down between the tough knuckles of driftwood. It is almost morning.

# John Krumberger
## DINING OUT

A man sings romantic ballads in the piano lounge swaying like a bear. He hits the high notes of "Danny Boy" and begins to weep.

It has rained for three days straight tearing the leaves off of the trees. Rain on the North Shore highway past Gooseberry Falls excites the pulse of the Baptism and Temperance Rivers. In the woods along the highway the trees are like widows who still speak of husbands.

Duluth is the last outpost here, the only city for miles and miles. The lake is an immense and anxious presence even when obscured by darkness. The singer stops weeping and begins the first verse of "Some Enchanted Evening." October leans like a blind man at the precipice of a cliff.

～

## THE QUAKER MEETING

Inside the Quaker meeting house people sit in silence and a small invisible stream flows just beneath the earth. One or two men are so old their hands move without sound; hair sparse and white like patches of snow on rough grass. I wonder about these old men, why they are so happy.

I cannot think of God or even loneliness. I watch the faces in these pews and the slender shoulders of a young woman across from me. I would like to reach across this room to touch her face. A Zen Master once said our whole lives pass by while our minds lie asleep in the outer world.

I think of a photograph of a train stopped in a small town in central Wisconsin. A crowd of people wait on the station platform holding packages. Some of them stand in light, some in shadow. The shadows creep down the roof like ivy climbing a fence. Each journey begins in silence, the mind calm, the body slipping from shadows. Snow falls on the road to farm land, a '58 DeSoto parked along the tracks, its motor running.

# Marilyn Krysl

BODY

My body is too many children, they are all hungry at once. As I write this one of them bangs my thigh with a doll. I say, *Stop that!* But my body is headstrong. When it doesn't get its way it throws a tantrum. Once it kicked a wall and broke three toes. In winter it sulks because it can't fly. And some days it won't put on its clothes no matter where we're going. It gets oily and sweats and sits in its mess, breathing, and I have to wash and comb it patiently and sing it little songs, and then it goes to the party

without me. I come later, alone. I tell it it's going to regret all that beaujolais. But my body is defiant, has another glass, and another, gets roaring. The next afternoon I have to phone and apologize. I say, *Please excuse my body. There is no excuse for its conduct, but now it regrets the greedy gobbling of hors d'oeuvres, those lies about your gracious wife.* Then I march it to the mirror in the bathroom and I make myself stern and say sharply, *I'm ashamed of you! When are you going to grow up?* And my body hangs its head. But I'm suspicious. Should I trust it?

When we have a dentist appointment my body hangs back. I am cheery. *Be brave,* I tell it. But my body is nervous, makes excuses. Then I have to say, *At your age! This is disgraceful!* It starts to sniffle, to grovel, to beg, *If only,* it says. In the end I drag it to the car. Slam the door and rev the motor. *Some day I'll wash my hands of you,* I say.

Then one night it sits down on the bed, strokes the cat. Is anything wrong? The cat jumps off, my body lies down, stares at the ceiling. And now I understand that it is sad. The other body it wants to be loved by has flown off to Bermuda with the redhaired stewardess, and now my body says it wants to die. So I sit down beside it. *Wouldn't you like to go for a walk?* I ask. *Shall I get you a glass of cold water? Want me to brush your hair?* But it turns away. Is it weeping?

204

It is weeping. Now its eyes are red, its face splotched, it is ugly. What can I say—it gives me pleasure and grief, and now it is weary, so heavy, its face sags, it doesn't care about the mirror anymore. It doesn't care about the public or about politics. It doesn't love music or admire the plastic arts. It is tired, it has stopped pretending. I will go out quietly and let it sleep.

⟳

## INCARNATE

—*for Charlie*

The day I heard you'd died, that day, toward evening, I was alone in the house, and I turned on the radio. What was there was music, a quiet jazz, sound to sway the body, and then I was dancing. Dancing alone, in that circle we call the spirit, that singular turning, that ceremony of one. I was alone, but I was not alone. I felt someone watching.

The body knows what's right and does that, if you let it. I began to undress then, doing it without thinking, turning, circling, alive on a strand of sound. I was unbound—as though a hand, reluctant, had let go of me. As though unwinding from myself one long strip of bleached linen.

Grief feels like a pulling apart of the net to let a soul fly out. We have to let the dead go. Maybe the dead have to let us go too. Dancing in my own skin at some point I understood: this was you releasing me, you giving me up, giving me back, returning me to my own flesh, its sweetness. You, who had once pointed out to me my own body, the way one child will hand another some treasure—a branch, a leaf, a stone—and say *Here, look at this. Hold this, feel this.*

# Greg Kuzma
## THE DESK

My father is chopping up the desk he built me when I was a kid to get smart leaning over looking at books he bought me so I could get out of town and be better than him, and not have to work for a living like he does, but sit around on my fat ass week after week, developing longer and longer arms so I can pat myself on the back, or reach all the way across country and pinch him now and then, just to see if he's still alive, which is getting him pissed off.

~

## WHY I WRITE

There are so many shoes in the closet hollering for new soles. My coat tails flap in the breeze trying to hang onto me, but soon I shall be gone. Leaves are falling into fishbowls out of which the fish have become the sparkle in the eyes of cats. The dead are planning vacations and I have been asked to design road maps for them. I who know nothing of darkness. My mother writes to ask what I am up to. I write her back. On the corner last night the mailbox put up a fuss over my fat envelope. The sun was just going down, it caught my breath, I felt young again, and ripe for celebration.

There are teeth in the darkness that are looking for mouths in which to get themselves fixed. I want to be their dentist. There are open roads down which buses are traveling, empty, the driver, with nothing to read, numbed by the white line. I want to be the fat paperback in his right hip pocket that keeps him propped up, uneven, painfully awake.

Yesterday the moon wore a monocle too big for it. Eight hundred and thirty-five persons died of cancer. Automobiles were flushed into rivers. Another day fell off the edge of our lives like ice off the face of a glacier.

Do I not need to make some report?

206

# Warren Lang

## BREAD

The bread rises in a cream colored bowl at the back of the stove. It rises slowly like the breathing of a small child sleeping. The woman who has made it has cleaned the counter of the fine grained flour and the clumps of dough. The kitchen looks as clean as a new car.

Gradually, the dough awakens. It opens its tiny mouths. It whispers, "I am your dead friends come back to feed you." No one hears. The sun pours in like a baker's smile. The dog yawns and stretches and walks toward the door.

∼

## SHOES

One day they leave me. They walk through the door, out onto the street. "Come back," I shout, but once they have started, they have no interest in returning.

I am worried. How will they do on their own? They are innocent of the world above the sidewalk. I imagine them at dusk searching for a place to rest. They walk into a sleazy hotel. The fat clerk does not care about my missing body. He gives them a room with a dim light and torn wallpaper. I can see them standing by the bed, tapping the floor, nervous about the long night, while I sit at home, afraid to take to the streets, shoeless and alone.

# Michelle Leigh
## SO YESTERDAY WAS BEAN DAY

So yesterday was bean day, devil day, and that's why in the early white morning the Dragon of the Heavens Temple next door boomed out five booms answered by a faroff single explosion and boomed five booms again. And that's why my daughter's friend's mother appeared at the door with two devil-masks, one red, one green, and a bag of peanuts for throwing about the house to get the devils out. And it must also be why today began gloomy and sort of moist, because probably devils were sulking and hiding in corners making heat which melted the snow, covering the sun with devil-clouds of gloom. And it's the first day of spring today, with all the devils gone off somewhere, all the beans swept up, and the sun emerging through ragged winter cloud-drifts, saying silly old devils, bean day gets you every time!

≈

## TEA

That man with the burnished Indian face. His eye catches mine, just past the warm wide shoulder of my lover who imagines no danger, no hunter nearby, his kind back to the door, innocent. The burnished man is a prologue, he sets the tone and the theme for the day. Later, alone with my lover's friend, it is not so surprising then, the extent to which he lets his light blue eyes see into me, while looking at my mouth for the shapes of beautiful kisses and dreams of Paris, seeing long nights and wet mornings in twisted sheets, with me: the smell of coffee bringing sad memories of other women, all lost, all gone, now ghosts in his blue gaze; and his eyes, his light blue eyes look at me. In his blue, in his sky-colored eyes and his small sharp mouth-corner, I see all this and I offer him tea.

∼

## I AM LOOKING FOR WORDS

I am looking for words that lack sweetness, dry words that rattle like spell-bones. I am looking for flat hard words that don't melt in the sun, old heavy words that don't fall down. I am looking for words that carry fast-moving rivers of dark meaning within them, words that can shoulder a burden, words that tilt like flying buttresses against cathedrals of thought, words that pull on the world like magnets, words that echo in the dead night.

# Roseann Lloyd
## REALITY AND ITS DURATION

At the end of the workshop, we're doing a meditation from Shakti Gawain, and we're supposed to picture something we want, and I'm going along with this idea, even though it's the same meditation exercise that made me laugh when Phebe wrote a poem about it, the one with the line *Pink is the color of the heart,* which is the line the workshop leader is saying right now, telling us to surround what we want in a pink bubble & there is no doubt in my mind as to whether I can do this, for my picture is so bright it radiates pinkness. It is my daughter in her new strawberry blond do, smiling at me in a yellow shirt & golden earrings, healthy, mentally healthy, & this is the way I want her—healthy & free—& as her bubble rises up out of the room floating away from me I see the balloons she used to set free, ten years ago when she was ten. How she loved the wind & sky & traveling clouds. She would take each helium balloon, tie it with a note, tied tight with string, *Hi, if you find this, write and tell me when & where.* One day we drove out to the Southdale parking lot, Sunday after closing when it was still light because parking lots are the best balloon release sites & she was getting frustrated because she'd been doing this for over a year & nobody had answered her yet so she was very focused every time, wanting an answer, printing the note with care, tying the string four times & I said I had to tell her something serious & it was hard for me & if I cried, not to be scared, I'd be o.k. & I said all that & she said, *What,* & she was scared, but doing her note anyway, & I went on to say I'd had to make a decision & my decision was that it wasn't safe for her to see her grandpa anymore because he molested me when I was a kid & I knew what that meant & and then I said, *He won't get help & he's a danger to you and your cousins* & she said, *What did he do?* & I said, *He made me take off my clothes & touched me in my private parts & and when you get older I'll tell you more if you want to know* & by this time I was crying & she was too & she turned to me & said *I love you, Mom,* but she was also checking out the front windshield at the tempting sky & so I said, *You know I love you, now maybe it's time for you to get out & let your balloon go* & she did—small girl in an empty lot, reaching up ex-

210

ultant as the red balloon was flying up & up & we both watched it lift—
me in the car, she in the wind—& a few weeks later she got her first
card back & all it said was *Hi, found your balloon* & the address was only
a short distance from our house & I'm feeling close to home now too when
my workshop leader announces *Let it go, let your pink bubble rise.* I have
no trouble seeing my bubble rise. I've had a lot of practice letting go of
people I love. I let her go now—my daughter—with her smiling, ris-
ing energy, & when she lands, she'll send me a postcard that tells me
where and when.

# Thomas Lux
## THE GAS STATION

I own a gas station. It's at the edge of the Mojave Desert. The only gas station within two hundred miles. It's a small place: one pump, oil, water. . . . I live in the back. Work on my cars a lot, you know, climb into the engine and tinker around even if everything is perfect. It's my life in there, the hood up, against the sun. Not much money, but enough. Yesterday a red lizard walked across the windshield of the old Ford I work on. I remember thinking I've never seen a lizard so red.

In the afternoon I had two customers. Ralph was one of them. He came by to fill up his truck. Then, about three o'clock, the convertible. Gas, oil, water, windshields. The driver wanted to use the men's room. The woman in the car was tearing her petticoats into bandages. (No one was wounded?) Also, there was a cello in the back seat. I watched them as they drove away. When I turned around my gas station was on fire. Flames blasted from the men's room door. He had started a fire in there! In minutes the flames reached the drums of gasoline on the other side of the pasteboard wall. When they went so did most of my gas station.

Two hours later I was picking through the ashes. It was almost dark before the sheriff came by. He wanted to know what happened. I told him. He said do you think they're across by now? I said yes. He said I'll go after them anyway. I said listen I want you to take a look at the carburetor of the old Ford. It was parked outside. He was touched. He did what I asked. Leaning on my car, he related a long story about the time he was nearly electrocuted by his own sunglasses. By midnight he gave me enough money to buy a new gas station. He was grateful that I didn't drag arson, and possibly other crimes, into his life. Out here, at the edge of the Mojave, we only give up when we're ruined, when a boot begins to look like a glass of water. . . .

~

## MY GRANDMOTHER'S FUNERAL

At least a hundred seabirds attended my grandmother's funeral. And we live over a hundred miles from the coast. They flew right into the Episcopal church and stayed for the entire service. No one said anything about them when it was over. We were all sitting around on folding chairs rented from the undertaker and no one said a word about the seabirds! Even the Reverend, who was once a prisoner of the Japanese, and whose eyes were tunneled deep into his head, didn't seem to mind. I watched him when a few of them perched on a special chalice. He didn't budge. It was harder for him but he knew as well as the rest of us that seabirds are imperturbable, and that they keep away the larger birds, the birds that sit on the coffin, making it almost impossible to carry. . . .

∿

## THE SWIMMER

When I jumped from the bow of the ocean liner I had three things in mind: one, that I'd swim desperately to a buoy a mile away and cling to it alone; two, that I'd be missed and the liner would swing around to pick me up; and three, the most important, that I could say I was the man who helped save his own life. But the liner didn't come back. As I swam toward the buoy I could see the people on the deck playing shuffleboard getting smaller and smaller. . . . And when I reached the buoy I was greeted by a Nazi U-Boat Commander! He said he'd been there since 1944. When he began to go for his slimy Luger I jumped in again and swam for the mainland. I swam at night and floated during the day. I ate nothing. My arms became wheels of salt. I swam under water. In shallow water I crawled on the bottom. Tiny openings, no larger than hairline fractures, began to appear in my memory. I was a white machine, swimming. Finally, on the fifth day, I reached a harbor. When it was dark enough I swam to the beach and slipped into a hotel, the man who saved his own life, the man who is an obvious liar.

# Morton Marcus
## LOST THINGS

Those little things we search for, find us—the misplaced key we unexplainably notice as we pass the kitchen table for the fifth or sixth time; the watch left in a pocket that days later reappears still ticking on a mantle or a windowsill, with arms raised in mock surrender at five of one.

Even our dead parents seek us out in sleep, and those love affairs, which ended so badly, search for us in pop tunes on car radios late at night, or in photographs which weren't there yesterday but this morning unaccountably appear in our bureau drawers.

There are some things, however, that fall so far inside us they cannot return without our help, like children in a tropical rain forest after an airline crash who must wait for us to undertake an expedition to rescue them.

Harnessed in cumbersome backpacks and strapped into oxygen tanks made of steel plates stippled with rivetheads like nineteenth century ship hulls, we forge into the jungle from the clapboard rivertown.

Soon our equipment litters the path behind us and we stagger on, gasping, barefooted, clothes shredded, as if pulled toward a destination we cannot resist.

Each day we are more frantic because time is running ahead of us and we fear that we'll never catch up.

In the end we find the children seated blank-eyed in a clearing or in a thatched hut, pounding husks with stones. They have grown so tall, so thin, their faces as gaunt and weary as our own, that we hardly recognize them.

Later we stand by the graves we have discovered in the underbrush. They are wild and overgrown, no longer visited by anyone and strewn with what the survivors identify as religious artifacts—keys, watches, combs, and yellowing photographs of us.

~

## THE GIRL WHO BECAME MY GRANDMOTHER

Every night after the household was asleep, the girl who would be my grandmother rode her stove through the forests of Lithuania.

She would return by dawn, her black hair gleaming with droplets of dew and her burlap sack filled with fog-webbed mushrooms and roots.

"It's true," my grandfather said. "At first I followed, but I could never keep up." He would hear the clanging and rusty squeakings fade into the trees and, with a sigh, he would go home.

He accepted the situation until the night she left in the kitchen, as if she rode a coach pulled by black horses of wind.

Grandfather followed in the rest of the house, standing in the doorway to the now-departed room, bellowing threats as if urging the house forward at greater speed.

He caught her outside Vilna, when she stopped to get her bearings, and the house slammed into the stalled kitchen, grandfather tumbling through the doorway and hitting his head on the leg of a table.

"And where do you think you're going this time, Lady," he groaned from the floor, rubbing his right ear.

The girl smiled down at him and, kneeling by his side, stroked his hair, but didn't say anything.

That was the last time the girl who would be my grandmother went on a nocturnal outing. Soon after, they left for America.

In Brooklyn, she rode from one day to the next in the house he built around her, watching the unchanging scene beyond the kitchen window.

It was then she became my grandmother, white-haired and smiling, never saying much of anything, even when the old man shouted from the other rooms. Not that he ever needed anything. He just wanted to be sure she was still there.

# Peter Markus
## STILL LIVES WITH WHISKEY BOTTLE

*Still Life #1: A Good Night's Sleep*

He had gone with his father into Detroit to look at used cars, though
halfway there his father had all of a sudden stopped the car in front of
a liquor store, and had got out and had gone inside without saying a word.
And when, a little while later, his father had come back outside to the
car carrying a brown paper sack, he didn't have to ask him what was
inside. Instead he silently watched his father reach his hand into the
bag and pull out a bottle, and after his father had unscrewed the cap and
had taken a drink, he noticed how the skin on his father's face seemed
to loosen its grip. And for the first time in a long while his father looked
like a man who had just awakened from a good night's sleep.

*Still Life #2: Broken Pieces*

It happened that on one too many nights in a row his father had come
home drunk, so drunk that the next morning the whole house stank of
liquor and smoke and urine, so on this one night his mother couldn't
take it any longer, and so she took his father's drunkenness into her own
hands, and she took all the bottles of beer and wine and whiskey still in
the fridge and in the kitchen cabinets, and she broke them out on the
back steps, one right after another, so that the sound of glass breaking
shattered the nighttime silence, and the windows of the neighbors'
houses all lit up, and curtains were pulled back, and from his own bed-
room window he watched it all: he saw his mother step outside into the
cold night air in her bare feet, her nightgown hanging loose around her
shoulders, and at first she smashed the bottles, but then, after a little
while, she dropped down onto her hands and knees, the shards of green
and brown and clear-colored glass shining up at her like a string of mis-
matched Christmas lights. And for a moment, as he stood there alone
in the darkness of his room, he believed that his mother had fallen onto

her knees to say a prayer, though he realized, finally, that she had simply begun to pick up all the broken pieces.

*Still Life #3: Whiskey Love*

One summer when he was twelve and his father was for a time not working, his mother had gone off to Michigan City, Indiana, for a few days to visit a dying aunt. This was the first time he had been left alone with his father for more than a couple of hours, and although he was twelve and had been told he was a boy too old to be crying, he cried when his mother left. The night before she left, his mother had cooked up enough food to last the weekend through—a cold chicken casserole, a chocolate cake, plus a freezer full of easy to fix frozen dinners—but he was already hungry and lonely even before the red brake lights on his mother's big-fendered Ford disappeared around the corner on the way to the freeway out of town. He stood there for a while by the side of the road, watching to see if his mother's car would come back home, though when it became clear to him that his mother wasn't turning back he went back inside the house to be alone with his father. Inside, his father was standing by the kitchen sink, staring out the window at the tiny patch of grass in the backyard. He didn't know what to say to his father now that the two of them had been left alone, and so he didn't say anything. He didn't say anything about the brown paper sack standing upright on the kitchen table, or the cigarette slowly burning down in his father's big-knuckled hand, or the fact that—in his mother's words—his father was trying to turn his house into a bar. He didn't say anything till the moment his father took the whiskey bottle out of its bag, and broke the seal, and then took a good long drink. And what he said then was, "What's it like?" And his father paused then, for a moment, and then he said, "Here. Go ahead. Take a drink," and he handed him the bottle. And when he had taken that first drink down he felt closer to his father than he'd ever before thought possible. Though he knew deep down that as soon as his mother returned home he would never forgive himself, or forgive his father, for the whiskey he mistook for love.

*Still Life #4: Lifeline*

All of that summer and into the fall, he saw men he'd known his whole life —good men, family men, hard-working men—searching the streets for work, sometimes relaxing, stoop-backed, over Formica-topped lunch-counters studying "Help Wanted" ads in the *Detroit Free Press,* though after a while, by wintertime, he watched hopeful gazes turn into lost stares looking vacantly into bottomless mugs of coffee, steam curling up around whiskered faces like hands offering comfort, a warm caress, a voice—a mother's, or a wife's—telling them not to worry, not to think. Some days he saw his father sitting among these men, or standing in a long, single-file line outside the town newsstand, shuffling from foot to foot as if work—not just papers—were being sold. But that was the year Michigan lost its jobs, lopped off like fingers in a punch-press, and in his neighborhood of shoebox-shaped bungalows built side by side in the cold, dark shadow of the town's lifeline—McLouth Steel—crudely-staked "For Sale" signs, dozens in a row, like gravestones, foretold the future of a town where only the dead were left to bury the dead.

# Debra Marquart
## GETTING READY

i'm the thousand-change girl, getting ready for school, standing in my bedroom ripping pants and shirts from my body, trying dresses and skirts. father, at the bottom of the steps, yelling, the bus is coming, here comes the bus. i'm wriggling into jeans—zippers grinding their teeth, buttons refusing their holes. my brother, dressed-in-five-minutes, stands in the hall, t-shirt and bookbag, saying what's the big problem. i'm kneeling in front of the closet, foraging for that great-lost-other-shoe. father, downstairs, offers advice. slacks, he's yelling, just put on some slacks. i'm in the mirror, matching earrings, nervous fingers putting the back to the front. downstairs, the bus is fuming in the yard, farm kids with cowlicks sitting in rows. everything's in a pile on the floor. after school, mother will scream, get upstairs and hang up that mess, but i don't care, i'm the thousand-change girl, looking good, trotting down the stairs now, ready for school. father, pulling back from the steps with disgust, yelling, it's about time, giving me the once over, saying, is *that* what you're wearing?

～

## MY FATHER TELLS THIS STORY ABOUT
## HIS BROTHER FRANK AND THE WICK
## (EVERY TIME I ASK HIM FOR MONEY)

your grandpa marquart, he was a tight sonofabitch you know every night he'd come to the bottom of the steps and yell up, frank, go to sleep, you're wasting my oil. because frank liked to read, he was always reading something, he wasn't much for farmwork, but he liked school and reading and just wasting his time on books. so grandpa thought he better put an end to all that laziness and sloth, frank was pretty much worthless when five o'clock chores rolled around. it was more work getting him out of bed than just doing the chores yourself. so this went

219

on for years, this grandpa coming to the bottom of the steps and yelling up, frank, go to sleep, you're wasting my oil. and frank, setting his book down, leaving it open to the last page he was reading, and rolling the wick down into the lamp and dousing the flame. so finally frank gets this town job and makes a little bit of money and the first thing he does is buys himself some oil right off, see, so that he can read as late as he pleases. then when grandpa comes to the steps at night and yells up, frank, go to sleep, you're wasting my oil, frank gets out of bed and goes to the top of the steps and yells back down. this is my oil, i bought this oil with my own money, and i will burn this oil however i see fit. but grandpa, he had a way, you know, of seeing how things broke down, how they divided up, because he yelled right back without even thinking, he said, but what about the wick. that's what he said, what about the wick? your grandfather, i'm telling you, now there was a tight man.

～

## SMALL TOWN CAFE

Tonight, while the husbands have gone home to their wives and the teenagers to their cars, only the two old bachelors full of gossip and coffee sit by the window and watch as cars roll by. The cook in greasy glasses has emerged from the cave of the kitchen, with a yellow fly swatter in her hand, bent to kill all winged intruders. I follow in white shoes wiping the steam of splatter from the tables with this wet rag. The owner smokes and watches from behind the counter. She has designer eyeglasses and fingernails, and a limp that even her mink won't let you forget. Coffee is ten cents, but if a new car pulls up, full of suits with briefcases, she will lift herself from the stool, limp across the room and whisper, *charge them twenty-five.*

# Kathleen McGookey
## INSTRUMENT FACTORY, BRAZIL

It's simple enough to give away the coins in your heart, when dust settles over a pool filled with mineral water and the dogs, those sleek guards, raise their inky noses to a silver saxophone moon. Beyond São Paulo, down a dirt road, men make French horns, flutes, and cymbals with the delicate precision of angels. Blue-suited, they sit at tables: one tests a saxophone, another welds the key of a flute. And each has tools on the table, a candle, a blue welding flame. Stacks and stacks of half-finished instruments crowd the factory aisles: bells of horns, all sizes, rows of French horns hung on a green metal rack, pyramids of tambourines and drums. I love to watch their mouths emerge, but I have closed my own against the men with their suit coats hung over their shoulders. Our guide runs his finger across my cheek, then down the elegant neck of a flute. And the slim scraps of brass, shaved off, curl like hair when they sweep the floors. Here, they use plastic for clarinets; even the good wood, when they can get it, rots in the sun. Behind us, a young boy plays scales in a testing room while vats for nickel and brass plating steam behind windows. And the workers walk with horns slung over their shoulders, the almost obscene curves shining in their closed hands.

≈

## SHYNESS

*—São Paulo, Brazil*

And so the men smile, and I smile back at them. And if I opened my mouth to the parrot? To the three big dogs that prowl my borrowed neighborhood at night? The policemen on horses patrol so we can feel safe; I hear hooves passing the house as I am coming out of sleep, not sure if the sound is a dream or a memory. Tell me how to open my mouth. I will do it, despite the parrot on the gate and this bad air. What I want to say, I can't: I simply smile, embarrassed, and adjust the neckline of my dress. The men smile back, lean forward, and help me order some fish. We can't dance in any of these rooms: there's not enough space around the white tables, no stained glass, and all of the statues are grimacing. Here, I am kissed more than I can stand. One man makes a game of grabbing my face between his huge hands and kissing my forehead. I blush. Of course I blush. Each day different men take me to their cars. But still, I have been forgotten, traveling so many hours toward the idea of music. So many hours with a bad taste in my mouth. If I keep my head down, low to my body, I think I can almost disappear.

# Jay Meek
## THE BEAUTIFUL AND INVISIBLE TREE
## THAT RISES THROUGH THE UNIVERSE
## FOR WHICH THE STARS ARE LEAVES

Afternoons, I sit on the cafe terrace, here in the mercantile district where only last week a general strike began. It was August. There was a parade. The marchers held banners with violently red lettering, and in their faces one could see the anger of a long-deferred surrender. Workers from far down the boulevard came up under the plane trees as if they were walking out of a wilderness that was still burning. Today, the waiter in his black vest and long white apron moves easily among the marble tables. When he brings my *express,* I unwrap the sugar cubes, deliberately, as if I were opening a small gift. He and I, we are blessed with consciousness. For us all, it is like a door that opens to an invisible community, but a door that is not true, so that we can see in its opening four white swans flying over the city wall, four white swans and the city burning.

When we lie down at night, we put aside our watchfulness and longing. Around us, the darkness shines. Perhaps one day, entering a tramontane village, we might find all that's lost to us, forms sheered off from their substances—sollerets and phaetons and mortsafes—still without rust in the rarefied air. Who can say? I have seen pictures of a man who carried inside him the incomplete boy of his twin, only the spine and shoulders visible on his chest as if his brother had dived into him. In the whole of the universe, who's to say the human form is right? Truly, we are capable of infinite variation, like the ocean our crossing takes small measure of, the whitecaps falling on one another like the shadows of a possible world.

~

MEDICI FOUNTAIN

In the Luxembourg Gardens, I unfold a map of Paris over my knee.
Light comes down through the trees and illuminates the leaves at the
bottom of the pool, over which the shadows of ripples sometimes pass.
I've just seen the Aphrodite of Melos, someone older than I supposed,
a woman given in to the weight of her body. Beside her were the young
nudes, Roman from the way they stood, with hands on their hips and
their hips thrust forward, their penises like the flames on votive can-
dles. They knew how beautiful they were, and yet they were not
altogether caught up in themselves. How much life I spend in con-
sciousness alone, mapping the joys I see: this fountain, a few iron chairs,
shadows of things. These touch me, wonderfully, and go on. Distance
cleaves to me, like the merry-go-round I can't quite make out through
the trees, here in the park where I've come to stand beside a moment
that is overwhelming.

～

## TRAVEL NOTES

I remember Cully: this is what happened there. As the captain turned our launch toward the dock, it was raining. In the rain, the Alps were blue. A man and woman sat together in front of the patisserie and watched a train passing on the hillside, toward Montreux. Seeing a chestnut tree in flower, I could hear everything thrum with the voice of its own kind, like that one tree in the rain, or even the most singular of poems, as it sounds. After we docked, a man and woman got off, but no one waved and no one met them. Then a man in a blue uniform drew our gangway onto the deck, and we pulled away. There was nothing more. I made a note of how life shimmered in the town.

We need poems to help us change, and to ease our knowing. Not that a poem should assume more than we know, but allow what we do not know; that it might give to our weakness; that it might take us in confidence; that it might enact itself in us; that it might raise us out of ourselves. Even nights when we take it lovingly in our hands, and ease it of its sound, the poem we give our breath to is already assured beyond changing: it is a record of movement accomplished, of hope followed through into knowing. Of flawed perfections. Of conditional joy.

Yes, I was at Cully, and I'll remember it not only for its resonance and the rain, but the pleasure I felt in discovering that whatever else it does, a poem will always make the sound of a poem. By this, it exempts itself from its own being, to hold us in mildness and quiet. Reading it, we can be at our best, without apology, and bear our lives in its song.

# W. S. Merwin
## THE PERMANENT COLLECTION

In a rich provincial city there is a museum as imposing and quite as large as any in the capital. The façade is immense and the portico dwarfs the visitor, seeming to fill the space between his usual size and his shrunken self with an echo. The style of the building is not obviously contemporary, though it could have been produced in no other age. It manages to suggest, with its general proportions, high columned halls, and open airy courts surrounded by enormous arcades, an entire classical tradition in which temple and palace are never completely distinguishable from each other. The approach to the building is lined on either side with marble pedestals, each of them empty. Across the top of the main portico there is a large panel for a name or inscription. It is blank.

The museum is referred to, in the literature supplied by the chamber of commerce, as The Permanent Collection—the gift of an anonymous donor. The terms of the donor's will stipulated that there should be no other designation. But publications for which the city administration cannot be held accountable reveal that the museum was the bequest of a local millionaire whose forbears, through several generations, had played a dominant role in the exploitation of that region. The name is common in those parts, on streets, banks, office buildings, bridges, housing developments, foundations. But the family—at least the direct line for which these have all been named—has died out. The last of the line was the builder and donor of the museum.

In his youth, according to the local historians, he had fallen in love with the daughter of another wealthy household, at a northern resort where both dynasties had summer houses. Only one portrait of her is known to have survived. It shows the girl at the time when they first met—already beautiful: slender, dark-haired, her expression gentle, delicate, remote. She had pretended not to notice his early, clumsy suit. During the first winters her name was coupled with one boy after another from the same schools which he attended. But one summer, perhaps out of mere indolence, she had paid him more attention, or at least had spent more time in his company than before, and their families had come to take the relation between them for granted—though neither of the young people did so. They were spoken of for a winter or so almost as though they were engaged. Between the assumption, which he met on all hands, of his future with her, and the secret barrenness of his hopes, he became aware of an abyss that would swallow everything he knew.

During college he had seen as much as possible of a succession of other girls. He had even formed attachments with several of them, lasting for a matter of months. But she was the one whom he tried not to want, and the longing for her grew with him. He proposed to her before he left college and she listened to him quietly and told him she wanted to wait. Then she had gone abroad with her family and he was not surprised when, shortly after their return, he received an announcement of her engagement to someone else.

They had continued to see each other, occasionally. She had had a daughter. He too had married—twice, once hilariously, both times disastrously. He had had no children.

Her marriage too had ended in divorce, after fifteen years. Her husband spent his summers on his own estate, and her daughter was sent to be with him in June. She herself had returned to visit her family, in the northern resort. There she had seen her former suitor again. There had been a second courtship, to which he deliberately imparted an air of casual urbanity that was as contrived—on his part—as the stillness of the breath above a trigger-finger. It worked. They were married during the following winter. Nothing is known of their life together. Outwardly it was placid. She died a year later, while swimming.

The entrance to the museum is guarded by wardens in plain dark uniforms without metal buttons or insignia of any kind. Inside the main portal is a vast hall, with another marble pedestal in the center, catching the light. It is empty, like those outside. In the walls on either side are tall niches, also containing nothing. Guards in the same featureless uniforms stand in pairs at each doorway, and at intervals along the corridors and in the arcades. There is a prescribed order for visiting the rooms, and the guards point the way.

And in each room there are more of the large pedestals, without statues or names. In some, besides, there are glass display cases, of different shapes and sizes, empty, and picture frames containing blank canvas on the walls. All along the arcades there are empty niches and pedestals, alternating, and in each of the courtyards there is an empty fountain. No one talks. It takes well over an hour to make the tour of the rooms and step out into the world again on the same side as the entrance but further along. From there one leaves by another walk flanked by empty pedestals. The donor lived to see the building completed, but the public was admitted only after his death.

Why did he want the visitors at all? Could he have foreseen those who come out from the building with a sigh of relief and a joke, or with a burst of indignation at the abuse of wealth or at the enormity of his egoism or with a yawn, a glance at a watch, a suggestion about eating? Could he have foreseen those who emerge from time to time in silence, with their faces shining?

～

## A GARDEN

You are a garden into which a bomb once fell and did not explode, during a war that happened before you can remember. It came down at night. It screamed, but there were so many screams. It was heard, but it was forgotten. It buried itself. It was searched for but it was given up. So much else had been buried alive.

Other bombs fell near it and exploded. You grew older. It slept among the roots of your trees, which fell around it like nets around a fish that supposedly had long since become extinct. In you the rain fell. In your earth the water found the dark egg with its little wings and inquired, but receiving no answer made camp beside it as beside the lightless stones. The ants came to decorate it with their tunnels. In time the grubs slept, leaning against it, and hatched out, hard and iridescent, and climbed away. You grew older, learning from the days and nights.

The tines of forks struck at it from above, and probed, in ignorance. You suffered. You suffer. You renew yourself. Friends gather and are made to feel at home. Babies are left, in their carriages, in your quiet shade. Children play on your grass and lovers lie there in the summer evenings. You grow older, with your seasons. You have become a haven. And one day when a child has been playing in you all afternoon, the pressure of a root or the nose of a mouse or the sleepless hunger of rust will be enough, suddenly, to obliterate all these years of peace, leaving in your place nothing but a crater rapidly filling with time. Then in vain will they look for your reason.

# John Minczeski
## MY NAME

*—for Victor Contoski*

My name arrived from Poland in 1910 stowed away in the engine room of a Swiss freighter. The cook took pity on it and every day brought sausages, berries, and milk. My name for two weeks was deafened by the sound of pistons and the turning of the twin screws. My name, without a passport or an extra change of clothes, without a toothbrush or a brown shopping bag, swam to Staten Island, barely missed being eaten by Sharks. My name didn't know English. It was taken in by potato farms and learned to drive trucks and drink beer. My name tripped over a cabbage and was cut in half by a harrow. Thus I was born. I have given it years of pain. My name has forgotten how to cry.

~

## TANGO

> M'illumino
> d'inmenso
>   —Giuseppe Ungaretti

Just outside Chicago, at the home of a dead architect, three of us sat at a round table on the brick patio. The sedum was in bloom, and on it the bees could not gorge themselves enough with the taste of October. The ivy covering the brick building beside us had turned a deeper rust than the brick itself, and in the night wind the hawthorns rasped against the bedroom windows. The colors were the same that poured out of Flora's mouth in the Botticelli, but it was fall, not *primavera,* and it was no allegory, just the three of us eating on the patio. As we ate, piano and saxophone blues unrolled on the tape player I brought. Warm enough to be comfortable, too late for flies and mosquitoes, the moment slowed down, almost stopped, the sun going down on the prairie. The tape clicked from Archie Shepp to Mary Lou Williams. We sat in an unbroken silence. What could we say to equal the moment? The blue of the sky came down, so blue it became black. We drank our wine, the candle burned down.

None of us expected anything more than to be there in that moment. The old wooden gate stood open leading to the driveway and overgrown yard beyond the candle's illuminated circle. We couldn't know that in a few years one of us would die—cancer or AIDS, it's all the same—the success of another's novel would let her live comfortably on a Vermont farm and continue writing, and one would be sitting in a motel room with ugly curtains in the sixth or seventh largest city in Minnesota. Beyond it all is that moment time stopped—I can't remember who brought the wine, it was simply there when the moment called for it.

And that was it. A moment lasted forever and it was gone like all good things in this world, but from somewhere it can return, like a tango, something that needs only music to revive it. A day it was good to be alive—or because it was a good day to die we were alive, and the earth beneath us continued falling through its orbit into Fall and beyond.

# Judith Minty

## IRONING

The pattern flows. Leaves and flowers blend, a river spinning over the cotton. It is my daughter's blouse. Green ripples under my fingers. Pink and blue blossom under the iron's steam. Tiny buds. The cement floor presses its back against the soles of my feet. The pipes gather pearls of moisture. I am a tree. I rise from the earth. I shade the ironing board. My hand passes back and forth, a branch in the wind. One sleeve, then the other.

Summer, but this basement remembers winter and holds loam to its heart. The water in these pipes wants to go underground, back to the dark. It is June, and my daughter sleeps in the heat of her dream. She is far from my belly now, on her white bed, still as a breath in the hospital wing. I have washed the blood from her blouse. Now this iron passes over a sleeve, it curls around a button. Colors intertwine, tangle. The petals blur. They bleed into leaves on the vines.

The car was thick with glass, little beads of glass, blue and yellow in the sun. The lace of slivers of glass, glistening on her skirt, under her bare feet. Glass clinging to her blouse, her skin. Glass in the upholstery, on the carpet, the dashboard. Prisms in the sun. A clink and tinkle like wind chimes when she stirred. Her hands gliding to her face. Glass glinting in her hair. Blood shining on the glass. Glass flowing, separating, as she stirred on the seat of the car.

I pass this iron over her blouse. Steam hisses. I hear her voice as she is lifted from the car. Steam rises from the flowers, the petals. The leaves. I am a tree. Her long hair matted with blood, the cut open on her scalp. My feet curl like roots on the floor. Sweat gathers on the pipes. I rustle over her blouse. Her hair unfurls on the pillow. The flowers blend, the leaves blur. My hand glides over the pattern, a river spinning. Her dream flows without sound. Steam hisses from the iron. Petals and leaves mingle pink and blue. Green. I am ironing her blouse. Only this motion is left.

# N. Scott Momaday

*from* The Strange and True Story of
My Life with Billy the Kid

## THE MAN IN BLACK

I rode across the snowfields in the moonlight, holding myself in steady relation to the stars. The black timber on either side lay flat against the slopes, running down before me into the bottom of the night. In the dusk I had seen rabbits—and once a fox, like the point of a flame, flickering among the trees. But now for miles I had seen nothing but the night. There were wolves about; I believed in them, for the near edge of their presence cut into the nerves of my horse, and our going on was quiet and cautious. And it was cold; the cold was absolute. At length nothing mattered, not even the wolves, because of the cold. At nine o'clock, perhaps, I saw the lights at Arroyo Seco.

The man sitting across the table from me was slight of build and rather unseemly in appearance. He affected the wearing of black, which in another, more imposing figure might have been dramatic, even ominous; but in this man it was an unremarkable aspect, save that it accentuated something that lay deeper than his appearance, a certain somberness, a touch of grief. It was as if the Angel of Death had long ago found out his name. His skin was nearly colorless, and his front teeth protruded to such an extent that his thin lips seemed never to come together. His eyes were blue, just the blue of water in milk, and devoid of expression, so that it was impossible to say what he was thinking—or indeed *that* he was thinking. Thought seemed somehow irrelevant to his real being, apart from his true nature. I have heard that certain organisms—sharks, for example—are virtually mindless, that they are creatures of pure instinct. So it was with this man, I believe. If a rational thought, or a whole emotion, had ever grown up inside of him, he should have suffered a great dislocation of himself in his mind and soul. Such was my impression; he should have been like a plate of glass that

233

is shattered upon a stone. But at the same time I had the sense that his instincts were nearly infallible. Nothing should ever take him by surprise—and no one, except perhaps himself. Only one principle motivated him, that of survival—his own mean and exclusive survival. For him there was no morality in the universe but that, neither choice nor question. And for that reason he was among the deadliest creatures on the face of the earth.

His hands were remarkably small and delicately formed. I have heard it said that they were like a woman's hands, and with respect to size and shape that is true. But they were rough, too, and marked by hard use. There was something like propriety in all their attitudes—and great utility; you looked at them and you thought at once of fine tools, precision instruments. They were steady and extraordinarily expressive. You could read this man in his hands as you could never read him in his eyes. His hands articulated him in the way that a leaf articulates the wind or the current of a stream. And yet they were nearly evasive, too, in their propriety.

There was no resonance in his voice, but it was thin and hard and flat—wood clacking lightly upon wood. He was ill at ease within the element of language; I believe that silence was his natural habitat. Notwithstanding, his speech was plain and direct—and disarmingly polite.

"Thank you for coming," he said.

"I will go with you," I replied.

And this is how it began; and this is the strange and true story of my life with Billy the Kid.

∼

## BILLY THE KID OFFERS A KINDNESS TO
## AN OLD MAN AT GLORIETA

He was a broken-down old man, a twist of rawhide. When you looked at him you had the sense that you were looking at a ruin, something of prehistoric character, like a shard of pottery or the remnant of an ancient wall. His face, especially, was an archaeology in itself. The shadows of epochs come and go in such a face.

He was a cowboy, he allowed. He had broken horses all his life, and not a few of them had broken him. And he had known men and women, good and bad—singular men and singular women. He was more than willing to talk about these and other things. We listened, Billy and I. The old man's real existence was at last invested in his stories; there he lived, and not elsewhere. He was nothing so much as the story of himself, the telling of a tale to which flesh was gathered incidentally. It was no wonder Billy liked him.

We passed the time of day with him, and he created us over and over again in his stories, fashioned us into myriad wonderful things that we should not otherwise have been. Now we were trick-shot artists in a Wild West Show, and the old man, his guns blazing, shot the buttons off our vests. Again we dined on the most exotic and delicious fruits in the golden palaces of the Orient. We were there at the Battle of the Wilderness, at the very point of the Bloody Angle, following the old man into legend. Christmas was coming on, and we were the Magi, the old man said. Laughing, we half believed him. And then it was time to go.

Billy fetched a plug of tobacco from his coat pocket, cut it in two with a jackknife, and gave the old man half. We said goodbye and left the old man there at Glorieta, before his fire. The leading edge of a dream was moving like a distant, migrant bird across his eyes.

Later, on the way to Santa Fe, I said to Billy:

"Say, amigo, I have never seen you chew tobacco."

"No, and it isn't likely that you ever will," he said. "I have no use for the weed."

Then, seeing that I was perplexed, he went on:

"I bought the tobacco at La Junta because I knew that we were coming this way and I hoped to see the old man, who is my true friend. He has a taste for it. And I offered him the half instead of the whole because he should prefer that I did not give him something outright; it pleased him that I should share something of my own with him. As it happens, I have thrown away my share, in which the ownership consists—it lies back there in a snowdrift. But that is an unimportant matter, a trivial conceit—and this the old man understands and appreciates more even than the tobacco itself."

He started to say something more, but apparently he thought better of it and fell silent. He seemed lost in thought, but it was impossible to say. This brief sojourn into language had been for him extraordinary, and he seemed spent, and indeed almost remorseful and contrite, as if he had squandered something of which he had too little in store. His eyes were precisely equal in color to the sky at that moment, and the sky was curdled with snow.

"Indeed we are the Magi," I said, but I said it softly, that his thoughts, whatever they were, should not be disturbed.

# Beverly Acuff Momoi
## IF SHE CAN'T HEAR YOU

*—for Aung San Suu Kyi, winner of the 1991 Nobel Peace Prize, living under house arrest in Myanmar since July 20, 1989\**

I ask each of them, nine boys, one girl, to make a list of leaders, of heroes. She says your name, sure and clear in her answer. The others laugh, say they never heard of you, ask how you can be a hero if no one knows your name. She tells us. She tells us you are from her country, you are the true leader of Burma. She calls it Burma, using the old name, not Myanmar as the paper calls it. A woman? they jeer. A woman can't be a leader. Yes. Yes, she can. She takes the chalk from them and writes your name on their list. Then she takes the eraser to make sure it stays.

Like young boys, the men of your country try to deny you. They make you into the other, tell your people you are not one of them, remind them your husband is British.

"Her permanent address is Oxford. If she wants to leave for her permanent address, she can leave."

"People think she should be reunited with her family."

"... when you see things with a cooler head ... I think she did overdo things."

"Her ideas of democracy and freedom ... were out of touch with the real Burmese situation."

You sit in your house of brick and shingle, refuse to leave your home country, wait out the days of your life. How long can you continue to hear only the words of your own making, to see only your own reflection, to reach out and touch only memory? How long before their words are true, before you truly are "out of touch with the real Burmese"? How long before you are no longer the mother of a young girl's dreams?

∼

*\*On July 10, 1995, Aung San Suu Kyi was released from house arrest. —ED.*

## INTIMATE LANGUAGE

I was learning the language . . . being with it every moment . . . I started to know the characters individually. Big, black curving ones that reached across my shoulders and hugged me. Squiggly ones that danced like overgrown children. Solemn, straight-arrow ones. Ones that sat in judgment. . . . Finally, they started sleeping with me, wrapping black, ropey arms around me, knee to back of knee, butt to belly. This was the language I loved. This was home.

# Frederick Morgan
## ELVES

The notion of living entities in human shape, intelligent but not human: look upon it as an experiment conducted upon the stuff of being. Shall they be smaller than we? Bushier, perhaps? What impulses bring about these particular condensations? To what extent do alien existences depend upon certain crystallizations of our own thought, perhaps upon our very words? Shall we postulate *elves,* speaking the word aloud so as to give life to a certain meaningful vibration? But then we have become responsible for them and must find them a bodily home. Is the preference for frail and exquisite manikins? Or elongated, wispy personages clad in forest green? Or small fat burly chaps with beards? "The elves hold their revels," I say. "They revel on the meadows in the moonlight." The stage is set; the action begins. Little whiskery creatures cavort in the pale gloam, guzzle beer from oaken kegs, kick off their britches and fart, and let their balls swing in the midnight breezes. These elves are from a vulgar tradition, which I happen to like.

"Eleven elves reveled on the level velvet veldt." I summoned them long ago: their existence is not in question. Secure in their borderland homes, they inhabit a climate well-adjusted to their several moods, and maintain a well-recognized pattern of activity—which is, to be sure, somewhat circumscribed and ritualistic. But there is a twelfth elf, a doubting Thomas, who observes them as they fulfill their moonlit rounds but himself neither moves nor speaks.

I go out by night and watch them occasionally, under a sky of indigo.

~

## PTERODACTYLS

I have always regarded them as friends. Somewhat grotesque, but dutiful in their comings and goings, and forming a necessary link in the chain of existence. I was therefore displeased, at age thirteen, to see one crumpled between the paws of a hulking apish brute and tossed to the waves below as if he were no more than the flimsy wreckage of an archaic and defective aeroplane. There was a structure here that merited more consideration.

It is true that one will occasionally, flying through an open window at night, seize a sleeping girl—naked or in filmy nightdress—and abscond with her to some distant mountain or inaccessible rooftop. But her fate is not desperate. He will usually bring her directly back to her own room and bed—after having set her down in that lonely place, stalked about her three or four times in awkward circles, and given her the once-over with his unblinking quizzical gaze. (Perhaps even, with his long bony beak, pecked gently once or twice at her nipples or belly button.)

Counterbalancing this foolishness, one must insist on their usefulness as messengers. Featherless birds, hovering between the serpent and the angel, they possess an intelligence which is more than vestigial but limits itself to immediate practicalities. Their lack of imagination is refreshing: without drama or self-aggrandizement they may bring tidings from above or below. When one of them comes looming down and settles himself before you, creaking and flapping—then takes an ungainly step and, cocking his ugly head, looks squarely into your eyes—you will know he brings a message that had best be heeded.

# Kristy Nielsen

*—from* The Language with One Word

## DURING THE LAST MONTHS

The woman must smile back at the face of death. Privately, she is unable to sing. Sometimes, alone, she clutches at the sheets, or presses her temples fiercely.

There is less and less of him to hold as summer intensifies around the humming house. She puts on weight, eating what he can no longer swallow as his bones reveal a series of graceful angles. Blue eyes startle against a lean face, all the life of the season held in a single blue jay.

He buys her a flurry of gifts. A six-month anniversary of the conversation when they decided. The last birthday. She goes to work heavier and heavier, laden with the pressure of time and the next symptom. She tells herself she can always do things later, meaning: *after.*

"The moon is full again," she says: *another month is gone.* Wondering: *will I remember this forever? Patio stones cool under my feet, the exact shade of this year's begonias, my love's collarbones, the voice like a summer blanket in winter, and the way I can almost make time stop as he watches night darken.*

"Come here," he says, patting the space next to him. "Come watch the moon with me," he says, meaning: *You will remember this forever.*

~

## BEFORE HE DIES

It is best to try in the morning. She makes her lips into fish and kisses along his spine, the old control panel. With swimming hands, she moves each kiss out over his back to spread the message: There is still love to be had in his body. He rolls toward her.

Death is a slipknot in the corner of the room he's beginning to see a way into. Life is this woman with rivers of yellow hair and mountains

241

that remind him of the whole planet. She beckons across the galaxy of the bed. "My love," she whispers.

Her certainty holds him there, and he carefully takes her continents in his hands. The Mediterranean spreads across her belly, places he's never been. He sails across to admire villages, caress the horizon gently.

The woman spins, she rotates, she holds gravity tight inside. Her body produces a hot disk. In love, she places the sun in his hands, but he knows he cannot hold it long.

At the edge of the bed, an angel strokes the cat with a gold-toned cloud, watching this exquisite human attempt.

Nothing is more precise than the light it radiates, and the light falls over him.

"Love," the angel says seductively. "All love."

～

## SLEEPING

It is a good sound that she makes, the growling off-key wail that seems to spiral out of her tailbone, powerful as a snake. And the movement is good too: it matches. She does not feel pretty.

In this way, she moves through the rooms, facing the expectation, the vision of him curled up on a chair with a magazine. "Hi," he says in that voice of old cotton and she strikes back like a snake. "You are gone." She moves into his space until it is hers again. She dumps out his bottles of pills and clears away the special foods. Removes the toothbrush, throws away ticket stubs and Chinese fortunes.

Crumpled up behind the door she finds a note. It is addressed to her. "Please don't disturb me," it says. "I am sleeping."

Later that night, curled away from his side of the bed, she cries again, again, again, knowing there is more she must do to let him go. As casual as a jay landing on a branch, she feels her love's hand against her back, the palm flat. This she allows for a moment and then rolls flat. "No," she admits, eyes open, hands moving over the whole bed. "I am alone," she chants, finally drifting to sleep. "I am alone again."

# Nina Nyhart

## THE BEECH TREE

My childhood has left me, stomped out like a sullen child into the back yard. I'm left here in the modern kitchen wondering what I did wrong.

But a child like that! Who can bear her moods!

It's late afternoon, dusk has wrapped itself around the beech tree, and the child, too, is walking around the trunk, shoulder to the bark, as if she needed to be touched, touched continuously.

~

## THE CATCH

Last night my mother appeared on Walnut Street wearing a skimpy white hospital gown, clutching a bunch of spring flowers—tulips and daffodils, white lilacs. She said It only hurts when I cough. I wanted to take home all the pieces of her, put her in a warm bed, bring her beef broth, put the flowers in a vase filled with fresh water. I said Get in the car, you'll catch your death. But she'd already caught it, light as a beach-ball, red and yellow, white and green.

# Monica Ochtrup
## NORDEN

Our daughter, Jennifer, comes home from her trip to West Germany. She has spent much of it, having found a home, in Norden, a mile and a half from the North Sea. Norden, Norddeich, Norderney. It is a music that continues. The town. The harbor preceded by the dyke. And the island in the sea. Cows. Boats. It does not stop. The town goes into the land goes into the sea comes into the land comes into the town and the people make a life by it.

In a house in Norden a child is born midwifed by his grandmother. He grows up, leaves the town for schooling, comes back. He will leave the town again, but meantime has his tools. With his father, the carpenter, he builds houses. The tool box he keeps near his bed. It is elaborate. Pulls up into many trays. His good friend the sculptor has also done his schooling and now for the past eighteen months looks for an apprenticeship. While the American is there, he finds it. The celebration that night in the Borka is noisy. The American lights her cigarette from a candle on the table. People look up. Conversation stops. When you take light from the candle a sailor dies at sea.

～

## THE TRUTH

There were two ways to get to my grandmother's house. One was to cross the railroad tracks and go on down the block past the white clapboard building where the tailor had his shop; turn right down the alley which turns again left and rutted up to Mrs. Shebetka's back door where you could stop, standing in view of my grandma's back porch. If you stood there in the summer, her neighbor's garden was mean and small, over-shadowed by a row of hot, horny sunflowers, tall as a grown man and grabbing for their share of the air. The row belonged to my grand-mother, widowed and fertile.

The other way was through the underpass along Highway 4, across Main Street and down a block of nothing to the alley; turn left past Bill Keyes' house and hope crazy old Bill won't come out; cut around my grandma's barn and up the skinny back walk where my grandpa died: pushed over by a huge stray dog, the walk being brick, it killed him.

Most often I went the first way, up to the back door. Go ahead. Kick it in. The smells of garlic and camphor will no longer assail you. The kitchen belongs to someone else now, but you wouldn't find the truth there anyway. Stick to the corner of Shebetka's house. Go on. Walk back out to the initial spot and stand, rooted. Do not move. Feel the sharp edge of that house's corner where wall meets wall. That's it. Turn right, now. Turn into the sunflowers. You are tall as a grown woman looking into your grandmother's gray-green eyes. In the yellow heat of the sunflower patch you are aware of her strength, the diffusion of countless spores flying thick in the air like fine dust swelling your nostrils. Breathe deep.

# Roger Pfingston
## DARWIN'S MIMOSA

When it started raining this morning I woke from a dream of something I'd read years ago, an experiment of Darwin's in which he played his bassoon to a mimosa plant to see if he could stimulate the feathery leaflets into movement.

It was warm and humid and my wife lay naked beside me with the sheets crumpled around her ankles. It was the beginning of what I knew would be one of those slow, sibilant, day-long rains, the gray threads nearly invisible unless looked at against dark foliage.

At seven A.M., under a black umbrella, I walked out to my backyard garden, a modest act of horticulture, nothing but potato plants, rows of lush green made greener still by the light of an overcast sky. As I stood at the edge of the garden I began to weep for no reason I could think of, and then for all the reasons I could think of. I felt for a moment like the Chinese poets who nurtured their sadness, usually with a little wine to help them along.

When I got back to the house my wife and I made love and then we made breakfast together. While we ate I told her about my dream and what a failure Darwin's experiment had been. She asked if my singing had produced any noticeable results.

"Singing?" I asked.

"I could've sworn I heard you singing to the garden early this morning," she said.

~

## GRADY MOURNS

Not old really, Grady wakes to a child's rapture of snow drifted deep as ocean waves, though nothing moves, even the wind seemingly frozen. He presses one fingertip to the ice-encrusted windowpane and holds it until the sting passes through his body like the aftershock of his father's grave.

Suddenly there are birds in the air, on the railing, their chatter like the voices of childhood friends. Grady considers stepping outside to ask about all the years, the times in between, most of all Stringtown Hill where he sledded, bumping airborne down to a broadside skid to keep from shooting the bank into Pigeon Creek.

At the sound of the door opening, the birds fly off in all directions, their songs and colors diminishing to a random note, a dark blur. Grady steps back as the wind returns, his face tingling with crystals of snow.

# Carol J. Pierman

## *from* The Naturalized Citizen

You take the E train uptown to the Modern. You are meeting your lover there to see the Matisse show and have lunch. Hung over from the night before, you close your eyes between stops. At 14th Street, you stare at the Philadelphia Cream Cheese ad. "The Cream of Cheese," it says— a plate of hors d'oeuvres garnished with pimentos. You smell the franks and sauerkraut boiling at the Nedick's down the platform and your stomach turns. At 42nd Street, dozens of men in beltless double-knit slacks and black shoes get off studying folded copies of the racing form. As the door closes, three black girls clatter down the steps, screaming, "Hold the door!" but the train pulls out. They pound on the sides. On the escalator at Fifth Avenue, commuters climb past, hitting the backs of your knees with briefcases, shopping bags. At the museum, your lover notices you are pale, suggests soup and a cup of coffee. You feel better already and mentally agree to anything. Later, you dream you meet Balzac in the sculpture garden, tending his statue, brushing snow from his shoulders.

≈

In front of the Pleasure Chest, a wino goes through a row of garbage cans. As you approach, he staggers toward you, shoves his face into yours, and rasps, "If I ever see you again, I'll cut your heart out." Gray stubble, old sores patch his red skin. You smell grease, and acid on his breath. You sidestep, and he lurches past. The next night you meet him again, scuffling toward 14th Street, head down, muttering to himself. You wonder if he'll recognize you. But he is deep in thought, a brown bag clutched to his chest. You turn the corner to go home and meet a mounted patrol. The horses roll their large heads, blowing at you. Saddles groan. After they pass, you still hear the sound of their tails, the regular swinging back and forth, like a scythe.

≈

You lie on the couch in your lover's studio. While she works, you stare out the window, down Vandam, toward the river. Rain soaks the black streets until they reflect like patent leather. Sodium lamps stain the rain orange, and a green and red Miller's sign in the corner deli blinks on and off in a dozen puddles. One block over, the traffic light makes a full cycle every fifty seconds. Overhead, planes in the final approach pass up the river, landing lights burning like flares. You count sixty-second intervals. You fall asleep counting, and when you awaken later, your lover kneels over you, shading your eyes with her hand.

～

It's St. Patrick's Day, and warm, so you leave work and go to the parade. You find a place along the park, where the crowd's thin and sun hits your back. The beginning is quiet, hushed as a hoard of New York pols walks up Fifth—Abe, Bella, O'Dwyer, Sutton. And then the drums and pipes crack off buildings, echoing up the avenue ahead of the bands. Police societies are first, rows of drummers swinging sticks high above their heads, then down at a stroke. A commander in a golden sash leads a unit in blue and green tartan. He spins a long silver baton, slowly in front, then brings it out to the side. They march rigid, eyes straight ahead. A kid in a prep school blazer, tie thrown over his shoulder, stands next to you on the curb. You look at him. He's got his hand inside his pants, jerking off. You stare for an instant, then move back to the park wall and jump up on it. A woman on his other side notices, and she wheels her baby off, down the street. Another police unit, in yellow and black kilts, marks time. The kid stands there, his back to you. If he comes, you can't tell.

# Jennifer M. Pierson
## WHAT MAKES ME INVISIBLE

I sit on the hard chair at the Mayflower Coffee Shop, my feet dangling, waiting, my head almost level with the table top, mother, elegantly smoking, inhaling and releasing her Pall Malls. I sip hot cocoa, bubbles of whipped cream on my spoon, dripping, and wipe my chin, my dress tied in the back with a perfect bow, my hair plain and clean. I know what's next, the boyfriend I'll meet, he'll sit by my mother, always they come later, a box as big as a t.v., in his arms. And he'll kiss her, she'll move her cheek to the side, and he'll join us, look to see that I like this, a good little girl, quiet, not begging.

The boyfriends are always bug-eyed and young, or old and used like the one with pennies glued to his tie, his sisters calling him their Baby Brother. And the box will sit on the floor like a bomb, its weight heavy on me, am I supposed to ask? guess? what I already know.

And I wait forever, mother not looking, only at the window, it's snowing or raining, I wish we could go, my cocoa's almost cold.

Then he arrives, Mark or Michael, his dark hair, his dark jacket, he's nervous, he hides the obvious. Sits down and he smiles, pats my head as mother elbows him, eyes me with her teeth fixed. Michael the Guardian Angel, Mark the Apostle, he slides the box over, I say slowly, "thanks," hate how life stops.

I sip more cocoa, don't want to be greedy, stare at the gold and white paper, the big ribbons. "Open it, sweetie." Mother's red lips part, her hand covers his arm, they whisper, make me invisible. The other tables are so noisy, the box is high. My fingers rip the ribbons off, the paper tears, its face stares at me, its blonde hair curled like Shirley Temple's, the one with the blue dress, it's velvet. It wears a straw hat with lavender flowers, black mary janes, white socks, its cheeks rosy, the pink words printed, "A Madame Alexandre Doll," my fifth.

≈

# THRIFT SHOP LADIES

They carry their long, heavy bosoms inside old sweaters and wear examples of excellent tweed. They are volunteers for Christ or the retarded or some hospital in which their husbands are on the Board. Some give orders, but no one is in charge. Some are not shy, they are too helpful. Their job is routine. Straighten the racks, rehang the shirts, see if anyone needs assistance with the awkward drawer marked "Table Linens."

At St. Albert's in Seattle, men weed through piles of warm suit jackets and beat-down shoes. They are generally ignored by the ladies. With no money to spend, the men drift back out into a cool environ, the dirty streets they call home. I've seen crazy women come in, too. They're nasty, shouting at the dingy yellow wall, or a stained chenille spread. They are toothless, and bulbous. There is a patina of elegance in the ladies and their trade, and the crazy women's yelling seems so unseemly. But they cannot ask them to leave. Not easily.

D.C.'s Junior League Shop ladies love to steal time away to look at a new load of donations. A large box arrives full of gowns from the 1930s. I can hear them sigh at the memory of their own youthful parties. One dress is a sea-green chiffon, embossed with seedpearls. They know they cannot fit into its slender waist. The beadwork on a pale peach number is ogled at, then hung reverently in a private corner.

The ladies in Geneva's Christ Child are good at figures, efficient. They carry calculators to divine the nickels and bills added in taxes. They are precise. The tablets they write upon are as faded and fragile as their slackened cheeks. They do not do a fast trade and their hours are few. Church rooms are for church business, much of the time. Lunch is a paper sack of sandwich, and coffee from the rectory above. While they eat, they chatter about the downpricing of summer goods. One remarks what good taste I have in dresses. When I exit with my purchases, I hear them argue over the quality of a new piece of costume jewelry. At three o'clock the lights go out and they go their separate ways.

# Holly Prado
## THE OWL TURNS HIS HEAD ALL THE WAY AROUND

I

some hunters come to our fire to get warm after being in the hills all day. two men and two half-grown boys—the boys silent in their heavy jackets and shoes, standing on one foot then the other, while the men talk about how fine the full moon looks, just coming up over the mountain. our fire is autumn—a scarecrow, a cave, birds flying. our corn and potatoes cook, deep in its coals. in the morning I gather rose hips—a bagful of them to make jam out of. each one comes off the branch with a tug, taking a little stem with it. I work in the sun, bending, a thorn now and then in my fingers, my hands sticky with orange from the hips that are soft and full. I put the bag next to me on the floor of the truck as we drive home, thinking of the fruit smell—the pressure of my hands. we stop for gas and another truck parks there that has two deer in the back, dead, being taken to the city. each deer has a tag tied to one of its ears.

II

the inside of my mouth is raw and every bite of the apple stings, but the taste is clean, sour, and the air gets cooler as we drive out of the desert. the sky is full of clouds. it's late afternoon, the time that I feel weakest. my energy settles back into my body and I want to think carefully, to hold my life as I held the small fish yesterday—we put him back into the lake after taking the hook out of his mouth. he was cold and moved in my hand and I could feel the murder and was happy when I saw him under the water again. there's a rainbow in the sky next to the sun, not an arc, but a cluster of pale red, orange, yellow, on to violet that is part of the clouds. I see that it's an omen, something special, and I narrow my eyes until it becomes circles of brightness, all gold, and then a dark circle appears on my left. my death, looking at me without recognizing

252

my shape. when I open my eyes the rainbow has moved higher and has thinned out to streaks of color. I feel suddenly sure of myself, as if I've been doing the right thing for a long time.

~

VISIT

I

marla gets off the plane and I see her walking fast, toward me, dressed in white and purple. we hug: I can feel that she's taller than I am, and I'm a little afraid of her. she's shouting that she can't believe she's in los angeles and saying, "shit, baby, shit, I'm not really here." I've dressed up, too, the way women do when they want to impress each other—a long skirt, earrings—but I feel as if she's not looking at me. a few people stare—she's waving her arms and her ass and I'm thinking about driving home on the long freeway with so much / nothing to say.

she likes my house. the wooden filing cabinet, the pink and green shawl on the old chest, the cat, the quilt, the flowers I picked for her, the windows, the lights outside on the hill. she's terribly tired and starts to really talk. the purple comes off. her nightgown is long and she tells me that her little boy didn't want her to come. "the first things I've done on my own—on my own—in ten years." I start to think of the ocean / picnics / shopping / going out with men like we were nineteen years old laughing and fussing with our hair. once, when we were in college, I stitched her into a dress—she was going to a dance and the dress was new and too big in the waist. when she came back to the room she was drunk, and I had to get the scissors and try to cut the stitches while she stumbled around, feeling sick to her stomach. we kept laughing and snipping and finally she threw up on her new shoes.

II

I've been out of the city for a month, camping around the west—
wyoming, colorado, utah—outside of any life except my own mov-
ing. I got comfortable in rain: crouched in leaves, or close to a fire,
or lying in the back of the pick-up truck with a tarp pitched over
me. I began to like the smell of myself.

at first, the wind scared me at night. once I couldn't sleep much, and kept
waking up from a dream about climbing a ladder, carrying a pail
of water. a wooden indian at the top said hello in a mechanical
voice. I woke up, rolled over in my sleeping bag, and the dream
changed: I walked into a room full of plants and flowers, all marked
and identified. I felt excited that I'd be able to know all of the
plants of the area—columbine, paint-brush, mariposa lily, all the
sages—I wanted to take a long time to look at everything. a woman
was there as a guide. she wore a beautiful, flowing dress, and the
room had the light of a greenhouse—generous, but filtered and
shadowy. I began to accept the wind after that.

back in the city, I had to think about my car, insurance bills, my land-
lady. I felt fat, after corn and potatoes for a month. staying inside
made me restless. when marla called and said she was coming, I
couldn't stand the thought of having her in the house that was al-
ready pushing in on me. but she's an image of myself that I sense
in mirrors, pieces of glass, clothes that fit even though we're not
the same size, handwriting, never thinking about it. I remember
a coyote howl / moan / bark. I heard the hollow of the roof of his
mouth. bones in his neck. how his paws felt on the rocks. I could
have looked into his throat and seen the shape of the enemy / lover
he was seeing.

III

I wake up in the middle of the night and marla's crying in her sleep. I know it's a bad dream, and I feel it moving into the room where I am, making the air stop and my shoulders cold. I get up—push myself out of my own sleep—and go into the bedroom. she doesn't wake up, but keeps making the sounds of trying to escape. I touch her face—it feels soft, like feathers or leaves, and she thanks me for coming in. "I've had this dream before."

in the morning I get up early and sit outside for awhile. it's going to be hot. the yard next door has just been watered and looks green, fresh. we'll drive to the ocean and let the tide get into us for the day. we can take some fruit / climb around the rocks to a cove that might not be crowded. when I hear marla in the kitchen, I get up, but my foot's asleep and it hurts when I walk. she stops making coffee to lean down and rub my leg until I can stand on it.

# David Ray
## THE LECTERN

When I was flying around on Ozark Airlines giving poetry readings at colleges, I had a bad habit of leaving stuff on lecterns. I was in kind of a trance after an hour of getting in touch with my own poems and sharing them.

Once I left my Timex watch, and later I called the poet-professor who had been my host and asked him if my watch had turned up.

"Yes," he said in a deadpan voice much like his prize-winning poems. "I have it."

He was a very glamorous poet. In with all the groups I was Out with. The critics loved him. Nobody could understand a thing.

I never knew what the hell contemporary poetry was, only that mine didn't give the critics enough to gnaw at. They went after the obscure stuff.

I asked the poet to send my watch along. It wouldn't cost him anything to send it, I pointed out, as our universities were connected by courier service.

The watch never arrived. Several years later I met the poet at a conference, and asked him if he still had my watch.

"Yes," he said, deadpan as ever.

"It's not worth much," I said, "but I'd still appreciate your sending it back to me."

"I'll mail it," he said, in a voice freighted with neutrality.

Another decade has now gone by. Now and then I see the poet's old poems in fashionable anthologies, where they are always included, just as mine are always left out.

He is still In. I am still Out. He still has my Timex.

≈

## MATURITY

How we looked forward to maturity! I'd one day be a grown up, a regular good man! In our little town, its main street like a string bean, there were two general stores, one with a gas station, the pumps angled, hypotenuse to a right angle.

And nine taverns. As a boy I would stand at the window at night and watch people come in and out of those taverns. There were three taverns I could see from my window. And after the taverns closed, I could hear arguments in the parking lots, and occasionally the screams of wives who were beaten. The couple in the shack next door to our house were very loud in their drunken violence, and I could actually hear the blows across her face or back before she let out her wails and groans and threats to leave him, though such threats seemed to bring on even heavier blows.

It must be fun, I thought, for both of them, and that's what I wanted to do when I grew up. I couldn't wait to get out there and start going to those taverns, drinking beer and breathing the blue smoke. I couldn't wait to get drunk and beat up on my wife. I couldn't wait to give up on such a bitch and go back to the tavern to meet a new woman. I couldn't wait to get a beerbelly and smokes of my own. I couldn't wait to have all that fun.

How we looked forward to maturity! I'd one day be a grown up, a regular good man for sure, welcome in the taverns. And in the meanwhile there was junior high, high school, and possibly even junior college. And getting my hands on the wheel of a car, the breasts of a woman, the slippery amber glass of a beer bottle.

# Dave Reddall
## IN THE PARK

He settled into the park bench and soon fell asleep, made drowsy by
lunch and the sun. Before long, he was having a lovely dream.

In the dream, it is 1954 and he has a good seat just behind first base
at Ebbets Field. The Dodgers are playing the Giants. Carl Furillo is at
bat. Furillo hits a blooper towards first, and here's where the dream
starts to go bad, for the umpire reaches up, bobbles the ball for a mo-
ment, then catches it and calls Furillo out. Everyone accepts this as nat-
ural and players are running on and off the field because Furillo's out
has ended the inning.

This ruling is a bit strange, but it isn't too important, because it is 1954,
the sun is warm and the infield grass is fresh and glowing in the light
of late afternoon. The seats are newly painted and, in the outfield, red
and yellow billboards sparkle against the cobalt sky. The basepaths re-
mind him of dirt roads that wend their way off into the country some-
where in a Currier and Ives print.

Still, there's the question of this new rule. Alvin Dark has just hit a
high fly ball which hangs suspended in the slackness of afternoon some-
where above Snider's waiting glove. Knowing that Snider will make the
catch, he turns to the man next to him to ask about the rule.

At that precise moment he awoke from his dream. It is not 1954
anymore. It is 1974. Worse yet, the man next to him turns out to be a
derelict, who has slumped against him in a stupor. Bits of lint are im-
paled on the derelict's whiskers and he is drooling on the sleeve of the
man's seersucker coat.

Behind him, on the grass, children throw a plastic football through
the thin sunshine and chill autumn air.

# John Calvin Rezmerski
ENTROPY

I am in a play, Shakespeare's *King John*, directed by a friend—he and I plan to do a scene for a class he is teaching. I will enter the room after he has started the class (I am playing King John and he the King of France) and we will begin the scene without announcing it first, with him still seated at his desk. I enter. We begin.

Seized by a whim, I abandon Shakespeare, speak my third line in contemporary paraphrase. On the fourth line, I throw in an ad-lib, because I have forgotten what the line is, exactly as it had been written. He tries to cover for me, but I forget my next line entirely, and he forgets what his next line is supposed to be. We try to cover, but fail.

The class doesn't even laugh. Embarrassed, he says we will have to use the text. I am not only embarrassed, but panic-stricken. I have not brought my copy of the text. He produces his, and asks someone in the class to lend us a copy.

Now neither of us can remember which act or scene we were supposed to be doing. I seem to remember it was act II, scene 3, but cannot find it. When I do, he remembers it was not scene 3, but scene 2, but cannot find it. When we finally find it in my borrowed copy, it is not the same scene we have been doing. I accidentally discover the first lines of what we have been doing in a masque written to appear between acts II and III. He tells me to do what is written there, so the class can get an idea of the feeling of the piece, anyway. The class is half asleep.

He starts Elizabethan background music on a phonograph, and I begin to read. I read well, until halfway into the piece, I realize it is not at all the same speech I have been doing in performances, that the King of France has been replaced by the King of Prussia, and that the lines keep getting more and more unfamiliar, not on the perquisites of power, but on the deaths of tyrants. By the end, I am stumbling over lines I have never seen before.

We think the borrowed copy I am using is perhaps a defective edition—act II has only one scene. We check against his copy. It has only one scene, too, but it also diverges from the scene we have been doing for so long. We decide to rescue the class session from being completely wasted, so we discuss the difficulty of establishing an authoritative text for Shakespeare, and of publishing definitive editions generally. Nobody seems to have a copy of *King John* on hand. Some copies are not even Shakespeare. One student has never heard of Shakespeare. We all agree that truly definitive editions are impossible, since change is inevitable over long periods of time.

～

## ORDERING

Here I am in the all-night restaurant again, sitting in a booth, just me and the menu, waiting for the arrival of the waitress and the bottomless coffee cup. I am studying to be one of the regulars. It is just after the busy time after the bars close, and the place is two-thirds full of people in various stages of intoxicated weariness and morose hunger.

A woman a few tables away says, "My pancakes are ice-cold."

I hear her clearly and my hearing is none too good. She says it again, leaning intimately toward the stiff man seated across from her, and raising her voice a decibel: "I said my pancakes are ice-cold."

In the booth behind me, a woman says to the woman with her, "Did you hear that?" The woman with her has been caught with her mouth full of hamburger, and must chew and swallow in ludicrous politeness for thirty seconds, which probably seem like five minutes to her, with her hand in a frantic flutter signifying that she intends to answer soon, then saying with the last bit of noisy gulp still in her mouth, "Did I hear what?"

"She said her pancakes are ice-cold."

"Who said?"

"She did. That woman over there."

"So why doesn't she send them back? Why should I care?"

"I just thought it was odd for her to announce it to everyone."

"She didn't announce it to me."

"If you didn't chew so loud, she would have."

Then the voice rises again, more in pitch than in volume: "They're really ice-cold." Still, it is an informative statement, not a complaint exactly, certainly not a protest.

From somewhere across the room (I am not sure from whom), a deep voice announces, "That's funny, mine are piping hot. Piping hot."

A chuckle passes from person to person around the perimeter of the restaurant. Even the glum man sitting under a blue hat in the corner smiles audibly behind his raised coffee cup.

Somebody else says, "My omelet is too runny," and a tablemate says, "Well. My salad is just right, so I ate it all up."

The laughter in the room is the laughter of an audience, but the fun is the fun of actors—real dinner theater.

The waitress steps up to take my order. Everyone is listening to hear what I will say, whether the play will continue or the mood will be broken. I am stuck. They are still riding on their guffaws as the waitress delivers her straight line: "What'll it be?"

The crowd titters at my silence.

Then I realize they are giggling because they already know that anything I say—anything that anyone says—will provide a new laugh.

"I'll have pancakes," I say. Laughter explodes, and as it subsides, the waitress seizes her cue.

"Hot cakes, or ice-cold?"

When the howling and whistling die down, she takes a curtain call at the kitchen door. We applaud again. I am part of the company. We are all regulars.

# George Roberts
## THE FACTS OF LIFE

Valerie is not in class again today. As we open our books she is outside, getting into a car with an older man. What is there in a short story like "Snake Boy" to challenge a beige Cadillac and a good-looking twenty-six-year-old guy?

The facts of life are . . . there is nothing, right now, that will draw her back into the classroom. The sweet smell of leather upholstery, Luther Van Dross crooning from the speakers, and the tingle rocketing along nerve passages as they drive away together, smiling, is all she knows or wants to know.

Valerie chooses to attend a different school today. She is learning the facts of life. And I am learning them as well.

～

## NIGHTMARE

You are walking down a long hallway. Your classroom is the last one on the left. The walls, newly painted, catch the light in a way you haven't noticed for years. The lingering smell of new paint hangs in the air like a word on the tip of your . . . like what was it you had to do before class begins . . .?

Your classroom is still the last one on the left . . . way down there in the raw light, but you don't want to get there yet because the children are waiting and you can't remember today's lesson. And this was the lesson that was finally going to do it, finally going to tip those scales inside your students from troubled indifference over to the giddy rush of questioning everything. . . .

You urge yourself to remain calm as the handle of your briefcase slips an inch from your sweating palm down into the crooked hook of your fingers. Your breath is coming in short little puffs. A noise is following you, the bass drum of your heart.

You stop and crawl inside your head with a flashlight to look for the lost lesson. The light jumps out into the darkness like a shout and bounces off freshly painted walls. There is an almost blinding whiteness, an emptiness with your name on it. All your books, your papers, are gone. Even your desk, the folders full of kids' work to be corrected and returned, gone. Nothing. . . . Only the hint of fresh paint hanging in the air. Your classroom is the last door on the left.

⟿

## OPENING UP

Each morning, before the bells begin ringing, I unlock my classroom door and enter. Like an old shopkeeper whose rituals are the currency of neighborhood conversation, I switch on the lamps, tune the radio to a station the kids will object to, turn slowly and allow my glance to rest here, then here around the room. . . .

But these are not the habit of an old man. Like the Navajo silversmith who pauses before his tools, humble before the unworked metal, to chant his thanks, I have done the same since the first day. . . .

And it is always the morning before a parade, floats poised in somber garages; a glow like that surrounding bread dough rising in a warm corner of the kitchen, and the golden smell of something like yeast.

The chairs under the tables dream of standing up and becoming politicians. The books repose on their shelves like those sharks discovered sleeping and docile by *National Geographic* photographers.

# W. R. Rodriguez
## JUSTICE

a youth grabbed an old woman's purse fat with tissues and aspirin and
such sundries as old women carry in sagging purses a desperate youth
nice enough not to beat her head bloody into the sidewalk as muggers
of the feeble often do for the fun of it i suppose and he ran up the hill
but one of the perennial watchers watched it all from her window the
purseless old woman in slow pursuit yelling such curses as it takes old
women a lifetime to learn but it was too dangerous too futile the silent
watcher knew to call the police who might come and rough up some-
one they did not like just for the fun of it i suppose or who would talk
polite and feel mad inside and roll their eyes because there was really
nothing they could do and there were murders and assaults to handle
so this silent angry watcher carelessly but carefully dropped flower pots
from her fourth floor windowsill garden one crashing before one behind
and the third hitting him on the head a geranium i suppose and closed
her window while the huffing grateful old woman looked up at the
heavens to thank the lord and walked off with her purse laughing when
she finally calmed down and leaving the youth to awaken in the blue
arms of the law and do you know two smiling cops walked up all those
stairs to warn the watcher that if she weren't more careful with her
plants she would get a ticket for littering i suppose

~

## THE MALTHUSIAN THEORY

like every longshot it seemed like a sureshot and his legs were so long
his stride so swift his torso so lean his need so great he scooped up the
stakes from the 534 east 138th street crapshoot and the race was on four
lucky gamblers in pursuit what the the hell do the losers care who gets
the money but it was their game too and it was once their money and
what else was there to do now that the game was over and the beer upset

264

so as he passed 530 east 138th street they took after him too he led by ten yards with eight lucky and unlucky gamblers after his ass and their friends took notice because what else was going on to take notice of and by 526 east 138th street he was twelve yards ahead and eight gamblers and eight lucky and unlucky but otherwise bored friends were hounding him and by 522 east 138th street sixteen acquaintances of theirs must've thought how can he do that to our acquaintances because they took off too while asking each other what did he do anyway and he was sprinting in fine form with thirty-two gamblers friends and lucky or unlucky but no longer bored acquaintances huffing and puffing and shouting and screaming hot on his trail which got everybody's attention so by 518 east 138th street he was still about five yards ahead of sixty-four gamblers friends acquaintances and lucky or unlucky but very excited pedestrians which got the attention of the official 138th street spectators who watch everything and see nothing and sixty-four of the fleetest official spectators joined the mob as our part of 138th street ran out of numbers and he turned the corner while one hundred twenty-eight not so fast spectators streamed out of their doorways making that two hundred fifty-six gamblers friends acquaintances pedestrians and lucky or unlucky fleet or not so fleet but no longer solemn official spectators rushing onto brook avenue to be joined by two hundred fifty six brook avenue strangers making five hundred and twelve gamblers friends acquaintances pedestrians fleet or not so fleet official spectators and lucky or unlucky brook avenue strangers who were met by five hundred twelve lucky or unlucky nondescripts from the mill brook projects making one thousand twenty-four in the curious crowd only twenty four of whom could actually see who got him first or who got the money when the ambulance carried him away which only goes to prove that the hunger of a crowd for entertainment quickly exceeds society's ability to produce amusement

# Dorien Ross
## RED SWEATSHIRT

Must I walk the exact path the turn occurred? 'The valley of the falling leaves' we named it, or I did and you walked on ahead. A plaid wool shirt looks stunning through falling leaves. Do you know that? Do you know what your back looked like to me that day? Like a kind of strength I never had inside me. And your work boots and your large hands. And our dog Bones, the black labrador mutt with one yellow eye, walking ahead of us or I should say loping ahead of us in this smoky blue day of Autumn. And of course there is that picture of me and the Bones in a field of summer daisies. My eyes look red from the way the Polaroid developed, but nonetheless . . . in my brave purple cape with my black hair flying, yes flying in the wind. And Bones with his bright pink tongue all the way out as he'd been running that field with a kind of madness only he was capable of. No. You had that same kind of madness. He was, even years down a road we never imagined, still in part your dog. The long slant of the afternoon sun was already upon us. Sooner, sooner than we ever thought, we were turning.

Saying goodbye to you in your red sweatshirt was the hardest thing I had ever done. Waving goodbye at the airport, your huge paw-like hand moving up and down, not side to side.

Earlier that day, we had driven from the cabin all the way to the airport. The ride, though four hours long, had been silent. I am leaving New York to go to California. Our dog, Bones, is sitting between us in the truck. The world outside feels hostile, for there has been no world outside us for seven years. The familiar is slipping away.

Outside the truck the snow is falling in swirls around the headlights and then into the pre-dawn darkness. The only sound is the swishing of the window wipers pushing the snow back over and over. The silence inside the truck is as large as the years we have lived together. Not a word is spoken all the way to the airport. The only sound is the swish swish swish of the wipers, the motor of the old truck, your heavy tense breathing, and the snow dissolving into the headlights with a hiss.

In the airport about to board the plane, I turn. You are standing there in a red sweatshirt and your hand is waving not side to side, but in small motions up and down like a child. You are crying.

Waving goodbye to you at the airport. Red sweatshirt. The cabin that I loved. The valley of the falling leaves. Your hand. All red sweatshirts made me weep, because you were wearing one that day.

# Vern Rutsala

## BROOM

Like the feather duster it feels incomplete, a creature only half evolved, and anxiously scurries everywhere trying to find the rest of itself.

~

## DUST MOP

This creature is some curious by-product in the evolution of the unicorn.

~

## IRONING BOARD

It can fold its legs like a crane and is thus clearly some variety of bird no more grotesque than the pelican or the stork or, for that matter, the crane. It has three legs, for better balance, an enormous flat bill, and lives, as near as we can tell, on nothing but heat. A great solitary and apparently sexless—you rarely see more than one at a time—it is extremely docile and willingly nests anywhere you put it with its three legs drawn up tightly against its bill.

~

## GETTING LOST

This is an activity which has about it the subtlety of Zen and can only be managed by thoroughly experienced travelers or, at the very least, long-time residents of a particular neighborhood. The simple aim, of course, is to get lost and in doing so experience those emotions of doubt and strangeness, alienation, and, yes, even panic which, for the experienced player, is especially exhilarating. The trick then is to accomplish this deftly within familiar surroundings, areas that are literally known like the back of your hand. The venerated masters are those who are capable of getting lost a few doors from their houses. All aspire, however, to achieve the truly legendary feats of that revered grand master who is reputed to have gotten lost every day for a year though he never left his easy chair. Such genuine mastery is humbling indeed, but needless to say it is also inspiring.

∽

## LYING

In that you can have any number of opponents this can be a very difficult endeavor, requiring as it does an intricate, double-entry method of keeping score. The truly excellent, of course, juggle their score cards with ease, knowing as they do so that the real problem lies elsewhere: In order to lie successfully you quite simply must know what the truth is. As philosophers have persistently told us this is no easy task, and, because of this, there is some reason to believe that the truly outstanding liar lies out of a strong sense of modesty.

∽

## SLEEPING

Though winners are rarely declared, this is an arduous contest similar, some feel, to boxing. This fact can be readily corroborated by simply looking at people who have just awakened. Look at their red and puffy eyes, the disheveled hair, the slow sore movements, and their generally dazed appearance. Occasionally, as well, there are those deep scars running across their cheeks. Clearly, if appearances don't lie, they have been engaged in some damaging and dangerous activity and furthermore have come out the losers. If it's not dangerous—and you still have doubts — why do we hear so often the phrase, *He died in his sleep*?

# Ira Sadoff
## HOPPER'S "NIGHTHAWKS" (1942)

Imagine a town where no one walks the streets. Where the sidewalks are swept clean as ceilings and the barber pole stands still as a corpse. There is no wind. The windows on the brick buildings are boarded up with doors, and a single light shines in the all-night diner while the rest of the town sits in its shadow.

In an hour it will be daylight. The busboy in the diner counts the empty stools and looks at his reflection in the coffee urns. On the radio the announcer says the allies have won another victory. There have been few casualties. A man with a wide-brimmed hat and the woman sitting next to him are drinking coffee or tea; on the other side of the counter a stranger watches them as though he had nowhere else to focus his eyes. He wonders if perhaps they are waiting for the morning buses to arrive, if they are expecting some member of their family to bring them important news. Or perhaps they will get on the bus themselves, ask the driver where he is going, and whatever his answer they will tell him it could not be far enough.

When the buses arrive at sunrise they are empty as hospital beds— the hum of the motor is distant as a voice coming from within the body. The man and woman have walked off to some dark street, while the stranger remains fixed in his chair. When he picks up the morning paper he is not surprised to read there would be no exchange of prisoners, the war would go on forever, the Cardinals would win the pennant, there would be no change in the weather.

~

## THE ROMANCE OF THE RACER

The race car driver was different. He made love with all his clothes on. Always the smell of grease, a trailing vapor of gasoline. He drove circles around me and when it was over I was tired and dizzy, his tongue in my mouth was a memory, a thin slice of dirt road. When he spoke he was like an engine idling, he could never talk fast enough; but whatever he said was unexpected. "I enjoy being sad," he once told me. "I wish there were more sadness in the world." In bed he was not much of a man: once was always enough.

He was an insomniac who read long books and never said a word about them. He took me to the opera and asked me not to raise my voice. He hummed arias he said had not been written yet. Once he took me to a party where all his former lovers were, and they never stopped talking about him. Two of them he still made love to on big occasions: the night before a race, the afternoon of Verdi's birthday. And when he took me home he was unusually cautious, driving way below the speed limit, stopping at intersections where he had the right of way. When he got into bed he curled up like a wheel; in the dark I could have sworn he was spinning. In the end, what he had to prove he could not, and we all loved him the more for it, at least for a little while. When I drove out of his driveway for the last time I did not look back; but on the road I had the feeling I was constantly being passed, no matter how fast I went, no matter how many cars were filled with whistling men.

~

## THREE DREAMS OF AN AMBITIOUS MAN

1.

At first you feel safe in the middle of a crowd. Then the magician calls you up to the stage. He tells you that he has chosen you to be his vase, that no matter how many buckets of water he pours down your throat, you will never have enough to drink. In the end you will discover the true meaning of thirst.

2.

You are driving on a superhighway and you press your foot all the way down on the accelerator. The speedometer says that you are breaking the speed limit, but the other cars all pass you by. The other drivers look familiar to you but you cannot place their faces. When you open the window and shout, "Do you remember me?" a tremendous wind rushes over your body, but no one answers you. You blow the horn but even you cannot hear it. In the middle of the highway the car seems to come to a halt; you try to open the doors but cannot.

3.

You and your wife are entertaining close friends. The atmosphere is gay and everyone has a lot to drink. You begin to speak uncontrollably, there is no way you can stop yourself. You admit things to your friends that you would never admit to yourself, that you have never found a job that suited you, you have never been able to tell people how you really feel about them. Your whole life has been a lie. At that moment it seems to you that you have revealed the most intimate details of your life; you feel like an extremely religious man confessing to a priest. You begin to see a dark curtain between yourself and the others in the room. When you are finally able to stop yourself you hear them talking about a subject totally unrelated to you, as if you had not yet entered the room. You shout, you jump up and down, but they do not recognize you. Through the curtain you can see your friend making love to your wife in the presence of his own wife. You want to stop them but you cannot rise out of your chair. You pull open the curtain, but behind that curtain is another curtain, and behind that another and still another. It never occurs to you that it is useless to go on.

# Nicholas Samaras
## EPISODE IN STASIS

I remember a visitors' garden, lavender magnolias walled-in by red brick. Through the veranda's glass doors, I could see her at a parasoled table, sitting with her back to me, in a white wicker chair on the court-yard tiles, looking out into the narrow green, her chestnut hair in a cascade down her floral robe, her tanned wrists tilted over the pale wicker arms—the white, medical name-tag on her wrist, clipping the air. For that long moment, I couldn't take my eyes from her and I couldn't step over the threshold or utter a sound to call her. I saw only her healthy, vibrant hair, her thin, silver-winged bracelets and my held, cut lily that would spot in a week, that would continue to breathe her oxygen and not remember her name. And then, she turned to see me, her face quiet, olive-dark eyes brightly alive, a spread of petals in her lap.

Immortality is the exact length of memory.

# Roy Scheele
## EMINENT DOMAIN

The house torn down now, a hole in the earth, with a snow fence thrown up around the cedars that kept the wind from it on the north, around what used to be the steps leading to its door. The freeway is coming, and the state has taken up squatter's rights. In the engineer's office a pin like a flag secures the place on a map.

There is a mind that delights in tearing down, that has never looked out a north bedroom window at the snow darkening the cedars, that could not imagine as many varieties of grass as have sprung up here, several feet tall, in little more than a month. One afternoon, stopping where the road dips down so that you look back up at the lot, I felt a delicious sweet coolness steal out from the grass to where I stood in the heat of the day. It was like a glimpse of a face at a window.

~

## A VISITATION

The preacher mounts the pulpit and begins to speak as the metal folds of the organ pipes behind him (the pious lungs of the choir just now seated) stare at the sides of the nave, speechless at its Moorish arches. This is a church architect's church, an anthology of effects, and the eloquence of the preacher is at home here. He thumps the Bible lightly to make a point (the Devil tallies it up), and my eyes wander up the walls to the sunlit windows.

It is a fine winter morning, the sky so bright it hurts to look at it from the dimness we sit in. He is talking about the Holy Spirit and our submission to the things of this world, when suddenly a shadow wheels and falls down the wall, then another, and I see two pigeons, their wings straining them upward over the courtyard, head for the belfry in the high tower I climbed to once, years ago, to look out over the city adrift in itself in the snow.

# Alison Seevak
## APPETITE

You try not to stare at the firemen in the check-out lines of grocery stores. Sure, you like their mustaches, the way their muscles swell subtly under tight navy t-shirts. What you really like, though, are their shopping carts brimming with bright cardboard boxes of capellini, jars of red sauce, sticks of french bread. You think of dalmations, of fire poles, of big pasta dinners back at the station house. You want a man with an appetite.

Your last boyfriend, the toxicologist, had a soul as thin and as blue as the skim milk he drank to keep his arteries from clogging. Sometimes you miss his curly head on your pillow and you want to weep. Then you remember the low-fat, individually wrapped slices of American cheese in his refrigerator, all the reasons it wouldn't have worked.

You want a man like your Uncle Morris, the patron saint of the roadside fruit and vegetable stand. He would boil up a dozen ears of Silver Queen for a perfect August supper, then sit across the kitchen table from your Auntie Tillie shaking salt onto buttery cobs. You want a man who delights in piles of White Lightning, Early Sunglow, Butter and Sugar. Someone who knows to pull back the leaves in search of juicy kernels, a man who likes to roll cornsilk between his long fingers.

He doesn't plant Best Boys, the man of your dreams. By July, the Early Girls topple his wire cages. He can't pick them fast enough. Someone's Italian grandmother told him to let them ripen in a brown paper bag on his kitchen counter. He plies you with gifts of salsa, green tomato relish, tomato panzenella.

This man lets you wear his bathrobe when he makes you huevos rancheros on Sunday mornings. He won't wash his hands for hours after he's been with you. You're a spice that sticks to his fingertips. You're garlic and ginger under his nails.

You're Cleopatra in his bed at night. The city steams, his air conditioner hisses. You imagine him hovering, a serf fanning you with an ostrich plume. "Oh, peel me a grape," you say, laughing. What you really want is chicken stew and fried green plantain from Rosita's across the street. This is a man who will pull on his jeans, dodge the yellow cabs and panhandlers of Broadway for you. Later, in the quiet dark, neither of you can wait. He pulls you on top of him. Nothing else matters, not the heat, not the red beans, not the yellow rice that will spill into the folds of his tangled sheets.

# Jeanne Shannon
## CONCERT BY THE SEA

*—Errol Garner: Recorded live at Carmel-by-the-Sea in 1955*

1957. A twilight in early April. Rain is falling on that old house on a lone-some backroad in Virginia. Rain is falling with little paw-clicks on the roof.

Erroll Garner is playing "I'll Remember April." *This lovely day will lengthen into evening.* It is the time of day once called "the gloaming."

I am sitting in my bedroom, waiting for my life to begin again. It stopped last August when he went away. *For love and spring last such a little while.* Rain fell all that long evening too.

Lilacs against my window are heavy with purple buds. I am twenty. When the rain ends, and the music, the song of the spring frogs in the stillness stops my heart.

In another room my parents are talking. About my childhood. About my growing up, going away. Going away forever.

The walls of my room are cocoa-colored. I chose the color. My father painted the walls, singing "In the Gloaming," a song he taught me long ago.

The walls are the color of the hot chocolate my mother used to make, winter mornings in another house on another backroad in Virginia.

I turn the record over. *The falling leaves drift by my window.* When sweet September comes I will go away, to find my life again. *The autumn leaves of red and gold.*

1993, and rain is falling in New Mexico. Rain is falling in the sub-urbs. Rain is falling with little paw-clicks on the roof.

The yellow music spilling into the room is "I'll Remember April." *Digitally remastered from the original 1955 recording.* It is always April. It is always yesterday; it is always now. *For love and spring last such a little while.*

My father is gone, his grave beneath the wild hop vines on a hilltop in Virginia. For years he would move in and out of consciousness, traveling between this world and the other. Then one June morning he did not return.

My mother is dying. She floats in and out of sleep, drifting between this world and the next. Do they meet somewhere when she goes traveling? *In the gloaming, oh, my darling.*

The nurse brings her hot cocoa on a tray, but she cannot drink it. It is the color of the walls of my old room.

Cold rain is falling on the firethorn, prickling the rooftops and the panes.

～

## SPELLING

Right in the middle of the geography lesson about coal mining in Virginia and Kentucky, Mr. Collins calls on Larry Bledsoe to spell "bituminous." "B-i-t-u" Larry starts out, then hesitates, then draws a deep breath and goes on: "n-i-m-u-s." Well, Lord, that's not right, Rhoda Sue Rasnick mutters, the minute before Mr. Collins calls on *her* to spell it. She sails right through, like she always does. It's hard to find a word in the geography book—or any other book—that she can't spell. Next he calls on Gaynelle Bates to spell "anthracite," and then has to call on two more pupils before Jimmy Ray Blankenship gets it right. Now that we're through with the spelling part, he's asking us what's the difference between bituminous and anthracite coal, and which kind does Southwest Virginia have. He doesn't say, "What kind of coal does your daddy mine?" He used to talk about our daddies working in the coal mines, but he doesn't anymore. Not since Rhoda Sue's daddy was killed in a slate fall at Number 9 Jenkins across the mountain in Kentucky, the week before her baby brother was born.

# Karl Shapiro
## THE BOURGEOIS POET

The bourgeois poet closes the door of his study and lights his pipe. Why am I in this box, he says to himself (although it is exactly as he planned). The bourgeois poet sits down at his inoffensive desk— a door with legs, a door turned table—and almost approves the careful disarray of books, papers, magazines, and such artifacts as thumbtacks. The bourgeois poet is already out of matches and gets up. It is too early in the morning for any definite emotion and the B.P. smokes. It is beautiful in the midlands: green fields and tawny fields, sorghum the color of red morocco bindings, distant new neighborhoods, cleanly and treeless, and the Veterans Hospital fronted with a shimmering Indian Summer tree. The Beep feels seasonal, placid as a melon, neat as a child's football lying under the tree, waiting for whose hands to pick it up.

≈

## THE LIVING ROOMS OF MY NEIGHBORS

The living rooms of my neighbors are like beauty parlors, like night-
club powder rooms, like international airport first-class lounges.
The bathrooms of my neighbors are like love nests—Dufy prints,
black Kleenex, furry towels, toilets so highly bred they fill and fall
without a sigh (why is there no bidet in so-clean America?). The
kitchens of my neighbors are like cars: what gleaming dials, what
toothy enamels, engines that click and purr, idling the hours away.
The basements of my neighbors are like kitchens: you could eat
off the floor. Look at the furnace, spotless as a breakfront, stand-
ing alone, prize piece, the god of the household.

But I'm no different. I arrange my books with a view to their appear-
ance. Some highbrow titles are prominently displayed. The desk
in my study is carefully littered; after some thought I hang a diploma
on the wall, only to take it down again. I sit at the window where
I can be seen. What do my neighbors think of me—I hope they
think of me. I fix the light to hit the books. I lean some rows one
way, some rows another.

A man's house is his stage. Others walk on to play their bit parts. Now
and again a soliloquy, a birth, an adultery.

The bars of my neighbors are various, ranging from none at all to the
nearly professional, leather stools, automatic coolers, a naked paint-
ing, a spittoon for show.

The businessman, the air-force captain, the professor with tenure—it's
a neighborhood with a sky.

# Charles Simic

## *from* The World Doesn't End

I was stolen by the gypsies. My parents stole me right back. Then the gypsies stole me again. This went on for some time. One minute I was in the caravan suckling the dark teat of my new mother, the next I sat at the long dining room table eating my breakfast with a silver spoon.

It was the first day of spring. One of my fathers was singing in the bathtub; the other one was painting a live sparrow the colors of a tropical bird.

∼

It was the epoch of the masters of levitation. Some evenings we saw solitary men and women floating above the dark tree tops. Could they have been sleeping or thinking? They made no attempt to navigate. The wind nudged them ever so slightly. We were afraid to speak, to breathe. Even the nightbirds were quiet. Later, we'd mention the little book clasped in the hands of the young woman, and the way that old man lost his hat to the cypresses.

In the morning there were not even clouds in the sky. We saw a few crows preen themselves at the edge of the road; the shirts raise their empty sleeves on the blind woman's clothesline.

∼

The city had fallen. We came to the window of a house drawn by a madman. The setting sun shone on a few abandoned machines of futility. "I remember," someone said, "how in ancient times one could turn a wolf into a human and then lecture it to one's heart's content."

～

O witches, O poverty! The two who with a sidelong glance measured the thinness of my neck through the bars of the birdcage I carried on my shoulder. . . .

They were far too young and elegant to be storybook witches. They wore low-cut party dresses, black seams in their stockings, lips thickly painted red.

The big-hearted trees offered their leaves by whispering armfuls over the winding path where the two eventually vanished.

I was left with my cage, its immense heaviness, its idiotic feeding dish, the even more absurd vanity mirror, and the faintly sounding silver bell.

# Thomas R. Smith
## PORTRAIT OF MY GERMAN GRANDPARENTS, 1952

I see them always in midsummer, the retired minister and his wife seated
before the house too small for their thirteen children. My grandfather
lifts his feathered head, as Red Cedar River breezes stir his few locks.
His decorum and poverty show in the black wool suit he wears even in
this heat; his collar is thin but freshly bleached. He seems to listen to a
quarreling in the trees, the petulance, perhaps, of angels thrown down.
He hardly knows this world anymore, and will not know the world it
is becoming, just as the grandchildren, grown up, will not be known.
The grass, so lantern-like on its sun-side, casts long afternoon shadows.
He raises his spotted hand to my grandmother's cheek. Her brow shines
as the sun breaks through the shade and washes the silver braids pinned
up. She is still robust, after all the comings and goings. But her old legs
are tired, folded under the rayon dress. She puts her thicker hand on his
and holds it there, feeling the slow winter pulse.

≈

SAND

1.

Sand knows how to escape my fist, rains with a sizzle on the stiff oak leaves of this deserted, wave-dazzled October beach. You and I have met before, you dirt so clean you leave no trace on the palm except the dry satisfaction of once having been kissed.

2.

The days and nights of our vanity escape like this sand, a young man's dream of being held forever in the flower between the thighs of girls now worn down to middle-aged women. All the rocks of the world are growing older and smaller, and we with them, our strength farther and farther away until we see it the size of a grain of sand.

3.

Yet each sand grain is also a treasure once locked in a mountain before it became a bead on a princess's necklace, before it came here, on this river shore, to open its silica heart. When a mountain grows tiny enough to kneel on a beach, we see in it the image from the moment of creation, a crystal flower toward which our hands try to lift it. . . .

～

## WINDY DAY AT KABEKONA

Only a picture window stands between us and the full force of gusts that lift the branches of the red pine. Draft under the cabin door rolls the rug resolutely into a tube despite our attempts to lay it flat.

Foot-high waves spume across the lake; near shore the color of the long, gleaming swells softens to a milky jade, warmer looking than it is, almost southern. But the drift of this world is northerly; lawn chairs are hurled into woodpiles, propellers of outboard motors scrape against stones. The door bangs loosely in its sill. Jackpines groan as if they could snap and fall.

There is something in all this fury that makes the day oceanic: We're near at any moment being swamped, drowned, pinned by wreckage. In the cloudless sky, the sun gleefully conducts the turbulence as though it were a Wagnerian opera. A gull white as our idea of angels hovers above the shore for a moment—fully awake—fighting the wind before being torn from its place.

# Terry Spohn
## WEDNESDAY AT THE BEACH

The accountants are wearing their last clothing today. It is Wednesday, a day of wars, hammering, a day of carpentry, a day of wind and motion, a hard day to speak in. The accountants, their disciplined lips like rubber bands, have finished downsizing the company. All these years of brown ties, bad complexions. All this time never looking anyone in the eye. All those brown shoes in the closets of the accountants, all those brown pants shiny in the seat. All those bedrooms at home with the shades pulled on Wednesday afternoon, dark as an undertaker's socks, dark as Hitler's tea passing through him. Wednesday is a widow with a bent neck at church in the afternoon.

Today the accountants are cleaning out their desks. This afternoon they will go to the beach—the uncountable sand blowing into their shoes, the blank sun. The sky is the deep blue of a baby's dream, half the moon tucked into it. Even now gulls are standing by, circling the empty beach like a gust of invoices.

∾

## PARENTS

Dogs raise their heads from sleep. The rabbit's paws are wet. In the first watery light of the morning a woman is climbing the rocks. She is barely a speck against the granite from the hotel balcony across the river where a man is sipping coffee and watching his wife braid her hair, each hand doing the other's work in the glass.

"I dreamt I was climbing a mountain," the man's wife says, her hands circling behind her head like moths. "There were bees everywhere around me. It was getting dark and the heat was leaving the rock."

"I'm going to shave," the man says, walking into the darkness. There is his face in the mirror, the skin like a mail pouch. It is his father's face, the same one the man always has in the morning. His father is getting old, and the first old fears are rising again like locusts after all these years.

The climber is still inching her way upward, her mother's letters scattered on the ground below, birds circling, her blonde hair like shortbread cooling in the sun. She doesn't intend to die.

# Deborah Stein
## BLUE SOCKS

All the socks I bought for mother to bring on my visits, tan soft cotton socks, "nothing too tight at the ankle" white sport socks, short argyle wool ones, maroons, and more tan and more white and another wool (any color), I bought excessively for her then—and underwear, robes, night-gowns. All the socks bought for her sitting around, lying down, socks to fit her swollen ankles and feet, feet bloated from cancer sweeping through to the liver, skin stretching her ankles and feet like fruits ready to burst with ripeness. Her favorite blue fluffy socks she wore like slippers, at night in bed, then days in bed. Thursday, the day she died, I massaged her tender feet through those blue socks, she asked me not to stop, "don't go yet," all the socks I brought, she died in the blue ones, all those socks I now wear, shrinking tan cotton socks in the dryer to fit my narrow feet, slim ankles, I wear all the socks, all those socks, mother cremated in her blue socks, I wear all the socks except her blue ones.

~

## ONE THOUSAND SATURDAYS

By early adolescence, I was deposited more and more at Grandma's. I spent what seems like a thousand Saturday mornings watching TV with her, she sewing and watching me. Grandma would pin and stitch and patch everything that Mama dropped off with me. With her mending pile draped on her lap, there'd always be ripped seams from Mama's short-sleeved cotton blouses. Torn where her broad shoulders pulled at the back like most single mothers who lug two babies and groceries and work, all on their own. When Grandma had a mastectomy she told me they caught the cancer early enough so it hadn't spread. She was mostly worried about those foam bra fillers. All those times I saw Grandma pulling through a final overhand stitch, biting the thread and stabbing the needle into her chest through the cashmere sweaters she always wore, even when the sun was out. Being the oldest, I was able to recall all Grandma's sewing tips by the time I reached twelve, a good age to start mending. It was no accident then when I pushed a pin into my budding bosom and discovered it would hurt.

# Robert Sund

*from* Bunch Grass

The ranchers are selling their wheat early this year, not holding over for a better price in the spring. Next year the government lifts restrictions on planting, and nobody is sure what will happen when wheat grows "fencerow to fencerow." This morning another man has come out from the Grain Growers to help us out. John and I haven't got time to cooper boxcars and handle trucks too.

At lunchtime, he takes his carpenter's apron off and sits on a grain door in the shade of a boxcar, resting before he eats. I go out to join him and notice a Bible resting on the ledge under the rear window of his car. He says he doesn't read it much, and because he is anxious not to appear narrowly Christian, I want to know more about him. He is sixty-five, about to retire; a lonely man, it seems. There is something unspoken in him. His eyes squint to keep out the bright sunlight falling now just where the boxcar's shadow stops. I say, "There's one thing in Mark that has always puzzled me." He turns to face me, and I continue. "Where Jesus says, 'To them that have shall be given, and from them that have not shall be taken away.' That always seemed cruel to me, but since the verb hasn't got an object (have what? have not what?) if you supply an object, it's really alive. Love. Money. Intelligence. Curiosity. Anything."

In the bleached countryside of his mind, suddenly a new season washes over; common plants begin to blossom. And now, ideas fly back and forth between us, like bees, their legs thickening with pollen.

In the next hour we talk a lot and I learn that he has been reading Rufus Jones, Meister Eckhart, and *The Cloud of Unknowing*. He nearly trembles with a new joy he kept hidden. His wife writes poetry, he tells me, and adds—thrusting years recklessly aside—"I've worked here sixteen years, one harvest to another. I've seen a lot of young men come and go, and never had a decent conversation. It's worse with the college kids. They don't think, most of them."

Trucks start coming in again, lunch is over. He puts his carpenter's apron on again, but before we part he invites me home to dinner this evening, careful not to spoil it by appearing as happy as he really is.

Back inside the elevator, I'd like to lie down somewhere in a cool, dark corner, and weep. What are people doing with their lives? What are they doing?

# Barbara Szerlip
A.K.A. MATA HARI

She suggested we meet for lunch the next day at Cafe Americaine. "Wear the black derby you have on," she added. "It's quite becoming."

I arrived early, ordered a beer and watched the crowd. A party of boisterous Swedes. Marussia, the actress starring in the Folies, was sharing wine with an English officer. A group of French merchants conferring on a business deal.

I remember she wore lavender, with an extraordinary amethyst at the throat. The boulevard afforded a lovely view of the Opera House, but she insisted on a corner table at the back.

When I turned to get my hat from the wall-hook behind me, there was another black derby beside it. "The one on the left, I'm certain," Marguerite offered. When we reached my room at the Grand Hotel, she lifted the sweatband, removed a thin paper, then tilted the hat rakishly on my brow. "A kiss," she said, bestowing one, and was off.

~

## THE NOMAD'S STORY

We would like to have heard his story, to have spent an afternoon with the details of another life, if he did not touch us too deeply or turn out to be simply a homeless bore.

We recognized him in these ways: that he traveled alone and for the most part unseen, moving through darkness like a swimmer in a cave of dreams. No map would suggest his way, no monument recall past journeys. He would make use of what he found, henna, walnut, pomegranate; he would be the one to weave gardens in the desert. At times he might allow himself to imagine destinations, as if one could ever recognize such a place upon arrival.

Perhaps we wanted him to speak of things far from here, and so to us, exotic. To explain how only on looking back could he understand where he had been, and how he traveled to learn not to look back. And when he did look, the memory altered. We imagined his eyes would moisten or recede behind a mist as he spoke of these things. How once, on a streetcorner, he had seen a man and realized, in that instant, it was himself—living a possible present that had been denied him when, at a previous crossroad, he bore east instead of north or west.

Perhaps we secretly hoped he would leave us some phrase or thought we could amuse our friends with later, a piece of wisdom culled from so many journeys. He would say: *For Everything We Have, There Is an Infinity We Cannot Have.* Or: *Passion without Compassion Is Meaningless.* Or: *What We Think We Leave behind Is Always Here with Us.*

In our romanticism we imagined that he alone, in the turbulence of cities, could understand the rhythms of planets and weather, experience distance, silence the timeless indifferent noise of wind in trees or an animal dying. He would remember the hundreds of small, seemingly unimportant things we had neither room nor time for. The secret ways of fear. The contradictions of desire. Departure's many faces. Surely he could describe for us the distant land of Sedra, whose language consists of musical notes. Or the lobby of Hotel Splendide, whose pillars and furniture are said to be carved from ice, roses suspended in perfect geometries beneath ice carpets.

We never heard his story. Perhaps, in truth, he was a businessman on holiday. Perhaps we endowed him with a history we dared not imagine as a future for ourselves, shaping our uncertainties to fit his face, his clothes. He was gone in a week. We never spoke with him, or knew his name.

⁓

## TERRA INCOGNITA

We've walked since morning, the landscape, as before, perfect sem-
blance of a boardwalk except for this: instead of bleached symmetrical
planks, it consists of the most elaborate inlaid parquet, intricate as an heir-
loom, and highly polished. How it can be maintained at the edge of the
sea without succumbing to salt and heat remains a mystery. And main-
tained by whom? We've yet to see a soul.

To our continuing right, the booths, shops, and rides. Gaudily-striped
canvas tents, ticket booths, arcades (Measure the Thrill of Your Kisses,
5¢), and ahead, pale shimmer of a roller coaster, silver in the sun.

How long since we've left the ship, two days, a week? Doubt eats at
us like a blight.

We've tried, at intervals, to push further inland, only to be met with
vegetation that seems to grow as fast as we cut, dulling our blades with
a thick ooze. A disturbingly feminine blossom—a rosy, vulvic affair
with pervasive scent—hangs in steamy clusters.

By day, the sky is oppressive, a thick, even wall of blue. "Will no one
arrive to polish the floors?" someone joked, but we were hours past jok-
ing, and the falsely cheerful calliope was beginning to run a cold edge
in my blood. Yesterday we lost one man to the vegetation and one to the
Museum of Sleep. . . .

Darkness comes as a slave. Tonight, again, we make camp on the
beach, the sand marked only by an occasional star-spined bird and our
own bootmarks. The moon is a perfect globe, its broken reflection on
the water like diamonds. And now Henderson, our level-headed young
navigator, is saying the configurations of stars and planets are unlike
any he's seen before, swears there's not a constellation he can recognize. . . .

# Ross Talarico
## HOME MOVIES

There is the blue sky, which can place us anywhere to begin. A roof suggests a whole civilization out of the rain. The smoke from the chimneys tells us all we need to know about the nature of the wind that blows the leaves from their branches, and then, the flag from the disbelief of its stillness. And yes, now we know the country in which the mother is holding her child. But when she waves, are we to suspect she is going somewhere, or that we, even at this moment, are just arriving?

In the background, on a street empty of soldiers, where neither victory nor defeat can be sensed, there is a car with its hood open. There are children, ignoring their playmates, who are staring into the lens, as men stare into each other's eyes hoping, someday, to see themselves. There is a dog, the same old dog, walking out of the picture, and men with extravagant gestures who know for the moment they are without speech. And coming up the sidewalk are the strangers we have come to know as ourselves, and a home, neither yours nor mine, to which we have returned, and a movie screen upon which the shadows of our fingers become the ghosts of animals we have tried to imitate.

# Thom Tammaro
## WALKING TO MY OFFICE
## ON EASTER SUNDAY MORNING

I move through the quiet morning, watching a cluster of blackbirds arc
and dive above me, vapor trails of jets, and below me the brown grass
and soggy trash revealed by melting snow. New buds and a few white
petals on an almond tree. Passing Our Redeemer Church, I read the
marquee, usually filled with times for daily worship and a quotation
from scripture, but today it says only "His work is done!" Then the end
of a hymn being sung and the final notes of the organ rising. And the
congregation pouring out in all their joy and the children in their Easter
pastels, colors we see when we close our eyes and imagine light. How
we long to be lifted, carried from this world by the spiraling energy of
the Psalms and wrapped in brilliant colors! Colors I long ago put away.

Arriving at my office building, I open the door someone has left un-
locked all night, and walk down the long hall to my office. Sliding the
key inside the brass knob, I open the door to the dark and empty room.
Something inside of me rising. No one to greet us on the long road. So
much work to be done.

~

## FEBRUARY, 1951

In the cold middle of the month, in the late gray sky afternoon, a young
man, six years from the war and four years from his wedding, steps
from the mill gate, which he will enter and exit for the next thirty-one
years of his working life, onto the frozen bricks of Factory Avenue. A
gust of winter wind whips his 6' 1" slender frame, sending flakes from
a patch of snow swirling around his body. Turning up the collar of his
olive-drab fatigue field coat which he will wear well beyond middle
age, he heads home, alone in the last light which has given in to steel-
gray clouds drifting across what is left of that Pennsylvania day.

A mile away a young wife, four years from her wedding, beautiful
in her thick Jane Russell hair and robust in her life, waits for him as she

will do every day—or night when he works the night shift—for the next thirty-one years. She is wearing a long-sleeved blue cotton print dress that her sister gave her and a black wool button-down sweater with pearl buttons that she received as a gift from him last Christmas. Coffee perks in a small tin pot with a broken glass stopper as it will for the next thirty-one years. She wipes a swirl of snow from the window pane and looks for his slender shadow coming up the street. She opens the door to a blast of winter air when she hears him step from the dirt path to the wooden porch and climb the steps to the front door. When they see each other they smile as they will for the next thirty-one years. He walks through, one hand clasping shut the collar of his fatigue field coat, the other wrapped around the handle of the black metal lunch pail which he will carry to and from work for the next thirty-one years. They pause, embrace: she, reaching her arms around his shoulders and standing tip-toe to reach his lips; he, bending down to meet her lips, letting go of his coat collar to wrap his free arm around her thin waist, drawing her to his body, the warm, black wool sweater pressing against the cold folds of his olive-drab coat. In the room above them, their first child, thin but never weak from a faulty heart, will sleep until nightfall. After they greet each other, he goes to the sink to wash away the day's work from his face and hands, then combs his brilliant black hair in a great sweep atop his head. They sit at the gray formica table where they will eat their meals for the next thirty-one years, the yeasty smells of the kitchen all around them.

Below their second story flat above the butcher shop, swirls of snow sweep along the empty streets. And then in late afternoon darkness, without word, quick and deliberate as deer moving to water, they move to love each other. Somewhere deep inside their bodies they offer themselves, priest and priestess, in the holy sacrifice of their love, body and blood, flesh and bone, to the host I am to be, while the last flicker of February light finds its way down the long corridors of their love toward the first glimmer of my life—a distant planet orbiting in its path deep inside their bodies, waiting to take its place among the constellations. And then there was evening, and there was morning, and another day. And day after day, their creation filled the firmament, floating to find his place in this watery world.

# Tony Towle
## THE REVIEW

### Part 1

The magic month of June, when I was born. Ducklings take their first swim in the nearby pond. Roses and strawberries grow wild. The cottages vibrate as portents of riot and jailbreak come down from the hills. By October the parks and the field are full of fog; as though there were clouds on the ground instead of in the sky. In October there is a lot of smoke. We may go up with it to the hot sun, or gradually disappear in the cool afternoon.

Things are established by July. The floors of the houses are spread with rushes; our machines have worked themselves to exhausted perfection. I have brought you here to see this. When you are close, I get dizzy and cannot breathe. I am not thinking about that. I am thinking that we roll around the sky like the planets. The sun shines on us, like them. Ants and beetles go quietly along the ground. And every day we sleep.

### Part 2

He is pried loose, but soon he is back, clinging to the bed. First there is the mother. Then there are friends, and a number of women. The setting, and its environs, are scrubbed and gleaming. Flowers are planted along the roads leading to the cities. There are dozens of new hotels and castles. Spring in the castles becomes a brilliant burst of color and gaiety. One is hardly conscious of the surrounding rhythm of life. We only know that on the next day there will be the same delightful things to do and that nothing will ever change.

*Part 3*

The snow covers all the earth. It falls faster and faster. We think sadly of the trees and the sunshine, the grass and the flowers. We go peacefully to sleep, first one side toward the sun, then the other.

The sun rolls down the sky in the afternoon, and falls into the sea with a restful hiss. The woods are calm and safe. A flurry of snow comes in the daytime, while we are walking.

# Alison Townsend
MUSES


Sometimes I can almost see them. A swirl of skirt or the flash of a red skirt as someone disappears at the edge of the forest. Pine branches which sway, then rest, still and resinous beneath a glass of noon.

It is easy to imagine I've dreamed them. Tall women, bearing jugs, carrying baskets. Tall women with strong, capable hands, bare feet, and a knowledge of silence. How to pass through the forest like a blown leaf, like a needle, like a ray of clear light which falls, shifts, and falls again.

Everything has a life of its own. And it is easy to imagine I've dreamed them, except for the meadow around me, suddenly humming; this pulse in my own throat; and the poppies, shaking, though there is no wind.

≈

# MY EX-HUSBAND ASKS ME
# WHO READS MY ROUGH DRAFTS

*—for David*

*No one,* I say, over Thanksgiving dinner at the Fess, the rhinestone ear-
rings I bought to please my lover brushing my cheeks like cool, knowl-
edgeable fingers. Then I amend that to: *Well, my writing group does, of
course. But mostly I read my own rough drafts now.* I don't know why he's
asking or what it matters, the two of us poised at opposite sides of the
table, polite and wary, but still family of a kind, thrown together this hol-
iday by circumstances too complicated to question.

Dinner arrives, with all the trimmings, and we talk of other things.
His job and mine. Econometric models for utility companies. The busi-
ness of selling books for a living. He wears the navy blue sweater with
the snowflake design I helped him pick out at Brooks Brothers. I wear
a bargain, teal green silk from Shopko that he has never seen, the weird
alchemy of divorce making strange what was once most familiar.

Pumpkin pie comes, followed by decaf—sweetened, with lots of
extra cream—and all the silly things we know about one another float,
unspoken, in the lamplight between us. We do not talk of the future.

But as he bends to sign his half of the check, I see again how he bent
at our kitchen table, going over my manuscripts, pencil in hand, teach-
ing himself about poetry because he loved me. And how it is for love's
sake, and because no one in our lives can ever really be replaced, that he
asks me this question I do not know how to answer, except with the
words of this poem, this rough draft I am still in the process of revising.

# C. W. Truesdale

EL GORDO

Some of us knew he would cause terrible problems once we had made good our escape. I, for one, secretly hoped that he would die a hero's death after cutting the throats of the border guards, one by one. He seemed impervious to their bullets—he had already taken about twenty and was moving ponderously toward the fanatical captain of the guards. The captain was trying desperately to throw the huge flywheel into reverse, so the train we had hijacked would back right into the machine guns of our pursuers. But Gordo's hands were already on his throat. Soon, he would wring the captain's neck like a chicken.

I had already promised the dying Gordo a suite of poems and already I knew, as the train slid down among the green hills and the banana plantations, that I would never escape him. He would steal into my darkest thoughts at night, the eternal Stranger, the Mad Rapist. His hard, fixed accusatory eyes would say, over and over, how I had used him, and El Gordo would reach up out of his particular hell with his powerful hands and wring my neck.

～

MIGUEL AND GENERAL ALEXANDER HAIG

Miguel, the Ecuadorian guerrilla, came into my mind the afternoon that President Reagan was shot in Washington. His Secretary of State—General Alexander Haig never wanted to be that. He wanted to be President. For a brief time that Monday in March 1980 many of us were under the delusion that he *was* President. He certainly sounded like it. He has the kind of mouth that slaughters language with authority. His eyes have the hard, fixed glare of the Congressional Medalist of Honor. He is contemptuous of politicians and might not have tolerated Speaker Tip O'Neill if the Vice President's jet had fallen out of the sky over Dallas or Amarillo. . . . The ghostly eminence of General Douglas MacArthur breathes in him and comes rumbling stentoriously out of that mouth. And like MacArthur he would probably cross the Rubicon of Constitutional Authority, if he could, and bring down the Republic in the name of the Republic, if he could.

Miguel Donoso Pareja would have recognized him immediately. "Ah, my friend," he would say, "Your General Haig is what poetry is all about. He is the School I attended and the University of my most awesome dreams. He is 'El Angel de la Guerra' and for him the apples fall down out of the trees and the birds are afraid to sing."

⟿

## SCHEHERAZADE

The translations at least survived, and the published travel essays, gorgeous stuff—meticulous descriptions of East African flora and fauna, of tribal chieftains and malicious obese slave-traders. *The Arabian Nights. The Perfumed Garden.* His account of the discovery of Lake Tanganyika and Speke's side-trip to what proved finally to be the true source of the White Nile, Victoria Nyasa. There was little she could have done about those.

It is easy to write him off. He could be vicious and uncompromising, a self-serving man, testy in companionships, and prone to disputation. In his later years, when they had cut off his funds, he gave way to drugs and alcohol, a waste of a man dying into beautiful elegant angry phrases. Africa was his obsession, his horror, his muse, his queen, and when Africa was denied to him by the Royal Geographical Society, the fragile empire of his brilliant intellect crumbled like the papers and the erotic pictures she fed into that pyre.

She burned him all. Every scrap of paper. All his notes. His meticulous diaries. His letters. His priceless collection of erotica. She reduced everything to the pure flame of her still girlish imagination: "If I were a man," she said as a girl, "I would be Richard Burton. Since I cannot be a man, I will cleave to Richard Burton the rest of my days." To her he was the one Great Man and by the Catholic God she never stopped believing in she fed him already dead, now and forever, world without end, to this pyre, the man of her dreams so many years before, before he had ever really come into what he was meant to be.

# Mark Vinz
## WIND CHILL

The voice on the radio is urgent. When you go outside, it says, exposed flesh will freeze in less than a minute. Minus sixty-five this morning, and it will get worse through the daylight hours—who knows how much worse when the wind comes up, when it really comes up. Records will fall. Can't you feel it, there in the dim light of the kitchen, small drafts creeping through every pore? Think of flesh, the voice whispers. Think of bare flesh, numbing, tightening. Think of records, what you'll tell the others, the ones who don't live here, the ones who'll never understand. Listen, says the fading voice, this is what we believe in. Listen: this is every-thing we know.

≈

## STILL LIFE: THE PLEASURES OF HOME

The locusts are back this year, and toward sunset the racket is beyond all toleration—like a giant bandsaw hidden in the tops of the elm trees. But soon it will be dark and there will be a few hours of silence again, broken only by the hiss of tires, a porch door slamming, a barking dog.

The humidity is back again too, the worst this summer it's ever been, worse than any of the old men can remember. There's a dull ring around the streetlight, so heavy it seems to be dripping, as the front porches slowly fill up with people and paper fans. The old women come out after putting away the dishes, and sit in metal lawn chairs, their legs far apart, their stockings rolled down below their knees. The front room windows are streaked with blue and white light from the TV sets, and now and then the angry voice of a child calls out from within the house.

Everyone is thinking about sleep, about damp, sticky sheets. Some-thing seems to be stirring out there in the dark fields. Heat lightning to the south. Perhaps tonight there will be a breeze.

≈

## LATE NIGHT CALLS

Sometimes when the phone rings late at night I think of my friend Jim. "Did I wake you?" he'd say, and even if he did, I'd never tell him. "Read me something you've written," he'd say. "I need to hear what you've been doing." So I'd read to him and he'd say, "Jesus, that's lovely," or "read it again, brother, this time slower—something's not quite right in those first few lines." And then, of course, he'd read to me—about the farm in Indiana or the old queens at the steam baths where he went sometimes or the Yei-bet-chi dancers he saw once on the way back to Gallup. How different we are, he'd joke, and then I'd try to joke about how late night phone calls usually mean bad news. And Jim would say, "You know I'm bad news, always have been," and we'd talk about what ailed us or writing in bus stations and all-night cafes, or when I was going to come down and see him.

There aren't many people you can call when you're not sleeping, you know. I've been waiting these last few years for someone else to phone late at night, to read poems or ask me to read what I've been working on—just because it needs to be heard. "Jesus," Jim would say, "this dying is hard work, isn't it."

# Tom Whalen
## SELF-SERVICE WÄSCHEREI

In the automated laundromat on Birmensdorferstrasse just past Gold-brunnenplatz the small table I sit at is yellow formica. Outside the window, cars and pedestrians pass, the latter mostly Swiss housewives and elderly men. To them I must appear a peculiar window display. The 9 tram crosses my window, its passengers staring amazed at my figure. There are nine washers here, each numbered, and four (numbered) dryers. They rest atop blue bases. The six-foot-tall dispenser, dark brown, features in its circular trays white soap powder and in yogurt cups liquid softener the blue of the sky at its most irreal. The street sweeper with his orange overalls and orange cart sweeps up the litter with his broom of twigs. How colorful Switzerland is! The floor consists of square tiles, the colored ones randomly dispersed. The walls and ceiling are white. I can't read the German, French, Italian, Romansch instructions, but the system is so practical I get it right on the first try. At the navy blue box (three types of blue!) I press the number of my washer (1) and feed the box the 5.50 francs it desires, then return to the table. The only other machine currently in operation is 9, before which a round-faced young woman wearing a Born-in-the-USA t-shirt stuffs her laundry. Now the two machines slosh and gurgle to one another, now one spins and hums and the other responds in kind. On their separate bases they shimmer and sing, these twin Merker Bianca BE 60's. A woman in black stares in as she pedals past. A mother pulls her child away. A gray-haired woman with crutches and sunglasses takes no notice. I cannot see what the young woman in the t-shirt is doing, because she is on the other side of the dispenser. At the end of thirty minutes, when their cycles are done, 1 croaks its conclusion which 9 repeats in sympathy. We cross paths, the young woman and I, with our wet bundles in our arms, which we load into our dryers, and now dryers 1 and 4 begin their half-hour dance, and the young woman and I hum and spin about, gurgle and slosh together. Outside the window, the fascinated trams pass by, the buses, the bicycles, the pedestrians, the days. Soon this cycle, too, will end, and she in the t-shirt and I with the pencil and notebook will gather our clothes from the dryers and go our separate ways with laundry fresh as flowers in our hands.

# Patricia Wilson
ORDER

I never knew how much you suffered, but at your funeral I read from the same Bible passage you had carried around with you for years, though I didn't know it until after. Candy pulled it out of your billfold, showed it to me. It was worn and had been cut out from what looked like an old church bulletin.

When I was a child I wrote to you in the grade school autograph book I found in your father's desk: *Dear Leonard, When you grow up I want to be your daughter*. I was 8 years old then. Still, having a lawyer's sense of order you were surprised.

I think when you knew you were dying you became more like a child. The responsible things mattered less: the time, what day it was, the headlines. *When I was a child I spoke as a child, I acted like a child. When I became a man I put away childish things*. You tried to remember what really happened, how it really looked, like how you remembered your aunt, your father's sister, dying in your family's dining room from ovarian cancer. You were eight years old then. "She turned orange," you told me, "just like that chair over there."

~

## YEARS

Now I don't think about them that often, his last hours, though I have cried in my dreams, awakening exhausted. Or I dream of clothing, that I'm wearing something he wore, a bright red nightshirt, a yellow cotton windbreaker. He says "Don't ruin that, it's mine." I apologize, "I thought you had died," feeling slightly foolish, like the time when as a teenager I spraypainted the basement walls of the house he had just bought and he pleaded, "Don't. I want it to be nice."

But I don't want to tell you how hard it was, how I sat next to his bed that night and listened to his breath, how I would put a pink moist sponge like a lollipop into his mouth when it got dry, how he wore diapers, took morphine every 15 minutes. Because death is like that, the entire plot, banal, terrifying, irreversible. So I picked up the phone, called work, said I'd be back Monday, we didn't expect him to die 'til next Friday at the earliest. Max on the receiving end of my call, and this is something I'll always love him for, continued to speak with me as if I were sane and not practicing some bizarre and idiosyncratic form of denial, merely said, "It's gonna be busy. Are you sure you're up for it?" I asked what was the restaurant critic Jeremy Iggers eating? "Just appetizers. Mushrooms and cheese curds."

It was the end of November, the horses outside running to keep warm. He died in the morning, the tape recorder playing a Lutheran hymn, "The King Is Coming," something he'd always believed in. Two men from the funeral home took him away in a maroon and gold bag, the colors of his U of M football uniform. Which didn't seem to mean that much until the next day when in my sister's house I saw a picture of the whole team, a page from the Sunday paper, framed, dated November 29, 1945, the year he was eighteen. He would have liked the symmetry, that between the team photo and his death there were exactly forty-five years.

# Linda Wing
## MORTALITY ANECDOTES

At my brother's house and I'm in the rec room losing a game of Trivial
Pursuit with my mother and Theresa Samborski. I haven't answered a
single question in the arts and literature category, which is supposed to
be my job, though I'm doing semi-okay in science. So I walk up the side
stairs to get a drink of water from the kitchen faucet, like half-time
where you go over your game plan. I'm dropping ice in a plastic tum-
bler and hear my father talking with Buck Blese's dad, in between poker
hands, their break too.

I've hardly ever heard my father say anything about the war. In the
third grade we were studying it and Mrs. Barton told us to go ask our
fathers about their mementos, if they had any, keepsakes. I remember
my dad looking at me, not looking at me, and it felt scary, and he said,
"Tell your teacher I kept nothing. I don't want to remember." He had
nightmares though, I knew that, about Africa and snipers, guns in trees,
even when I was little I was sure he remembered but he would never
let me hear him talk about it, if he talked.

So I'm running water over ice in my brother's kitchen, and my dad
and Mr. Blese had both lived then and they're talking, about first days
and big boats. Ships. You're supposed to call it a ship. My father's sense-
of-humor complaining about the army. What they're supposed to carry,
each day, on their backs. How much it weighs: candy, pictures, bullets.
And he says, on top of it all, they've issued us extra mattress covers, du-
plicates, and how often do we even see a mattress? but carry this twice,
and then, he says, "The first guy I see get it, I learn what the extra mat-
tress cover is for, and they put him in there, and seal and ship him. That
next morning first thing, I got out on the street, and sold my mattress
cover to an Arab." Me, I'm running the water pretty slow and quiet and
it's not the noise but the poker player that sees me too casual and atten-
tive in the kitchen, says, "What are you doing?" "Getting water." And
he says, "We'll wait."

My father never told me anything deliberately, as far as I can tell, or
maybe even himself. I know that finally he left some things with Michael

on the after-work front porch because you can't go until you've set your story in someone's hands.

So I never heard my father say this personally. Michael asked him—he knew medals didn't matter, none of that, but if he came home with anything he was glad for, proud of, and my father answered him yes, "yes," he said, "they would have us line up, firing, and I always shot my gun into the air. I hope, I believe, best of my knowledge, I never killed anyone."

∼

## THE NEWS

The news goes by so fast this month. Andrea and I come home, September 1993 with paper sacks full of clean laundry, unfold hot thick bleach smells. The world is a ring of blue air, fresh socks, ten o'clock Saturday television. Lead story the one-year anniversary of Officer Haaf's death at Pizza Shack, and now the trial, jury selection. But justice is so different from repair.

Andrea and I talk about being younger, thin pipe legs and knowing everything, fishing in the Mississippi River versus growing up next to weapons technology in California, a major target. And she says all the kids understood radiation, knew that darker clothing absorbed more of it, and that if you died wearing a paisley blouse you went down wearing that pattern forever, its design burning deep through your skin.

Gee, I say, to the very last, California understands fashion, maybe, or perhaps just a clearer perception of sudden death, earthquakes and all. Taking the time, the forethought, to die beautiful. The white heat of a tough job.

Something ought to be cloud simple, like deer. September, Third Precinct, Pizza Shack, traffic in the everyday daylight, years since a school desk, hands over head saved us from bombs. Candles burn an intersection vigil, news interviews and posters, the moment in which we are raising new children.

And hoping they live beautiful, or at least die with purpose.

# Warren Woessner
## MAGGIE MAY

*—Rod Stewart, 1971*

"You led me away from home, just to save you from bein' alone." Pinball did that in the fall of 1971 and well into the spring. Psychedelia slowly fading, blown away with the initial violent energy of the antiwar movement. Friends drifting in and out of town. "I suppose I should collect my books and get on back to school." Mostly out.

We smoked and drank at the communal glass table, working on one long, never-ending poem of lights and flashes. Good pinball anthem, Maggie May, pulsing long song with pauses and rushes and frantic edges, just like a good game moved, the machine running hot then cold then hot. Keeping it up with George and Ed and Paul. I haven't had such a coherent group of men friends since, and not being a hunter or sports freak, probably never will.

We were always looking for a good machine, a level machine, one we could play and play, cigarettes burning out where stainless steel meets glass. Hearts and Spades, Mini-Pool, Subway, and Dimension. A good machine is hard to find, impossible today. Straight drop. Paul throwing away nickels and pennies as he hunted his pockets for one more dime.

Girl friends and wives left behind to their own devices. "You stole my soul, that's a pain I can do without." Living in a handful of bars, night and day. Getting better. Machines playing dead, rolling over and spreading their legs. Free balls racking up with electric thocks. Playing forever on the thin edge between cold and drunk, the rhythm beyond the work of school, work and words. Playing for an hour on one dime, no need to ever walk away but we did.

Along with the co-ops, communes, cadres, and affinity groups, my group broke up too. I'm not sure what gravity, binding energy or need pulled us together and held us there those months and then let go as suddenly to send us spinning away into our separate versions of reality but I can't complain. "I'll get on back home, one of these days," Rod sang in that song. That day came. I hope we all made it.

# James Wright
## TO CAROLEE COOMBS-STACY,
## WHO SET MY VERSES TO MUSIC

One afternoon a few years ago, in a mountain forest in upstate New York, I strayed from the beaten path and made my way slowly and alone through the brush. The little shrubs and bushes and saplings were not particularly dense, and I suppose I could have broken into a run if I had cared to. But there is something about a slow solitary walk that gives me the feeling of having become a moving root. If I could only make myself stand still long enough, I would turn into a tree. I wonder what kind of leaf I would bear.

Ordinarily a city-dweller, as I have become, hears nothing at all when he first arrives in some comparatively unspoiled natural place. I guess the drumming of urban sounds has made his ears temporarily insensitive. But after about fifteen minutes, one begins to be aware of the sounds of the forest. The birds, the insects, the breezes, the occasional movements of invisible animals (not always invisible—I saw a porcupine there once, rooting among dead leaves—he glanced at me over his shoulder of calm patience and, for all I knew, welcome—he was very fine) foraging or perhaps just turning over in their afternoon sleep—these made a rich music of their own.

But on my afternoon, I walked slowly, and paused, and stood still, and walked on slowly, further and further into the places of the trees, and paused, and walked slowly, and paused, and listened. And even after quite a long time, I heard nothing at all. I even resorted to an old device, honored by dead men who lie down among trees. I stood absolutely still, and closed my eyes, and listened and listened. And still I heard nothing.

When I opened my eyes, a doe was standing only a few feet away from me. She was dappled with fragments broken off from a birch tree. She stood utterly still. So did I. I didn't want to startle her, of course, but it was strange to realize that she didn't want to startle me either. Always when I walk in woods I become aware of being observed—never with hostility. I even enjoy the presences and the observations of snakes.

Extraordinarily beautiful, they are charming. The reserved and dignified serpents have received a bad press from western mythologies and religions. No, never with hostility: but with interest and even concern.

The doe and I stood and looked at each other. Usually a doe, when she appears, will fix you with her eyes. But this particular doe, ravishing as she was in her little dappling clear clouds of sunlight and golden brown fur, gazed not only into my eyes but over my whole body. And still she did not move.

And neither did I.

We stood for a long strange time. I was aware that we were communing without fear. We stood so long, that it occurred to me to listen yet again for sounds from the rest of the forest. And still I heard nothing.

And then I heard something. It was not a sound made by any animal or flower or wind known to me. It was music, and yet it seemed to pass almost beyond sound itself. It was movement. It was full of silences. I closed my eyes to cherish it all the more. The doe stood there, close as ever. I kept my eyes closed. I listened and listened and listened.

When I opened my eyes, I saw something that I would not have believed if it had been told me by somebody else. The doe stood there, her posture unchanged—and she had closed her eyes.

As I realized what was happening, a quiver went over and through my entire body.

All this while I had assumed that the doe and I were standing face to face, each waiting for the other to make a sound. But now I knew that, whatever it was I heard, the doe was listening to it, too.

After another short time, the music passed away into its own secret silences. The doe and I looked at each other with what came close to being a spoken farewell and blessing. Then each of us slowly, without a hint of panic or distrust, turned in the forest and slowly walked our separate ways. She may have stopped for a moment and looked back at me, as the creatures sometimes do. I do not know what she did. I simply walked away in a different direction. I had thought we were listening for each other. But I believed then, and I believe now, that somehow the doe and I were listening to the same thing, that it was something no other creature could have heard.

I still wonder what it sounded like to the doe.

You were far away, Carolee, on your own mountain-side near Santa Fe, your delicate white hands wakening the dark wood and ivory of your piano, the strange heavy instrument heavy and deep with life as a moving root; and your full throat utterly alive, molding and molding my dumb language till the words became leaves.

And you and the doe and I, three listeners to your music, none of us entirely sure if any other creature had heard.

∾

## THE WHEELING GOSPEL TABERNACLE

Homer Rhodeheaver, who was the evangelist Billy Sunday's psalmodist and shill at the offertory, did something in the year of Our Lord 1925 that made both of my parents almost ecstatic with happiness all the rest of their lives, until they died within a few months of each other in 1973.

Just as the Reverend Doctor Sunday was admonishing the congregation in congress assembled with his customary warning that they warn't no virtue in the clinking of shekels, a wicked sound; just as the Reverend Doctor was in full oratorical blossoming cry in praise of each silken soft certain rustle of one twenty-dollar bill against another in the wicker collection plate; just as the former semi-professional baseball player of the Lord God Almighty Lord of Hosts was advising how as "Bruthern, a twenty don't take up no more room in that there plate than a wun"—it happened.

One of Doctor Sunday's locally hired ushers glided to the minister's side and with ghostly discretion reported to the evangelical ear that the cops from Pittsburgh had just left Weirton, West Virginia, and were hurtling down the West Virginia Route 40 in their Prohibition-style armored Cord cars, bound to catch Homer Rhodeheaver in full song. He was wanted in Pittsburgh on a paternity charge.

By the time the Pittsburgh cops burst into the Wheeling Gospel Tabernacle, it was as empty and dark as the waiting room of a speakeasy. Where had the brethren gone? Some thought that Doctor Sunday ascended. I lean toward the opinion that the two laborers in the vineyards of the Lord skinned the populace of Benwood down the river the next day, and that possibly Homer had time between hymns to make some lonely widow happy.

The year was 1925. My mother and father got one of their chances to laugh like hell for the sheer joy of laughter before the Great Depression began.

They were younger than I am this year. I was born two years after Homer Rhodeheaver and Billy Sunday appeared to run up their crusading flag near the blast furnace down the Ohio River for what was surely a one-night stand.

For all I know, my mother and father loved each other in 1925. For all I know, Homer Rhodeheaver is still in full flight from the Paternity Squad of the Pittsburgh Police Department. For all I know, Homer Rhodeheaver really was a glorious singer of the great hymns down home. For all I know, he carried a better tune than he knew. Women heard him in Pittsburgh. Maybe women heard him in the Wheeling Gospel Tabernacle. Maybe Jehovah was drowsing, and Eros heard the prayer and figured that love after all was love, no matter what language a man sing it in, so what the hell.

Little I know. I can pitch a pretty fair tune myself, for all I know.

~

# TWO MOMENTS IN VENICE

## *I. Under the Canals*

All one needs to do is follow the sound of water.

An old man appeared suddenly around a corner. He entered a square very slowly, for all his quick appearance. He carried a middle-sized wooden ladder on his shoulder and a small curious net in one hand. A chimney sweep, Annie said. Maybe he was. With his coat elbows and his crushed hat scuffled enough, he could have prowled his way up and down the insides of these silvery, rotten walls.

But I am sure of the green moon-slime on his shoes and, until I hear otherwise, I will half believe that he had just climbed up some of those odd stairs out of a nearby canal. How can I know what he was doing underwater? The very streets of the city are water; and what magnificent and unseemly things must sway underneath its roads; the perfect skeleton of a haughty cat, his bone tail curled around his ribs and crusted with salt three centuries ago; even a chimney, swept free, till this hour passes, of all the webs they weave so stoutly down there, the dark green spiders under the water who have more than all the time they need.

## *II. City of Evenings.*

It is still too early for evening, and the smoke of early September is gathering on the waves of the Giudecca Canal outside my room. Steamers, motorboats, trash scows are moving past in large numbers, and gondolas are going home. In a little while we too will meet the twilight and move through it on a vaporetto toward the Lido, the seaward island with its long beach and its immense hotel, its memories of Aschenbach and his harrowing vision of perfection, of Byron on horseback in the moonlight, and the muted shadows of old Venetians drifting as silently as possible in flight from the barbarians, drifting as far away as the island of Torcello, taking refuge, as Ruskin said, like the Israelites of old, a refuge from the sword in the paths of the sea. Maybe Torcello was nothing much for the princes of the sea to find, but the old Venetians discovered the true shape of evening, and now it is almost evening.

⌇

## THE FRUITS OF THE SEASON

It is a fresh morning of late August in Padua. After the night's rain, the sun is emerging just enough so far to begin warming the grapes, melons, peaches, nectarines, and the other fruits that will soon fill this vast square. Women and children in bright flower-print dresses are already beginning to amble from stall to stall.

At the very end of the square I can see the azure and golden face of the town clock on the Torre dell'Orologio.

A baker with white flour sprinkled all over his boots just drifted across the extreme right corner of my eye.

And yet—to my left I can see the entire front length of the Palazzo della Ragione, on whose second floor the community has arranged a huge exhibit of paintings, the enduring fruits of five hundred years.

And spread below the faces of those peculiarly tender and fierce angels, the men and women and their children are still arriving from the countryside, arranging for our slow ambling choice the heaps of grapes, melons, peaches, nectarines, and all the other fruits of the season in a glory that will not last too long.

But they will last long enough. I would rather live my life than not live it. The grapes in a smallish stall are as huge and purple as smoke. I have just eaten one. I have eaten the first fruit of the season, and I am in love.

# Gary Young

Jimmy Rattcliffe played Jesus Christ in a farce at the Little Theatre. He played Santa Claus, the Easter Bunny, and at last, the Savior. Near the back of the hall a man cried out, sinner, Satan, blasphemer, and no one knew if he was part of the play or not. After the show, the man waited for Jimmy, and beat him to death in the parking lot. He and Jimmy had grown up together; they'd known each other all their lives. I had only been home two days, and the world was lost already.

~

One night, when I certain she was leaving me, I invented a man I thought my wife might love, and then I tried to be that man. I pulled her to me in the darkness. I kissed her, and she kissed me back. I'm wet, she said. Then she said, what is this? And I felt it too. My nose was bleeding; somehow I'd covered both our faces with blood. This is just like you, she said. You couldn't have planned it better if you'd tried.

~

The burning house turned our night clothes yellow. Standing at the curb, my brother batted ashes with his hand. We had a puppy, and my mother shouted, where's the dog, and then, my God, where's Cathy? I remember the sound of breaking glass, and walls too hot to touch. I remember pulling my sister from her bed, and leading her out into the world again. I did not wonder, then, how I'd found her, or how my mother could have turned so easily to send me back into the smoke and flames. It was my house; I knew where I was. I could find my way even in the dark.

# Lila Zeiger
## A PAIR OF PANTY HOSE

1.

No, they are not rubber, although they seem to extend themselves to fit many a situation. They start out rather small and shapeless, but become much larger and taller with daily wear. It is only with use that they stretch and walk and run, and even dance. Most of them come in what we call "flesh tones," but these shades vary considerably and are also subject to fading.

Their lives are dearly bought, for while they are somewhat adaptable, they are also vulnerable to every stress and accident. Painstaking research is always under way to make them stronger, but at this time it is still impossible to predict which of them will go quite early, if not almost immediately, and which will last a reasonable time. It is sheer chance.

We require of them only that they do their jobs smoothly and efficiently, without sagging or breaking under the strain. They are often considered best if unobtrusive. Random tears, holes, and wrinkles in their soft exteriors are therefore embarrassing and unpleasant.

What happens to them after they are no longer useful (and thus discarded) no one can say for certain.

2.

It had been coming on for some time now. The panty hose were getting really pissed about their name. That word panty, for example. A cutesy throwback to the twenties? Panty—a suggestive plosive, signifying heavy breathing—but just a little. Hose—watering, putting out the fire.

So the panty hose were trying on some new names. Like The Siamese Twins—connected from waist to crotch—the poor mindless couple so attached after all this time that one just couldn't make a move without the other.

Like Clit Cuddlers. Especially with those chaste little white cotton liners, sliding softly back and forth, to and fro, side to side. The smooth lid on the tiny kettle, loose enough to move a little with the simmer, tight enough to be self-absorbed.

And there were other names, put on for a while—like Up Tight or Shin Skins or Tease for Two. Even names that came with slogans, like The Adaptables (We Adjust to the Thrust) or Two Blind Mice (See How They Run).

By now, the panty hose were getting worn out with the stress. They decided that life was too short for so many changes. So they embraced the truly original, comforting themselves with the knowledge that hose is a hose is a hose. . . .

∼

## THINGS WE NEED TO KNOW ABOUT THE PICNIC:

1. Who conceived the idea of the picnic, and by whom?
2. On what continent did the picnic take place?
3. Is this the picnic that was rained out next Sunday?
4. When did the ants discover the picnic?
5. What well-known film maker invented Saran Wrap?
6. Who forgot the flatbröd for the paté?
7. Was there a body of water nearby, a fen, or a drinking fountain?
8. At what time did the discussion on "What is Poetry" roll down the hill?
9. Did we eat cold duck or drink cold duck?
10. Was the black spot on his thigh a tick or a malignant melanoma?
11. Who forgot the children?
12. When will the picnic end, and in what way?
13. Did the leaves notice how badly we were crushing the grass?
14. Were we continually aware that the words *picnicked* and *picnicking* have a *k* in them?
15. Could we explain why?
16. Did the women at the picnic have vaginal orgasms or clitoral orgasms?
17. How come only the men could urinate on the fire?
18. Why does God allow that green coating around the hard-boiled egg yolks?
19. Who forgot the sun?
20.

# Alan Ziegler
## THE GUEST

I am lost and knock on the nearest door to ask directions. There's a crowd, a party going on. I'm about to apologize for interrupting but everyone at the party treats me as if my arrival had been highly anticipated. This woman embracing me—do I know her? And this man slapping my back—is he an old roommate from school? They are listening to music I love, and offer me shrimp with lobster sauce, my favorite. Is this in my honor? Did I do something worthy without being aware of it? I decide to relax and enjoy; why analyze and maybe spoil it? I sit back, and one by one they come to me. "It was nothing," I hear myself saying—at least I am telling the truth.

Later, a teary woman makes her way through the crowd. She calls me inconsiderate and curses at me. I don't know how to respond, so I say nothing. She leaves, and everyone is quiet. The host comes over and says softly with a tinge of bitterness, "You know, you shouldn't have ignored her all night. It was hard enough for her to come. Sometimes you can be such a bastard."

~

## WOOLWORTH'S PARAKEETS

Hundreds of Woolworth's are closing and thousands of generic parakeets will be released on noon of the last day. Scrawny blue and green ten-dollar birds will scatter in downtown Las Vegas, uptown New York City, and suburban Lynbrook. They will be freed from their group homes, where they sleep, leaning on each other like passengers on a midnight train in India. These are not the cream of the exotic bird crop; they are bred for volume, their mark-up too low to help keep Woolworth's in flight. If you see one in your neighborhood, coax it home with seeds and love. Let it fly freely around the house, offer it food off your plate, teach it the words you've longed someone to say to you, and love it like you love the America that once was.

# Harriet Zinnes
## THE FALL

It came suddenly. You had created it. It had not been there before. This moment so rich so without anxiety. There it was hanging in the sky like a full moon. Without blight without history. You had made it so. Your voyage had led it to it. Its presence in the folds of history an illumination. Without past without events without margins of personal error. There it was. Rich beautiful contained. Nothing was needed now. Not even remorse. No guilt surely. It was all there. Suddenly in fullness. Suddenly it fit into the scheme of things. The daily scheme of things. It was unblemished too. Like silk cloths from India. Tapestries from China. It had come from distant worlds. At any rate you needn't have tried to discover from exactly where. It was no longer on the horizon. It was there. Round full as if never seen before. No longer forbidden. An event. An apotheosis but not abstract. Terribly real alive corporeal fathomable incarnate even worthy yes worthy. But when lightning struck it vanished. No bereavement really. What came so suddenly left suddenly. How should it be mourned? Isn't there practice in expectation? Long periods of rehearsal for purposes of mourning? But it came so suddenly. You had created it. Lightning struck and it was gone. No one set up a mourning period. There was no need. A vision created. A vision disappeared. Another event to be discarded. Only the fig tree remained and you had not created that. But who had planted the fig tree in that northern garden?

~

## I CAN HELP YOU SPEAK YOUR NAME

I can help you speak your name. And the names of the birds with flap-ping wings, and of those that perch silently on trees, their eyes open wide. I can help you speak the names of the many oaks, of the bark that folds over and over the different species of the birches. I can lead you back to the ravines. I can lead you where you want to go when you are free and easy walking in your boots through the long grasses. I can give you to yourself where your heart is and where your lungs open to the air, that air you breathe when you look down from the hills and see the moving reeds and name each one. I can help you speak your name.

# CONTRIBUTORS' NOTES

## NELSON ALGREN (1909–1981)

Nelson Algren published many works of fiction, including *A Walk on the Wild Side* and *The Man with the Golden Arm*, both of which were made into successful movies. Some of Algren's best writing lies in his short story collection, *The Neon Wilderness*. Algren was a city kid, whose epigraph for *Chicago: City on the Make* is a quote from Baudelaire: "I love thee, infamous city. . . ." As Ross Macdonald said of him: "Algren's hell burns with a passion for heaven."

∾

## SHERWOOD ANDERSON (1876–1941)

Sherwood Anderson, an Indiana businessman who ran away to become a writer in Chicago, was one of the loosely-knit group who helped create what he called "a robin's-egg Renaissance." In his *Memoirs* he writes of his struggle to work not with the language of books, but with "the language of the streets, of American towns and cities, the language of the factories and warehouses where I had worked, of laborers' rooming houses, the saloons, the farms." His most lyrical writing can perhaps be found in his collection of stories dating from that period, *Winesburg, Ohio*.

∾

## KAY BOYLE (1902–1993)

One of the most prolific writers of a prolific generation, Kay Boyle published two dozen works of fiction, half a dozen books of poetry, and several collections of non-fiction. She grew up in St. Paul, Minnesota, and spent several decades abroad, including a stint as foreign correspondent for *The New Yorker*. Returning to America in the sixties, she taught for nearly twenty years at San Francisco State University.

∾

## GELETT BURGESS (1866–1951)

Best known perhaps for his children's book, *The Purple Cow*, Gelett Burgess was a well-known satirist at the turn of the century, who, in San Francisco—along with a group of friends calling themselves "Les Jeunes"—published the *Lark*, one of the first and best of the little magazines of the nineties. *Are You a Bromide?* is another of his works, an account of "Sulphites" and "Bromides," which presages by more than half a century Julio Cortázar's *Historias de Cronopios y de Famas.*

∼

## WILLIAM FAULKNER (1897–1962)

As a young man, residing for a time in New Orleans, William Faulkner made a stab at newspaper writing. His work appeared in the Sunday supplement of the *Times-Picayune*. He also published sketches—such as the one included here—as well as poetry in the *Double Dealer*, before turning his hand to the fiction that would later win him the Nobel Prize for Literature.

∼

## NATHANIEL HAWTHORNE (1804–1864)

For the modern reader Nathaniel Hawthorne needs no introduction. Yet at the time he wrote his *American Notebooks* he was largely unknown. Even so, some of his most lyrical prose can be found in the *Notebooks*. His short stories are also masterpieces of craftsmanship. One place he worked, a small house with a great view of the Massachusetts Berkshires, still stands today on the grounds of Tanglewood, the summer home of the Boston Symphony Orchestra.

∼

## JANE HEAP (1887–1964)

For many years, working and living with Margaret Anderson, Jane Heap co-edited the *Little Review*. Her arrival at the magazine in the spring of 1916 was, according to Anderson, "the most interesting thing that ever happened to the magazine." Her influence—as well as Anderson's—on the development of modern literature is only now, at the end of the century, starting to be examined.

∼

## LAFCADIO HEARN (1850–1904)

Born in Ireland, Lafcadio Hearn lived for many years in New Orleans, working as a journalist. In later life he emigrated to Japan, married a Japanese woman, and became a professor of literature at the University of Tokyo. His comments on the prose poem can be found in his *Life and Literature*, particularly "Studies of Extraordinary Prose," and "The Prose of Small Things."

∽

## ERNEST HEMINGWAY (1899–1961)

While living in Paris, Ernest Hemingway took writing lessons from Ezra Pound in exchange for boxing lessons. At about this same time Hemingway published a series of sketches, "In Our Time," in the *Little Review*'s "Expatriate Number." These sketches were published by Bill Bird's Three Mountains Press in a tiny edition, and then went on to become the so-called "interchapters" of Hemingway's first short story collection, also entitled *In Our Time*.

∽

## FENTON JOHNSON (1888–1958)

Fenton Johnson grew up in Chicago and, in 1918, after finishing college, began publishing the *Favorite Magazine*, "the first and only weekly magazine published by and for colored people." In the twenties he founded the Reconciliation Movement, to improve relations between blacks and whites. His poems included here were reportedly part of a lost manuscript entitled "African Nights." Another unpublished manuscript, "The Daily Grind: 41 WPA Poems," can be found in the Fisk University Library Special Collections.

∽

## WALTER LOWENFELS (1897–1976)

Walter Lowenfels arrived in Paris in 1926, after first trying out the family butter business, and in a few years founded, along with Michael Fraenkel, a small press, Carrefour. Here Lowenfels published, among other works, his *Elegy in the Manner of a Requiem in Memory of D. H. Lawrence*, which he called an "operatic poem." Lowenfels stayed active in small-press publishing, and he is one example of the close connection between the literary world of the twenties and that of the sixties. This connection remains, as yet, an area ripe for further investigation.

∽

## ROBERT MCALMON (1895–1956)

A central figure in the literary world of the twenties, Robert McAlmon formed Contact Editions, which published early work by many expatriate writers. His *Being Geniuses Together, 1920–1930*, with supplementary material by Kay Boyle, is one of the most interesting chronicles of the era. Several years after the prose poem "Village" appeared, McAlmon published a novel by the same name—though unlike the poem, it isn't written in the first person.

~

## KENNETH PATCHEN (1911–1972)

Kenneth Patchen's work in poetry, prose, and art is too voluminous to catalog here. Living in San Francisco, though unconnected with the Beats, and "against a conspiracy of silence of the whole of literary America, Patchen has become the laureate of the doomed youth of the Third World War." So wrote Kenneth Rexroth at the end of the fifties.

~

## GERTRUDE STEIN (1874–1946)

Gertrude Stein's *Tender Buttons* first appeared in 1914. One cogent summation of its influence was expressed by Bob Brown: "At the time *Tender Buttons* was published I had to read it because positively there was nothing else in America to read. No *transition* back in 1914, no Joyce, no Cummings, no Kay Boyle, just a peep of Sandburg, no tricky little magazines of word experiment. . . . Gertrude Stein gave me a big kick. . . . That's the way you feel when you're tired to death finishing up the final paragraph of a three hundred page thriller and some blond angel slips in on a pink cloud with a cooling case of champagne. Sprays your scorched writing tonsils with it. Stein's book sprayed mine. It was a case of champagne to me in a time of dire need."

~

## H. D. THOREAU (1817–1862)

Henry David Thoreau's *Journal* stretches on for fourteen volumes. Much of his published writing was drawn from this rich source. The landscape around Concord even now has the same mystical quality that filled Thoreau's life and work.

~

JEAN TOOMER (1894–1967)

Jean Toomer's work first appeared in little magazines, including the *Double Dealer* in New Orleans. One of the earliest writers to document the realities of Southern black life, his poems and sketches were published together as *Cane* (1923). Toomer was enormously influential in the Harlem Renaissance—though he remained uncomfortable as an icon. He later became an active disciple of G. I. Gurdjieff.

∼

WALT WHITMAN (1819–1892)

Though he's best known for *Leaves of Grass*, some of Walt Whitman's finest writing is to be found in his prose, of which *Specimen Days* is an incomparable example. Whitman wrote a lot of prose before he first published any poetry; in fact, for years he made a living as a newspaperman. Thus he began a tradition, the newspaper-man-of-letters, which was continued by Lafcadio Hearn. Whitman remains the most important figure in the history of the American prose poem.

∼

WILLIAM CARLOS WILLIAMS (1883–1963)

William Carlos Williams's work is filled with poetic experimentation. *Spring and All*, for example, is a work of alternating prose and poetry. Williams refers in his autobiography to having been intrigued, in college (together with H. D.), by a work of early French literature, *Aucassin et Nicolette*, which is itself a combination of alternating verse and prose. Williams's epic poem *Paterson* incorporates prose into it, such as a letter from the young Allen Ginsberg to Dr. Williams, the famous physician-poet. Above all, Williams's experiments have as their substrate the American language. As he once said, "Let speech be the rule."

~

THE PARTY TRAIN

DUANE ACKERSON has edited several prose poem anthologies for Dragon Fly Press, including *A Prose Poem Anthology* (1970) and *Works: Edson, Benedikt, Ackerson* (1972). His poetry, prose-poetry, and fiction have appeared in numerous anthologies.

STEVEN AJAY has published two books with New Rivers Press: *Abracadabra* and *The Whales Are Burning*. He has traveled widely in India. He lives in Berkeley, California and teaches at California College of Arts and Crafts.

ROBERT ALEXANDER lives in Madison, Wisconsin. He has published a book of prose poems, *White Pine Sucker River* (New Rivers Press, 1993), and he is currently working on a Civil War narrative about the battle of Five Forks, Virginia.

BERT ALMON was born in Texas in 1943 and has lived in Canada since 1968. He has published seven collections of poetry. His most recent book, *Earth Prime* (Brick Books), won the Writers' Guild of Alberta Award for Poetry in 1995.

JACK ANDERSON, a poet and dance critic, is the author of eight books of poetry and six books of dance history and criticism.

DANIEL BACHHUBER has published poems in the *Christian Science Monitor, Iowa Review,* and *Southern Poetry Review.* He currently lives in St. Paul with his wife and son, where he works as a Montessori school teacher.

MICHAEL BENEDIKT has published five collections of poetry, including *The Badminton at Great Barrington* (University of Pittsburgh Press, 1980) and *Night Cries* (Wesleyan Press, 1976). A former poetry editor of *Paris Review*, he has taught at Bennington, Sarah Lawrence, Vassar, Hampshire College, and Boston University.

JOHN BENNETT's latest books are *Bodo*, a novel from Smith Publishers, and *The Names We Go By*, short stories from December Press.

CAROL BERGÉ has received grants in fiction from both the New York State Council on the Arts and the National Endowment for the Arts. She is an antique dealer in Santa Fe, writes for art and antiques magazines, rehabs houses, takes long walks, and is now sixty-six.

CASSIA BERMAN has been publishing, giving poetry readings, and teaching workshops for over twenty-five years. She lives in Woodstock, New York, where she also teaches t'ai chi, qi gong, and workshops on women's spirituality.

After two years as an Air Corps cryptographer in India and the Western Pacific, ROGER K. BLAKELY returned to teach English, American Literature, and Art History at his alma mater, Macalester College. His two poems in this anthology were originally published in *North from Duluth* (New Rivers Press, 1982).

DOUGLAS BLAZEK's most recent book is *We Sleep as the Dream Weaves Outside Our Minds* (1994), and he has work in a 1995 issue of *Zyzzyva*.

ROBERT BLY's most recent books of poetry include *What Have I ever Lost by Dying?: Collected Prose Poems* (Harper Collins); *Gratitude to Old Teachers* (Boa Editions); and *Meditations on the Insatiable Soul* (Harper Collins). He lives in Minneapolis, Minnesota.

MICHAEL BOWDEN's work has appeared in a variety of magazines, journals, and anthologies, including the *Pushcart Prize*. He was awarded a Creative Writing Fellowship in poetry from the Arizona Commission on the Arts in 1995.

JANE BROX's *Here and Nowhere Else: Late Seasons of a Farm and Its Family* was published by Beacon Press in June, 1995. She lives in Merrimack Valley of Massachusetts.

ANITA OLACHEA BUCCI has lived in Italy for the past twenty-five years, working mainly as a translator of literary and scientific manuscripts. The book, *The Dynamics of Ambiguity*, published in 1993 by Springer-Verlag (Heidelberg), is her most recent large-scale translation.

MICHAEL CAREY farms outside Farragut, Iowa. His poetry books include: *Nishnabotna*, *Honest Effort*, and *The Noise the Earth Makes*. He is also the author of a teaching manual entitled *Poetry: Starting from Scratch*.

SIV CEDERING is the author of three novels, six books for children, nine collections of poetry, plus three unproduced screenplays. She has just written, illustrated, and composed the music for seven television programs for children.

MAXINE CHERNOFF is the author of five books of poems, two books of short stories, and two novels. She is an associate professor of creative writing at San Francisco State University.

RICK CHRISTMAN's first collection of fiction, *Falling in Love at the End of the World*, was published by New Rivers Press in 1994. His second collection, *Men Without Children*, is in its final stages.

Three collections of prose poems by KIRBY CONGDON are motorcycle-cult poems, *Dream-Work* (Brooklyn, NY: Cycle Press, 1970); *Fantoccini: A Little Book of Memories* (Los Angeles: Little Caesar Press, 1981); and *Novels*, which is still in progress.

OLGA COSTOPOULOS was born in Alberta and now teaches and writes in Edmonton. She has published widely in Canadian poetry magazines. Her first collection of poems, *Muskoxen and Goat Songs*, has just been published by Ekstasis Editions in Victoria, British Columbia.

LORNA CROZIER is the author of many books of poetry, the last two of which, *The Garden Going On without Us* and *Angels of Flesh, Angels of Silence*, were both nominated for Canada's Governor General's Award. She lives in Saanichton, British Columbia.

PHILIP DACEY, a native of St. Louis, Missouri, has lived in southwestern Minnesota since 1970.

KAREN DALE received her MFA from UCI where she was awarded the Academy of American Poets College Prize. The poems here are from her book, *Until Morning*, for which she is seeking a publisher. Credits include *Threepenny Review* and *Greensboro Review*.

JULIE DEARBORN received her M.A. in Creative Writing from San Francisco State University and is currently living in San Francisco.

DIANE DI PRIMA is the author of thirty-two books of poetry and prose. She lives in San Francisco, where she is writing her autobiography for Viking Press.

JOSEPH DUEMER is the recipient of two NEA Poetry Fellowships and is the author, most recently, of *Static* (Owl Creek), and the co-editor of *Dog Music* (St. Martin's Press).

STEPHEN DUNNING has published widely in literary magazines and anthologies. He lives in Ann Arbor, Michigan.

STUART DYBEK is the author of two collections of stories and a book of poems, all of which include prose poems and short stories.

RUSSELL EDSON has published seven collections of prose poems from which a selected poems, *The Tunnel*, was published by Oberlin College Press.

HEID ERDRICH grew up in North Dakota, where her mother, a member of the Turtle Mountain Chippewa tribe, and her father, a German immigrant born in Minnesota, taught at a BIA boarding school. She attended Dartmouth College and Johns Hopkins University, and she now lives and writes in St. Paul.

DAVE ETTER's *Selected* Poems was published by Spoon River Poetry Press in 1987. He lives in Elburn, Illinois.

ROLAND FLINT, originally from North Dakota, has been teaching at Georgetown University in Washington, D.C., for twenty-six years. He has published six books of poetry and three chapbooks.

JENNIFER FOOTMAN lives in Brompton, Ontario, Canada.

CAROLYN FORCHÉ is the author of several books of poetry, including *Gathering the Tribes* (Yale University Press) and *The Country Between Us* (Harper and Row).

SESSHU FOSTER, author of *Angry Days* (West End Press), grew up in the Chicano barrios of East Los Angeles. He was the editor of *Invocation L.A.: Urban Multicultural Poetry* (West End Press), winner of an American Book Award. He currently lives in Iowa City, where he is attending the Writer's Workshop at the University of Iowa.

RICHARD FROST has published two collections with Ohio University Press and two chapbooks, *Jazz for Kirby* (State Street Press) and *The Family Way* (The Devil's Millhopper Press). His new collection, *Neighbor Blood*, will be published by Sarabande Books in 1996.

MAUREEN GIBBON writes poetry and fiction. Her poetry manuscript, *Kicking Horse My True Husband*, was finalist in the National Poetry Series in 1994 and 1995.

REGINALD GIBBONS is the author of four books of poems, including *Maybe It Was So* (University of Chicago Press), the novel *Sweetbitter*, and a collection of very short fiction, *Five Pears or Peaches*, both from Broken Moon Press. He has been editor of *Tri-Quarterly Magazine* since 1981.

ALLEN GINSBERG is a member of the American Institute of Arts and Letters and co-founder of the Jack Kerouac School of Disembodied Poetics at the Naropa

Institute. He has published many collections of poetry; forthcoming from HarperCollins is *Journals 1954–1958,* edited by Gordon Ball. He is a Distinguished Professor at Brooklyn College.

DIANE GLANCY is Associate Professor of English at Macalester College in St. Paul. Her third collection of short stories, *Monkey Secret*, was published in 1995 by TriQuarterly/ Northwestern University Press, and her first novel, *Pushing the Bear*, about the 1838 Trail of Tears, is forthcoming from Harcourt Brace in 1996.

PAULA GOLDMAN's work has appeared in many literary periodicals, including *The North American Review, Kansas Quarterly*, and *Poet Lore*. She has an M.A. degree in Journalism from Marquette University and is completing her MFA in Writing at Vermont College.

MIRIAM GOODMAN's poetry has been published in several anthologies, and she is the author of two collections of poetry. Her third book, *Commercial Traveller*, will be published in 1996 by Garden Street Press. She now lives in Cambridge, Massachusetts.

KEITH GUNDERSON has published several books of poetry, including *A Continued Interest in the Sun and Sea & Inland Missing the Sea* (Nodin Press), and has recently finished *Baja Journal*. He teaches philosophy at the University of Minnesota.

S. C. HAHN is a Nebraska native who remembers the names of most Kansas towns he has visited. He works as a technical editor and lives in Madison, Wisconsin.

DONALD HALL lives alone on a farm in New Hampshire. His books of poetry include *Old and New Poems, The One Day*, and *The Museum of Clear Ideas*.

KATHERINE HARER's book, *Hubba Hubba*, was the winner of the Slipstream Poetry Chapbook Contest for 1994 and is her fourth small press collection. She teaches at Skyline Community College just south of San Francisco and publishes regularly in literary journals.

MARIE HARRIS is a freelance writer and editor. Her collection of prose poems, *Weasel in the Turkey Pen*, was published in 1993 by Hanging Loose Press.

JIM HARRISON is a poet and novelist living in northern Michigan.

PENNY HARTER's recent books of poems include *Stages and Views* (Katydid Books), *Grandmother's Milk* (Singular Speech Press), and *Shadow Play* (Simon & Schuster). She lives in Santa Fe, New Mexico.

PETER HARVEY (1968–1992), a writer of both fiction and poetry, grew up around the beaches of southern California. In 1990 he received a degree in English and Creative Writing from the University of Massachusetts-Boston, where he published work in several issues of the student literary magazine and served on its editorial board.

JIM HAZARD is a poet and journalist who lives in Shorewood, Wisconsin. While not writing, he busies himself with playing the silver cornet and cooking.

TOM HENNEN's *Selected Poems, 1963–1983* was published by Prairie Gate Press. He lives at the Sand Lake Refuge in Columbia, South Dakota.

MICHAEL HETTICH's most recent book of poetry is *Immaculate Bright Rooms*, published in October 1994 by March St. Press. He teaches English and Creative Writing at Miami-Dade Community College in Miami, Florida.

JIM HEYNEN's most recent collection of short-short stories is *The One-Room Schoolhouse* (Knopf hardcover, 1993; Vintage paper, 1994). He is currently at work on a new collection of stories tentatively titled *Ordinary Sins*. He lives in St. Paul, Minnesota, with his wife, Sally Williams.

GORDON HICKEY has a master's degree from the University of Wisconsin-Milwaukee and is a reporter for the *Richmond Times-Dispatch* in Richmond, Virginia.

MICHAEL HOGAN lives in Guadalajara, Mexico.

BILL HOLM was born and still lives in Minneota, Minnesota. He teaches at Southwest State University in Marshall and is author of six books, most recently *Landscape of Ghosts* (with photographs by Bob Firth).

BROOKE HORVATH teaches at Kent State University and is the author of two poetry collections: *In a Neighborhood of Dying Light* and *Consolation at Ground Zero*.

DAVID IGNATOW has published fifteen books of poetry. A recent collection, *I Have a Name*, is scheduled for 1996 publication. His honors include a Bollingen Prize, a Wallace Stevens Fellowship, a Robert Frost Medal, and the John Steinbeck Award. He is Professor Emeritus, City University of New York, and Senior Lecturer, retired, Columbia University.

LOUIS JENKINS's most recent book, *Nice Fish: New and Selected Poems*, won the 1995 Minnesota Book Award for poetry. He lives in Duluth, Minnesota.

JIM JOHNSON lives and writes in Duluth and Isabella, Minnesota. His book, *Wolves*, was a Minnesota Voices Project winner.

PETER JOHNSON teaches creative writing at Providence College in Providence, Rhode Island, and is editor of *The Prose Poem: An International Journal*. His prose poems are being translated into Chinese for the Chinese journal, *The World of the Prose Poem*.

SYBIL KOLLAR lives in Brooklyn, New York.

MARY A. KONCEL has published in many literary magazines. She lives in Worthington, Massachusetts.

ELLEN KORT lives in Appleton, Wisconsin.

JOHN KRUMBERGER has a Ph.D. in psychology from the University of Minnesota and works as a psychologist in St. Paul. He was a 1989-90 Loft Mentor winner in poetry. His poems have appeared in numerous literary journals.

MARILYN KRYSL's latest books are *What We Have to Live With* and *Midwife*. When she's not teaching at the University of Colorado, Boulder, she works for Peace Brigade International.

GREG KUZMA's *Selected Poems* is due from Carnegie Mellon Press in 1996. Orchises will publish *What Poetry Is All About*, a poe-biz chronicle, in 1997.

Besides teaching English and eastern philosophy at University of Wisconsin-Stout, WARREN LANG enjoys acting and playing blues harmonica. His wife, Marion, and two grown sons, Ben and Dan, are a constant source of inspiration and support.

MICHELLE LEIGH is a writer, poet, and illustrator who has lived in Africa, Europe, North and South America, and Asia. She currently divides her time between a two hundred seventy-year-old farmhouse in Connecticut and northern Japan.

ROSEANN LLOYD's first collection of poetry is titled *Tap Dancing for Big Mom* (New Rivers Press, 1986). She collaborated with Richard Solly on *JourneyNotes: Writing for Recovery and Spiritual Growth* (Ballentine Books, 1992) and co-edited (with Deborah Keenan) *Looking for Home: Women Writing about Exile* (Milkweed Editions).

THOMAS LUX lives in Bronxville, New York.

MORTON MARCUS, author of six books of poetry and a novel, has poems in over sixty anthologies. He lives in Santa Cruz, California.

PETER MARKUS lives and works in Detroit, Michigan. Other poems from his "Still Lives with Whiskey" series have appeared in *The Prose Poem: An International Journal*.

DEBRA MARQUART's book of poems, *Everything's a Verb*—a Minnesota Voices Project winner—was published by New Rivers Press in 1995. She is an assistant professor of English at Iowa State University in Ames, Iowa.

KATHLEEN MCGOOKEY's prose poems have appeared in *Epoch*, *The Prose Poem*, and *The Prose Poem: An International Journal*. She lives in Allegan, Michigan.

JAY MEEK teaches at the University of North Dakota in Grand Forks. Carnegie Mellon University Press published *Windows*, his collection of prose poems, in 1994.

W. S. MERWIN, poet and translator, has published many books, including a collection of prose poems, *The Miner's Pale Children* (Athenaeum, 1970). He currently lives in Hawaii.

JOHN MINCZESKI is the author of two poetry collections, *The Spiders* and *Reconstruction of Light*, both from New Rivers Press. He is the recipient of fellowships from the National Endowment for the Arts and The Bush Foundation.

JUDITH MINTY is the author of four full-length collections of poetry and two chapbooks. She also writes fiction. She lives in northern Michigan.

N. SCOTT MOMADAY is a poet, novelist, painter, playwright, and storyteller, who lives and teaches in Tucson, Arizona. He has received a Pulitzer Prize and is a member of the Kiowa Gourd Dance Society.

BEVERLY ACUFF MOMOI's poems have appeared in various literary journals. She lives in St. Cloud, Minnesota.

FREDERICK MORGAN's *Poems for Paula* is due to be published by Story Line Press in October 1995. He is editor of *The Hudson Review*.

KRISTY NIELSEN's work has been published in many journals, including *Mid-American Review*, *The Prose Poem: An International Journal*, *The Illinois Review*, *Spoon River Poetry Review*, and *Kalliope*. She lives in Mountain View, California.

NINA NYHART has two collections of poems from Alice James Books: *Openers* and *French for Soldiers*. She lives in Brookline, Massachusetts.

MONICA OCHTRUP received a Loft-McKnight Award of Distinction for prose poems appearing in her New Rivers Press collection, *Pieces from the Long Afternoon*. She lives in St. Paul, Minnesota.

ROGER PFINGSTON teaches English and photography in Bloomington, Indiana. His book of poems and stories, *Something Iridescent*, is available from Barnwood Press.

CAROL J. PIERMAN is an essayist and author of two collections of poetry, including *The Naturalized Citizen* published by New Rivers Press. She is on the faculty of the University of Alabama in Tuscaloosa.

JENNIFER M. PIERSON was raised in New York by nuns and a Broadway mother. She "seeks the underlying experience of spirit." She lives beside a park in Washington, D.C.

HOLLY PRADO has had six books published. Her first, *Nothing Breaks Off at the Edge*, was published by New Rivers Press in 1976, "a wonderful encouragement."

DAVID RAY is the author of several books of poetry, including *Wool Highways and Other Poems* (Helicon Nine Editions, 1993) and *The Tramp's Cup* (Chariton Review Press, 1978). He lives in Kansas City, Missouri.

DAVE REDDALL lives in Provincetown, Massachusetts.

JOHN CALVIN REZMERSKI lives in Eagle Lake, Minnesota, teaches at Gustavus Adolphus College, and is the author of seven books of poems and editor of *The Frederick Manfred Reader*, which will be published by Holy Cow! Press in October 1995.

GEORGE ROBERTS lives in Minneapolis, Minnesota, gets up early each morning to write, and teaches at North High School, a few blocks from his home.

W. R. RODRIGUEZ is the author of *the shoe shine parlor poems et al* (Ghost Pony Press). He has completed its sequel, *the concrete pastures of the beautiful bronx*. He lives in Madison, Wisconsin.

DORIEN ROSS is a writer and psychologist. Her first novel, *Returning to A*, will be published by City Lights in October 1995. Her short stories and essays have been published in *Best American Essays*, *Tikkun*, and other journals and anthologies. She lives in New York City.

VERN RUTSALA's ninth book, *Little-Known Sports*, a collection of prose poems, received the Juniper Prize from the University of Massachusetts Press. He lives in Portland, Oregon.

IRA SADOFF's *An Ira Sadoff Reader* was published by the University Press of New England. David Godine will be publishing *Delicious: New and Selected Poems.* He lives in Hallowell, Maine.

NICHOLAS SAMARAS's first book of poetry, *Hands of the Saddlemaker*, won the Yale Series of Younger Poets Award. Currently he teaches at Saint Leo College in Florida and has completed his second collection of poetry.

ROY SCHEELE's poems have been widely published in journals, little magazines, and anthologies. He is Poet-in-Residence at Doane College in Crete, Nebraska.

ALISON SEEVAK, a short story writer and essayist, grew up in New Jersey and makes her home in Albany, California. She works as a program evaluator for a public health policy institute.

JEANNE SHANNON is a poet, essayist, and fiction writer. She grew up in the "coal country" of southwestern Virginia, and still draws upon her memories of the Appalachian region in her work. She lives in Albuquerque, New Mexico, where she has edited and published two poetry magazines, *Blackberry* and *Wildflower.*

KARL SHAPIRO has published many books of poetry, including *Collected Poems: 1940–1978* (Random House, 1978). He has received many awards, including a Pulitzer Prize, and now lives and teaches in Davis, California.

CHARLES SIMIC's first volume of poetry was published in 1967 and fifteen others have followed. His most recent book of poems is *A Wedding in Hell* from Harcourt Brace. Simic won a Pulitzer Prize for Poetry in 1990. He lives in New Hampshire.

THOMAS R. SMITH's books of poetry are *Keeping the Star* (New Rivers Press, 1988) and *Horse of Earth* (Holy Cow! Press, 1994). He lives in Minneapolis, Minnesota.

TERRY SPOHN's work has appeared in the *North American Review*, *Mississippi Review*, *Ascent*, *Dreams & Secrets*, and other places. He lives in Waukesha, Wisconsin.

DEBORAH STEIN was born in West Virginia, grew up in Seattle, and now lives in Minneapolis, Minnesota. She is the author of *Colors: Inspirations for a Culturally Diverse World* and editor of *From Inside Volume I, An Anthology of Writing by Incarcerated Women.*

ROBERT SUND lives in La Conner, Washington.

BARBARA SZERLIP is a two-time National Endowment for the Arts Writing Fellow. She was raised on the East Coast, lives on the West Coast, and is torn between fiction and non-fiction.

ROSS TALARICO has published two recent books: *Spreading the Word: Poetry and the Survival of Community in America* (Duke University Press, 1995) and *Hearts and Times: The Literature of Memory* (Karois Press, Academy Chicago Publishers, 1992). He is currently Professor of Writing and Communication at National University in San Diego, California.

THOM TAMMARO lives and works in Moorhead, Minnesota. He is the author of *When the Italians Came to My Hometown*, a collection of poems (Spoon River Poetry Press, 1995) and has co-edited (with Mark Vinz) *Inheriting the Land: Contemporary Voices from the Midwest* (1993) and *Imagining Home: Writing from the Midwest* (1995), both published by the University of Minnesota Press.

TONY TOWLE lives in New York City.

ALISON TOWNSEND is a poet, essayist, and teacher whose work has appeared in many magazines, journals, and anthologies. She lives in Madison, Wisconsin, where she works as a manager at Borders Book Shop and teaches.

C. W. TRUESDALE is a poet, essayist, and fiction writer who lives in Minneapolis, Minnesota. He has been publisher of New Rivers Press since 1968.

MARK VINZ has published two books of prose poems with New Rivers Press: *The Weird Kid* and *Late Night Calls* as well as many other books of poetry. He teaches at Moorhead State University in Moorhead, Minnesota, and is editor of Dacotah Territory Press.

TOM WHALEN's prose poems and fiction have appeared in numerous journals. When not in New Orleans, he teaches literature and film at the University of Stuttgart in Germany.

PATRICIA WILSON moved to New Orleans, Louisiana from Minneapolis, Minnesota, in 1994. She is currently working on a book of poems.

LINDA WING's poems have appeared in a variety of regional and national publications. Her chapbook, *Lover's Leap,* was published by Poetry Harbor in 1995. She lives in Minneapolis, Minnesota.

WARREN WOESSNER is the Senior Editor of *Abraxas* magazine. Collections of his poetry are forthcoming from BkMk Press (*Green Flash*) and Poetry Harbor Press (*Clear to Chukchi*). He is a lawyer and lives in Minneapolis, Minnesota.

JAMES WRIGHT was born in Martins Ferry, Ohio in 1927 and received a Ph.D. from the University of Washington in Seattle. His first book, *The Green Wall*, won the Yale Series of Younger Poets Award in 1954. He won the Pulitzer Prize for Poetry in 1972 and published many collections of poetry and translations until his death in 1980. Three books were published posthumously.

GARY YOUNG's most recent books are *The Dream of a Moral Life* and *Wherever I Looked*. He is editor of Greenhouse Review Press and lives in Santa Cruz, California.

LILA ZEIGER, author of *The Way to Castle Garden* (State Street Press), has been widely published in magazines and anthologies since her first poems appeared in *The Paris Review*. She directs the writing program in an AIDS Day Treatment Center in New York City.

ALAN ZIEGLER's books include *So Much To Do* (poems) and *The Green Grass of Flatbush* (stories). His work has appeared in *The New Yorker* and *The Paris Review*. He teaches at Columbia University in New York City.

HARRIET ZINNES is a poet and essayist who has appeared in a great many magazines and other publications over the years. She is Professor Emerita of English at Queens College. She lives in New York City.

# ACKNOWLEDGMENTS

Some of the material in this collection is in the public domain. Every effort has been made to identify ownership of copyrights; any additions or corrections should be reported to New Rivers Press for inclusion in future editions. We would like to thank the following writers, agencies, and publishers for permission to reprint these original works. Unless otherwise indicated, all works (except those in the public domain) are used by permission of the author.

Nathaniel Hawthorne: "Autumnal Characteristics" is reprinted from *The American Notebooks*, ed. Claude M. Simpson (Ohio State Univ. Press, 1972).

H. D. Thoreau: "Walking" was first published in the *Atlantic Monthly,* and has been reprinted many times.

Walt Whitman: All selections are from *Specimen Days* (Rees Welsh & Co., 1882–83), reprinted in his *Collected Prose*.

Lafcadio Hearn: "Spring Phantoms" was first published in the New Orleans *Item* and was reprinted in *Fantastics and Other Fancies,* ed. Charles Woodward Hutson (Houghton Mifflin, 1914).

Gelett Burgess: "The Confessions of a Yellster" first appeared in the *Lark*.

Gertrude Stein: All selections are from *Tender Buttons* (Claire Marie, 1914).

William Carlos Williams: "The Delicacies," from *Collected Poems: 1909–1939*, Vol. 1, Copyright © 1938 by New Directions Publishing Corp., reprinted by permission of New Directions Publishing Corp. "A Matisse," from *Imaginations*, Copyright © 1970 by Florence H. Williams, reprinted by permission of New Directions Publishing Corp. "Exultation," from *Collected Poems: 1939–1962*, Vol. 2, Copyright © 1941 by William Carlos Williams, reprinted by permission of New Directions Publishing Corp. Excerpt from "For Bill Bird" (which first appeared in *Contact*), Copyright © 1941 by Paul H. and William Eric Williams, reprinted by permission of New Directions Publishing Corp., agent.

Jane Heap: "White" first appeared in the *Little Review*, and was reprinted in *The Little Review Anthology*, ed. Margaret Anderson (Hermitage House, 1953).

Fenton Johnson: All selections first appeared in *Others*.

Robert McAlmon: "Village" first appeared in *Contact*, and was included in *Explorations* (Egoist Press, 1921).

Jean Toomer: "Karintha" is reprinted from *Cane* with the permission of Liveright Publishing Corporation. Copyright © 1923 by Boni & Liveright, renewed 1951 by Jean Toomer.

Ernest Hemingway: "L'Envoi" is reprinted with permission of Scribners, a division of Simon & Schuster Inc., from *In Our Time*, Copyright © 1925 Charles Scribner's Sons. Copyright renewed 1953 by Ernest Hemingway.

Kay Boyle: "Monastery" and "Whore Street" were published in *This Quarter*; "January 24, New York" is from *365 Days*, ed. Kay Boyle, Laurence Vail, and Nina Conarain (Harcourt Brace, 1936). These poems are reprinted by permission of the Watkins/Loomis Agency.

William Faulkner: "The Priest" was first published in the *Double Dealer* and is reprinted from *New Orleans Sketches,* Copyright © 1958 by Rutgers University. It is used by permission of Sheldon Abend, Agent.

Sherwood Anderson: "The Lame One" was first published in *Lyric America: An Anthology of American Poetry, 1630–1930*, edited by Alfred Kreymborg, 1930. Reprinted by permission of Harold Ober Associates Incorporated. Copyright © 1925 by The Liveright Publishing Company. Renewed 1963 by Eleanor Copenhaver Anderson.

Kenneth Patchen: All selections are from *The Collected Poems of Kenneth Patchen*, Copyright © 1949, 1957 by New Directions Publishing Corp., reprinted by permission of New Directions Publishing Corp.

Nelson Algren: "Nobody Knows Where O'Connor Went" is from *Chicago: City on the Make*. Reprinted by permission of Donadio & Ashworth, Inc. Copyright © 1951 by Nelson Algren.

Walter Lowenfels: "Jukebox in the Coalfields" from *Some Deaths*. Copyright © 1964 by Walter Lowenfels. Published by Jonathan Williams, the Nantahala Foundation, Highlands, N.C., 1964. Reprinted by permission of Manna Lowenfels, Literary Executrix.

∼

Duane Ackerson: "Fire" originally appeared in *A Prose Poem Anthology* (Dragon Fly Press, 1970). "The Minus Touch" originally appeared in *Pebble*. Both poems are reprinted from *Weathering* (West Coast Poetry Review, 1973).

Robert Alexander: "At the Party," "Finding Token Creek," and "A Joe Pass Guitar Solo" are reprinted with permission from *White Pine Sucker River* (New Rivers Press, 1993).

Bert Almon: "The Clematis Seminar" was first published in *Canadian Literature*.

Jack Anderson: "The Party Train" is reprinted from *City Joys* (Release Press, 1975). "Return to Work" is reprinted from *Toward the Liberation of the Left Hand* (Univ. of Pittsburgh Press, 1977). "The Somnabulists' Hotel" first appeared in *The Prose Poem: An International Journal*.

Michael Benedikt: "The Voyage of Self-Discovery" is reprinted from *Night Cries* (Wesleyan Press, 1976) by permission of the author.

John Bennett: "Postage Due" originally appeared in *Crazy Girl on the Bus* (Vagabond Press, 1979).

Carol Bergé: "Grey, or Turtle, Song" and "Timepiece (Michigan), or, A Moebius Trip ..." are reprinted from *Timepieces* (Fault Publications, 1977).

Cassia Berman: "Noumenon" was first published in *Lillabulero*.

Roger K. Blakely: "Icebergs" and "Perfectionist" first appeared in *North From Duluth* (New Rivers Press, 1981).

Robert Bly: "The Dead Seal" from *The Morning Glory* (Harper & Row, 1975), Copyright © 1975 by Robert Bly, "Snow Falling on Snow" from *This Body is Made of Camphor and Gopherwood* (Harper & Row, 1977), Copyright © 1977 by Robert Bly, and "The Exhausted Bug" from *Gratitude to Old Teachers* (Boa Editions Limited, 1993), Copyright © 1993 by Robert Bly, are reprinted by permission of Robert Bly. "Warning to the Reader" from *What Have I Ever Lost by Dying*, Copyright © 1992 by Robert Bly, is reprinted by permission of HarperCollins Publishers, Inc.

Jane Brox: "Apple Boxes" was originally published in *The Georgia Review* and "White Pine" was originally published in *The Gettysburg Review*. Both are reprinted from *Here and Nowhere Else* by permission of Beacon Press, Copyright ©1995 by Jane Brox.

Michael Carey: "The Darkening Hills," originally published by *Poet & Critic*, is from *Honest Effort* (Mid-Prairie Books, 1995). "The Dead Center" and "Translations" are from *Nishnabotna* (Mid-Prairie Books, 1995). "How Grandma and Grandpa Met" is from *The Noise the Earth Makes* (Pterodactyl Press, 1987 and 1990) and is reprinted with permission from Foundation Books, Lincoln, NE.

Siv Cedering: "In the Museum of Natural History" and "The Juggler" first appeared in *The Juggler* (Sagarin Press, 1977). "The Juggler" is reprinted from *Letters from the Floating World* by permission of The University of Pittsburgh Press, Copyright ©1984.

Maxine Chernoff: "A Vegetable Emergency," "High Rise," "An Abridged Bestiary," and "Sailing" are reprinted from *Leap Year Day: New and Selected Poems* (Another Chicago Press, 1990).

Rick Christman: "Asylum" is reprinted from *Falling in Love at the End of the World* (New Rivers Press, 1994).

Kirby Congdon: "The Motorcycle Social Club" is reprinted from *Dream-Work* (Cycle Press, 1970).

Olga Costopoulos: "Club Sandwiches" originally appeared in *Nimrod*.

Lorna Crozier: "Home Care" is reprinted from *Inventing the Hawk* (1992), and "Quitting Smoking" is reprinted from *Angels of Flesh, Angels of Silence* (1988). Both are used by permission of McClelland & Stewart, Toronto.

Philip Dacey: "The Elephant" is reprinted with permission from *Night Shift at the Crucifix Factory* (University of Iowa Press, 1991). "The Operation" is reprinted with permission from *How I Escaped From the Labyrinth and Other Poems* (Carnegie-Mellon University Press, 1977).

Joseph Duemer: "A Theory of Language" was first publised in *Mosaic*.

Stephen Dunning: "You Might Say . . . This Is the Story of My Life," first appeared in *Men & Women: Together & Alone* (The Spirit That Moves Us Press, 1988).

Stuart Dybek: "Belly Button" first appeared in *The Seattle Review*. "Confession" first appeared in *Manoa*. "Hometown" first appeared in *Poetry Now*.

Russell Edson: "The Breakfast That Came to Dinner" and "The Family Monkey" are reprinted from *The Clam Theatre*, Copyright ©1973 by Russell Edson, Wesleyan University Press by permission of University Press of New England. "Mr. & Mrs. Duck Dinner" and "The Explosion at the Club" are reprinted from *The*

*Intuitive Journey and Other Works* (Harper & Row), Copyright ©1976 Russell Edson, by permission of the author.

Heid Erdrich: "Boyfriend" was first published in *City Pages* (Baltimore, MD).

Dave Etter: "Baseball" and "Grain Elevator" were published first in *Home State* and then in *Selected Poems* (Spoon River Poetry Press, 1987).

Roland Flint: "Paint," "Sabbatical," and "His Oyster" are reprinted from *Resuming Green: Selected Poems, 1965–1982* (The Dial Press, 1983).

Carolyn Forché: "Ancapagari" is reprinted from *Gathering the Tribes*, with permission of Yale University Press, Copyright © 1976 by Carolyn Forché. "The Colonel," reprinted from *The Country between Us*, Copyright © 1981 by Carolyn Forché, is used by permission of HarperCollins Publishers, Inc.

Sesshu Foster: "'5 kids slept in the car . . .'" first appeared in the *Kenyon Review*.

Richard Frost: "A Bird of Some Kind" appeared in *Confrontation*. "Burro" was first published in *Resurgence*. "The Roof" originally appeared in *Slow Dancer*.

Reginald Gibbons: "On Belmont" is reprinted from *Five Pears or Peaches* by permission of Broken Moon Press. Copyright © 1991 Reginald Gibbons.

Allen Ginsberg: "A Supermarket in California," Copyright © 1955 by Allen Ginsberg, copyright renewed, and "The Bricklayer's Lunch Hour," Copyright © 1947 by Allen Ginsberg, are reprinted from *Collected Poems, 1947–1980*, by permission of HarperCollins Publishers, Inc.

Diane Glancy: "War Horse II" was published in *The West Pole* (Minnesota Center for Book Arts).

Miriam Goodman: "Shopping Trip" originally appeared in *The Prose Poem: An International Journal*.

Keith Gunderson: "Number One Man on the Sit-down Power Mowers at Lakewood Cemetery" is reprinted from *To See a Thing: Rhythms, Typographs, and Prose Poems* (Nodin Press, 1975).

Donald Hall: "Flies" from *Old and New Poems*. Copyright © 1990 Donald Hall. Reprinted by permission of Ticknor & Fields/ Houghton Mifflin, Co. All rights reserved.

Katherine Harer: "Frida Kahlo & Diego Rivera" has appeared in *Five Fingers Review* and *The San Francisco Bay Guardian*. "Frida Kahlo & Nick Muray" first appeared in the *Berkeley Poetry Review*.

Marie Harris: "Airborne" and "Louis Antoine de Bougainville" are reprinted with permission from *Weasel in the Turkey Pen* (Hanging Loose Press, 1993). "Tent Circus" first appeared in *Hanging Loose Magazine*.

Peter Harvey: "Liquid Dominoes" and "Salome" are reprinted by permission of Jay and Elaine Harvey.

Jim Hazard: Selections from "The Snow Crazy Copybook" are reprinted from *A Hive of Souls: Selected Poems, 1968–1976* (Crossing Press, 1977).

Tom Hennen: "Crawling Out the Window" appeared in *Selected Poems: 1963–1983* (Prairie Gate Press).

Jim Heynen: "The Man Who Kept Cigars in His Cap" is reprinted from *The Man Who Kept Cigars in his Cap* by permission of Graywolf Press, Saint Paul, MN. Copyright © 1979 by Jim Heynen.

Michael Hogan: "The Message of Onan" and "A Nursing Mother on the Dorchester–Harvard Train" are reprinted from *A Lion at a Cocktail Party* (Gallimaufry, 1978).

Bill Holm: "Brahms' Capriccio . . ." first appeared in *The Dead Get By With Everything* (Milkweed, 1991). "Girl Eating Rice" appeared in *Weber Studies*.

Brooke Horvath: "Abrasion" originally appeared in *The Denver Quarterly*. "The Woman in the Peter Pan Collar" first appeared in the chapbook *In the Neighborhood of Dying Light,* which was included in the chapbook anthology *Men and Women/Women and Men* (Bottom Dog Press).

David Ignatow: "An Account in the Present Tense of How It all Happened," " 'I am standing on the soft . . .' ", " 'I sink back upon the ground . . .' ", and "Cockroaches" are from *New and Collected Poems, 1970–1985*, Copyright ©1986 David Ignatow, Wesleyan University Press, reprinted by permission of University Press of New England.

Louis Jenkins: "Basketball," "Frost Flowers," and "Library," were originally published in *An Almost Human Gesture* (The Eighties Press & Ally Press, 1987).

Mary A. Koncel: "Come Back, Elvis, Come Back to Holyoke" first appeared in *The Illinois Review*.

Ellen Kort: "Sea Turtle" previously appeared in *Columbia Pacific Review* and in *Dreaming History* (Prairie Oak Press).

John Krumberger: "The Quaker Meeting" first appeared in *The Menomonie Review*.
Marilyn Krysl: "Body" and "Incarnate" are reprinted from *What We Have To Live With* (Teal Press, 1989).

Greg Kuzma: "The Desk" and "Why I Write" were originally published in *A Horse of a Different Color* (Illuminati, 1983).

Thomas Lux: "The Gas Station," "My Grandmother's Funeral," and "The Swimmer" are reprinted from *Memory's Handgrenade* (Pym-Randall, 1972).

Morton Marcus: "Lost Things" first appeared in *The World*.

Peter Markus: Parts I & II of "Still Lives with Whiskey Bottle" appeared previously in *Verve*.

Debra Marquart: "Getting Ready," "My Father tells this Story . . . ," and "Small Town Cafe" originally appeared in *Everything's a Verb* (New Rivers Press, 1995).

Jay Meek: "The Beautiful and Invisible Tree," "Medici Fountain," and "Travel Notes" first appeared in *Windows* (Carnegie Mellon Press, 1994).

W. S. Merwin: "A Garden" and "The Permanent Collection" are reprinted from *The Miner's Pale Children* by permission of Georges Borchardt, Inc. Copyright © 1970 by W. S. Merwin.

John Minczeski: "My Name" was originally published in *The Spiders* (New Rivers Press, 1979).

Judith Minty: "Ironing" from *Dancing the Fault* (University of Florida Press, 1991) is reprinted by permission of the author and the publisher.

N. Scott Momaday: "The Man in Black" and "Billy the Kid Offers a Kindness" are reprinted from *In the Presence of the Sun* with permission of St. Martin's Press, Inc., New York, NY. Copyright © 1992 N. Scott Momaday.

Frederick Morgan: "Elves" and "Pterdodactyls" are reprinted by permission from *Poems of the Two Worlds* (University of Illinois Press, 1977).

Kristy Nielsen: "The Language with One Word" is reprinted by permission from *Kalliope*.

Nina Nyhart: "The Catch" first appeared in *Tampa Review* (Spring 1995).

Monica Ochtrup: "The Truth" first appeared in *Warm Journal*. "The Truth" and "Norden" are reprinted from *Pieces of the Long Afternoon* (New Rivers Press, 1991).

Roger Pfingston: "Darwin's Mimosa" originally appeared in *Paragraph Magazine*. "Grady Mourns" is reprinted from *Grady's Lunch* (Matchbook Press, 1988).

Carol J. Pierman: All selections from "The Naturalized Citizen" are reprinted from *The Naturalized Citizen* (New Rivers Press, 1981).

Holly Prado: "The Owl Turns His Head All the Way Around" and "Visit" were originally published in *Nothing Breaks Off at the Edge* (New Rivers Press, 1976).

Dave Reddall: "In the Park" is reprinted from *The Vagabond Anthology (1966–1977)*, ed. John Bennett (Vagabond Press, 1978).

Vern Rutsala: "Broom," "Dust Mop," "Ironing Board," "Getting Lost," "Lying," and "Sleeping" previously appeared in *Little-Known Sports* (U-Mass Press, 1994).

Ira Sadoff: "The Romance of the Racer" is reprinted from *Palm Reading in Winter* (Houghton Mifflin, 1978); "Three Dreams of an Ambitious Man" and "Hopper's 'Nighthawks' (1942)" are from *Settling Down* (Houghton Mifflin, 1975). All are reprinted by permission of the author.

Roy Scheele: "Eminent Domain" and "A Visitation" first appeared in *Fifty-Four Prose Poems*, eds. Greg Kuzma and Duane Ackerson (Best Cellar Press, 1974).

Jeanne Shannon: "Spelling" first appeared in *The Sow's Ear*.

Karl Shapiro: "The Bourgeois Poet" and "The Living Rooms of My Neighbors" are reprinted from *Collected Poems: 1940–1978* (Random House, 1978). Copyright © 1978, renewed 1985 by Karl Shapiro, and appear by arrangement with Wieser & Wieser, Inc., 118 East 25th Street, New York, NY 10010.

Charles Simic: Excerpts from *The World Without End*, Copyright © 1989 by Charles Simic, are reprinted by permission of Harcourt Brace & Company.

Thomas R. Smith: "Portrait of My German Grandparents, 1952," is reprinted from *Keeping the Star* (New Rivers Press, 1988). "Windy Day at Kabekona" originally appeared in *The Prose-Poem: An International Journal*.

Deborah Stein: "One Thousand Saturdays" first appeared in *Paragraph Magazine*. Robert Sund's untitled poem is reprinted with permission from *Bunch Grass* (Univ. of Washington Press, 1969).

Barbara Szerlip: "a.k.a. Mata Hari," "The Nomad's Story," and "Terra Incognita," first appeared in *The Ugliest Woman in the World and Other Histories* (Gallimaufry Press, 1978).

Ross Talarico: "Home Movies" previously appeared in *Fifty-Four Prose Poems*, ed. Greg Kuzma and Duane Ackerson (Best Cellar Press, 1974).

Thom Tammaro: "Walking to My Office on Easter Sunday Morning" first appeared in *The Sun: A Magazine of Ideas*. "February, 1951" is reprinted with permission from *North Dakota Quarterly*.

Tony Towle: "The Review" first appeared in *Mother*.

Alison Townsend: "Muses" originally appeared in *Pinchpenny*.

C.W. Truesdale: "Miguel and General Alexander Haig" is an excerpt of an essay which appeared in *Walt Whitman: The Measure of His Song* (Holy Cow! Press, 1982).

Mark Vinz: "Wind Chill," "Still Life: The Pleasures of Home," and "Late Night Calls" are reprinted with permission from *Late Night Calls* (New Rivers Press, 1992).

Linda Wing: "Mortality Anecdotes" and "The News" are reprinted from *Lovers Leap* (Poetry Harbor, 1995).

Warren Woessner: "Maggie May" first appeared in *Abraxas*.

James Wright: "To Carolee Coombs-Stacy, Who Set My Verses to Music" first appeared in the *Paris Review*, and is reprinted by permission of Anne Wright. All other selections are from *Above the River: The Complete Poems* by James Wright. Copyright © 1990 by Anne Wright. Reprinted by permission of Farrar, Straus & Giroux, Inc.

Gary Young: "'Jimmy Ratcliffe . . .'" first appeared in *Hubbub*. "'One night . . .'" first appeared in *Quarterly West*.

Lila Zeiger: "Things We Need to Know about the Picnic" originally appeared in *Exquisite Corpse*.

Alan Ziegler: "The Guest" first appeared in *So Much to Do* (Release Press, 1981).

∾

Finally, the editors of *The Party Train* would like to call attention to some previous collections of the prose poem:

"A Little Anthology of the Poem in Prose," ed. Charles Henri Ford, *New Directions* 14 (1953).

*A Prose Poem Anthology*, ed. Duane Ackerson (Dragon Flying Press, 1970).

*Fifty-Four Prose Poems*, ed. Greg Kuzma and Duane Ackerson, *Pebble*, No. 11 (July, 1974).

*Imperial Messages: One Hundred Modern Parables*, ed. Howard Schwartz (Avon, 1976).

*The Prose Poem: An International Anthology*, ed. Michael Benedikt (Dell, 1976).

*Models of the Universe: An Anthology of the Prose Poem*, ed. Stuart Friebert and David Young (Oberlin College Press, 1995).